WOMEN COMPOSERS, CONDUCTORS, AND MUSICIANS OF THE TWENTIETH CENTURY:

Selected Biographies

by

JANE WEINER LEPAGE

The Scarecrow Press, Inc.
Metuchen, N.J., & London
1980

Library of Congress Cataloging in Publication Data

LePage, Jane Weiner, 1931-
Women composers, conductors, and musicians of the twentieth century.

Includes index.
1. Women musicians--Biography. I. Title.
ML82.L46 780'.92'2 [B] 80-12162
ISBN 0-8108-1298-3

Manufactured in the United States of America

Dedicated to my husband,
William E. LePage

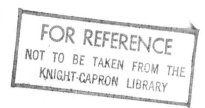

CONTENTS

ACKNOWLEDGMENTS

It was an inspiring experience to work with the composers, conductors, and musicians presented in this book. Their willingness to share personal experiences as well as their attention to detail and authenticity made possible a thoroughly documented publication. To these women I am deeply grateful.

I wish to thank Denise Restout, director of The Landowska Center and assistant and companion for twenty-six years to Madame Wanda Landowska, for her priceless time and contributions.

Also, thanks go to Mr. Charles Seeger, husband of the late Ruth Crawford (Seeger), who died before we could meet and to the music critics, both in America and Europe, for their supportive reviews which added depth and validity to the book.

My research was facilitated by many library staffs and I am especially grateful to the staff at North Adams State College, Williams College, Bennington College and the New York City Library.

I wish to acknowledge my colleagues Dr. Kathy Heiligmann and Dr. Ellen Schiff, Suzanne Kemper, Research Librarian, and the support staff at North Adams State College, without whose help the book could not have been completed.

My total absorption in my research, writing, and interviewing was thoughtfully supported by my husband and family. Special thanks to my daughter Jane Weiner for researching, to her and my daughter Renay LePage for their help in interviewing, and to my daughter-in-law Susan Weiner for her research in Canada.

Jane Weiner LePage

PREFACE

The more I researched and interviewed, the more the plan of this book changed, until it took the form of the present volume. Reference books and textbooks generally have dismissed women composers and conductors in a few sentences. My primary focus is to make readily available the contributions and accomplishments of some of the gifted women musicians of the twentieth century. The role of women in the arts has been neglected, and accurate historical information must be collected if we are to preserve their achievements for posterity.

Ideally, there should be no need to separate the sexes; merit should be based solely on artistic ability. Unfortunately, this has not happened, even though recorded history shows that women have been composing since the third century. The societal structure did not provide for public presentation or documentation of their work. A few compositions written by women were performed and published under the names of their brothers or husbands, or under male pseudonyms. The talents of many women have never been preserved or shared with the world. Society has been the loser because of its failure to recognize these talented and creative women. Negativism should not be accepted, but I do not fault society for its past history. The important issue is to swiftly eliminate the inequities.

My research, interviewing, and writing will continue in hopes of publishing a second volume in order to document the contributions of all those women not mentioned in this book.

VICTORIA BOND

Conductor, Composer

In 1977, Victoria Bond, America's most promising professional orchestral conductor, became the first woman to be awarded a Doctorate of Musical Arts Degree in Orchestral Conducting from Juilliard School of Music. Dr. Bond is bright, talented, articulate and a youthful, beautiful person who is recognized as both a conductor and composer. Her accomplishments are varied, and she has received excellent reviews and press coverage throughout the United States. There are various roads to the conductor's podium, and Dr. Bond's biography gives an insight to the road she has traveled, a road that has built a new and exciting flexible model, and reflects an image based on intellect and confidence.

Victoria Bond was born of a musically talented family in Los Angeles, California, in 1949. Her physician father had sung professionally with the New York City Opera, her mother was a concert pianist, and all the grandparents were professional musicians including her grandfather, Samuel Epstein, who was a composer and conductor. As a child genius with inventive ingenuity, she began playing the piano at age three, and was composing variations on songs in elementary school, as well as composing musical stories on the piano before she could notate them.

Her life was to be profoundly influenced as a teenager through the efforts of one of her early music teachers who invited her to conduct one of his many community orchestras. "Of all the bizarre things, the orchestra happened to be the Senior Citizens Orchestra of Los Angeles, California." It was an absolutely incredible experience; she remembers being terribly nervous beforehand because she had never stood before a full orchestra and conducted Schubert's Unfinished Symphony.

I had no idea if I would remember everything I had

VICTORIA BOND
(Photo by Christian Steiner)

> studied for weeks and weeks before or whether it would be lost in a flush of nerves--but when I conducted, something magical happened--it was as though I had conducted all my life, and I felt completely natural and relaxed and became part of the music. This was a revealing experience that was the turning point in my career, many of the senior citizens had been members of prestigious instrumental groups, and they felt I had great potential as a conductor. Until this time I had never thought seriously of conducting as a career.

Victoria Bond was a composing major at the University of Southern California and received her Bachelor of Arts Degree with honors. She was a student of Ingolf Dahl and Ellis Kohs and did orchestrating and arranging for many film composers. She had the opportunity to conduct some of her own compositions and fully realized that she must study conducting if she were to command respect of the musicians and bring to fruition all aspects of any composition.

Music critic Irving Kolodin, a family friend, convinced her to do graduate work at Juilliard School of Music where she majored in both conducting and composition. She received scholarships from 1972-1977 and fellowships from 1973-1977. Bond studied composition with Roger Sessions and Vincent Persichetti. Some cynicism greeted her unheard-of bid for a position in the conducting program; however, she was accepted and trained under such notable master teachers as Sixten Ehrling, Jean Morel, Pierre Boulez, and Herbert von Karajan.

Dr. Bond learned to be a precise thinker and to get to the heart of problems in complex modern music, under the tutorage of Boulez, whom she respects and admires. Herbert von Karajan taught a master class at Juilliard and encouraged her in her conducting. Bond learned an extraordinary concept of sound from him, as well as the importance of developing the technique of listening. Other influential teachers included Paul Glass, Darius Milhaud, and Jacob Druckman, all master artists and active in the development of twentieth century music.

Victoria Bond acquired an extensive background and developed exciting techniques and skills that have placed her among the young contemporary leaders in America. She was assistant conductor of the Juilliard Orchestra and Contemporary Music Ensemble, and recipient of the Victor Herbert Conducting Award for outstanding achievement. One of Bond's early conducting teachers suggested she not seriously consider conducting as a career, because when she married her husband wouldn't let her go to rehearsals. What nonsense! Bond's handsome, New York attorney husband of several years, Stephan Peskin, is an avid supporter of her conducting career and regularly shares commuting duties with her so they can be together as much as possible. They represent the contemporary concept of supportive marriage.

Bond received a conducting scholarship to Aspen Music Festival in 1973 and studied under Otto Werner Mueller and Herbert Blomstedt. This festival is held each summer, and in terms of performance and of performer-training, is rivaled in this country only by Tanglewood in Massachusetts. During this festival, there is a conference on contemporary music, founded by Darius Milhaud, and directed the past eight years by Richard Dufallo.

In August 1974, Ms. Bond was assistant conductor at the Cabrillo Music Festival at Aptos, California. The theme of this contemporary music festival was Women Composers. Through Ms. Bond's tireless efforts, a variety of women composers were afforded an opportunity to have their music performed. The festival programmed a composition by Netty Simons, The Pied Piper of Hamelin (an allegorical setting of the familiar fairy tale), using contemporary musical techniques as sound-effect devices. The versatility of Bond was most evident not only by her conducting performance, but also by her talents as a composer. Performed during the festival were her compositions Suite aux Troubadours, for voice and five instrumentalists, and C. A. G. E. D., for strings. She both conducted and sang the first composition, which superbly reflected the troubadours and trouvères of France during the 11th through 14th centuries. She comments on C. A. G. E. D. below:

> The letters C. A. G. E. D. represent all of the open strings on all the stringed instruments and are the basis for the motive on which the entire piece is built. The opening section comprises a statement by each of the strings of this motive.
>
> The letters also suggested to me the image of a caged animal, and the movements of the piece can be thought as:
>
> 1. An animal pacing the length of his cage;

bored and aimless; tracing circles around the confines of his prison; rhythmically swaying back and forth; panting and staring out of the bars.
2. An animal, such as an ape or any of the more intelligent zoo inmates, leaning against the bars of his cage; gazing wistfully out at those who stare at him, helpless and mute, and painfully aware of his confinement. The Dylan Thomas quote: "Time held me green and dying, though I sang in my chains like the sea" to me, aptly frames this thought.
3. This movement is involved with frustration and rage. The confined one shaking the bars of his cage; trembling with enormous temper; aggressive, hostile and violent, the futility of his rebellion only serves to further inflame his anger.

These ideas, although they came to me in terms of animals in the zoo, could also be applied to human prisoners as well. My immediate experience of seeing prisoners is non-existent, and although it is moving to read about them, it does not tear at one's gut the way actually seeing someone or some creature in a situation such as this does. So let it remain that this piece is essentially about any living creature, confined against its will to a life of imprisonment.

One needs to reflect and express admiration to Maestra Bond for her concerted effort in the development and presentation of the 1974 Cabrillo Music Festival. In addition to all that has been presented concerning her total contributions, she also presented verbal recognition to works by women composers of the past, including the noted Clara Schumann's Piano Variations on a Theme by Robert Schumann. This composition was included on the program and performed by Dennis R. Davies, director of the festival. Victoria Bond never disappointed musical circles with her inexhaustible contributions for this festival.

On August 19, 1974, Jack Benson wrote a review in the Santa Cruz Sentinel (Santa Cruz, California), which is partially reprinted here*:

Victoria Bond Steals Cabrillo Festival's Opening Concert

Before the concert began, Manuel Santana, President

*Reprinted by permission of the publisher.

of the Cabrillo Guild of Music, spoke briefly of a new direction the festival would take this season in an effort to involve the entire community.

One such break with the past was immediately apparent in the program: Of seven composers listed, the first five were women. Furthermore, the performing musicians were predominantly female, one of whom really stole the show. This was Victoria Bond, a charming young lady whose musical talents seem boundless.

After a pleasant, introspective reading by Davies of a set of piano variations which Clara Schumann wrote on a theme by her famous husband, Miss Bond appeared on stage carrying a lute. Accompanying herself, she sang a song composed by a 16th century duchess named Leonora Orsina.

Miss Bond's voice was rich and strong. She sang the first without ornamentation and then repeated it with the vocal embellishment characteristic of the period in music.

Next, she went to the piano and, again accompanying herself, sang Larime Mie, a sacred song by Barbara Strozzi, adopted daughter of the 17th Century poet Giulio Strozzi.

This was only the beginning, however, for now Miss Bond took stage to combine her talents as a singer and instrumentalist with those of composer and conductor.

She actually sang while conducting her own Suite aux Troubadours, a group of medieval songs and dances which she had recomposed in modern musical syntax using an ensemble of violin, cello, lute, oboe and flute. The scoring was sparse and clean and the performances excellent.

The talented Victoria Bond authored a sensitive and provocative article, "Closet Composers: A Portrait of Doriana Gray," published in the International Musician, July 1975. She eloquently related the unfortunate plight of creative women and the pressures of society. The following are excerpts*:

"To be ladylike" was the goal instilled in most young women, and being an artist meant the uncomfortable and often unrewarding climb away from the

*Reprinted by permission of the publisher.

ordinary. It also meant long hours spent alone, which involved the curtailment of many social functions long cherished as the sole responsibility of women. When you are immersed in the bringing to life of an idea, most other daily considerations seem trivial by comparison. It was a dangerous thing for a woman to realize her own creative potential because someone had to be relied on to "mind the home" and if it was not she, then who would do it? Thus it became her "Divine Mission" to aid and support others whose mission was somehow considered to be more important than her own.

I have never known an intelligent mind, either male or female, at any age, not to be investigative and aggressive. The passive personality is one with less desire to probe, and this is not a biological, but a psychological factor. I know fully as many passive men as passive women.

Until we know the whole picture, we cannot criticize the details. The past does not necessarily predict the future. As we grow to greater realization of ourselves and our potential creativity, we begin to understand that the mind is not restricted by the body. We may learn through experience, but if what we create is no more than a recreation of our mundane existence, then our expressive palette is extremely limited. Unlike the actor, a creative artist is not typecast by his or her physical self. A woman is no more limited to expressing her "femaleness" than Toulouse Lautrec was to drawing his misshapen body. The realm of imagination goes far beyond the known realm.

It is necessary to re-evaluate ourselves as women and creators, and to encourage those whose courage has been shaken. This year marks the first International Women's Year, designed by the United Nations to call attention to the creative talents of women which have been overlooked, unsung and generally ignored, for so long.

Ms. Bond's composition Conversation Pieces was performed in a concert in the Summergarden of the Museum of Modern Art on August 15, 1975. The composition is scored for viola and vibraphone producing an electrifying tonal combination. Conversation Piece tingled the ears and left a lasting impression with the audience; new, different, and evocative timbre was displayed in this work by violist Karen Phillips and vibes player Martin Kluger. The composition was easily rated number one on the program which included: Caoltro for flute and piano, and Three Pieces for clarinet and piano by Daria Semegen, O Aderyn Purby/Clair Polin, and Daysongs by Nancy Laird Chance.

Victoria Bond offers the following personal comments on Conversation Piece, and reflects on the development from a composer's point of view:

> Conversation Piece was written as a theme and seven variations. The theme is stated as a recitative by the viola with the vibraphone as accompanist. The first variation is a cadenza for vibraphone solo, in which the use of the pedal speed is treated as an ornament in much the same way that the use of vibrato, both slow and fast, was treated in the viola's recitative. A duet follows in which the vibraphone has the melodic interest and the viola accompanies. Variation Three isolated a passage from the vibraphone cadenza which is played in augmentation by the viola in its highest register while the vibraphone, in its lowest register, rushes about with a nervous series of ascending figures. Variation Four is a cadenza for solo viola in which a question, stated fortissimo and agitatio in the upper register is answered by a tranquillo pianissimo in the low register. This conversation becomes quite animated until the roles are reversed. The cadenza concludes with arpeggio figures which lead into Variation Five which is titled: "Changing surfaces over a deep stillness." The viola begins the hypnotic, repetitive figures as an accompaniment to the vibraphone's recitative. The two exchange roles and the vibraphone's repeated notes lead into Variation Six which is a series of canons based on the motives of the theme. Variation Seven is a fast dance movement of a light-hearted and joking nature, suggestive of jazz improvisation.

Victoria Bond conducted a program with the Columbia University Orchestra of New Orchestral Work by female composers in 1975. The concert included the world premiere of Elizabeth Lutyens's Karinina, a chamber work for solo viola and eleven wind and percussion instruments. One leading music critic considered it the best piece of music programmed and the best performance. Other works included Julia Smith's Concerto for Piano and Orchestra, Grete von Zieritz's Concerto for Flute, Clarinet, Bassoon and Orchestra, Jean Eichelberger Ivey's Testament of Eve, and Germaine Tailleferre's Overture for Orchestra. The program received funding from the National Federation of Music Clubs.

Ms. Bond's compositions have been performed throughout the country and she has received many excellent reviews. She considers each piece a separate world in itself, and it never happens twice the same way. Composing is marvelously unpredictable according to Bond and sometimes results from literary, visual, improvising, or performing experiences. When asked about her style, she gave an impish grin, laughed and said, "In the words of Louis Armstrong, 'You blows what's you is.' " Sonata for Cello and Piano, composed by Bond in 1971, was conceived as a work in one continuous movement for the purpose of exploring the possibilities of change and evolution without reaching a conclusive resting point or cadence until the very end of the piece. The piece is ten minutes in length and has been recorded by Ms. Bond, with Gilberto Mungia on cello, on Laurel-Protone Records (2451 Nichols Canyon, Los Angeles, California 90046. No. LP-13).

Having prepared for a dual career as composer-conductor, Victoria Bond was offered many guest conducting appearances even before her doctorate degree was conferred. Her talent with the baton was quickly recognized as the result of the quality of her musical experiences and the long arduous hours devoted to the study and development of her creative ability. Bond believes that conducting is really a question of stamina and being able to stand the hard knocks that are dealt when nobody believes in you. Few people are willing to take the first step and take a chance on an unknown commodity. A conductor must have 100 percent faith in her ability to do what she wants to do. The work is the great satisfaction; success is purely a by-product. One must enjoy the conducting, the study, the rehearsals and the daily living with music. Performance is only the tip of the iceberg.

Victoria Bond was appointed guest conductor of the Aspen Music Festival in 1975 and was Assistant Conductor of the Opera Department. She conducted several inspiring concerts including the Colorado premiere of Ingolf Dahl's

Saxophone Concerto with Harvey Pittel as soloist. Professor Dahl was one of Bond's former composition teachers.

In 1977 Victoria Bond returned to Evergreen, Colorado, to conduct several programs as Assistant Conductor of the Colorado Philharmonic. The season was most rewarding in terms of making music and working with people to help them give the best possible performance. Her composition Equinox, originally a ballet score commissioned by the Pennsylvania Ballet and choreographed by Denverite Lynne Taylor, received its premiere performance as a concert suite. Orchestrated for full orchestra, it is published by Seesaw Music. Robert Micklin, reviewing this ballet for Newsday (Nassau edition) in November 1977, called this ballet "The Ostensible Showpiece of the Pennsylvania Ballet New York six-day engagement." He felt that Bond's music "had bite and direction." The ballet was inspired by the concept of duality found in the writings of Hermann Hesse and, more particularly, by his medieval story of Narcissus and Goldmund, in which spirit and flesh are personified by two different men. The monk, dedicated to life of the spirit, discovers in one of his students the gift for life in the world and helps him begin his journey. By opposite paths, they reach the same destination.

Victoria Bond is in the position of launching a prestigious career, including music director of the New Amsterdam Symphony Orchestra in New York, and a conducting position with one of America's leading symphony orchestras. Her responsibilities as conducting assistant for the Pittsburgh Symphony Orchestra and music director/conductor of the Pittsburgh Youth Symphony Orchestra mark a milestone in the history of music. Never before has a woman been appointed to these positions with a major symphony orchestra. Dr. Bond is proficient, and her ability is recognized even in the conservative musical institutions, a rare good omen for women conductors of the future.

The year 1978 was an especially tremendous one for Maestra Bond who covered all Pittsburgh rehearsals of the Pittsburgh Symphony and was in charge of all conducting, rehearsals, personnel, and programming for the Pittsburgh Youth Symphony Orchestra. This orchestra has a membership of more than one hundred musicians ranging in age from early teens to early twenties.

Maestra Bond has been accepted on her own merits, and musicians are unprejudiced when they work under a conductor who is intelligent, knows how to listen, and focuses so intensely that nothing escapes her attention. The sex of the conductor is not important, only the ability to musically communicate is rated, and obviously Bond scores in the top percentile. Victoria Bond still continues her successful composing career and received commissions from both the Theater Dance Collection and Fairmont State College in 1978. Bond, like all successful composers, has gone through many phases: harmonies achieved via the twelve tone row, tonal idioms, aleatoric passages, improvisation, and at times a bit of neoclassicism. She continues to search and seek new tonal combinations and forms that can best express her ideas.

On Sunday December 3, 1978, Maestra Bond conducted The New Amsterdam Symphony Orchestra in an American Opera Gala. The audience was mesmerized by the expressiveness of the conductor; each movement sparked with creativity and the orchestra responded to the smallest movement of her hand. The entire concert was conducted with sensitivity toward every detail. The program included The King's Breakfast (1973) by Joyce Barthelson, The Shepherdess and the Chimneysweep (1962) music by Julia Smith, and The Nightingale and the Rose by Margaret Garwood.

All great conductors build their reputation on visibility and verbal support at a certain level from the musical community. Victoria Bond established her credentials while still in graduate school, and they are seriously respected by the musical establishment. She is perhaps the epitome of the twentieth-century enlightened woman. She is well educated, a cultured woman, fine musician, respected composer, and talented conductor. She is fluent in languages and an accomplished scholar. She is articulate and compassionate and enjoys conversation. She is an avid environmentalist and has several hobbies including horseback riding, hiking, dancing and cooking. Based on the brilliance of her achievements, Victoria Bond could become the first permanent woman conductor of a major symphony orchestra in the United States.

Partial List of Compositions

1967 Pastorale, woodwinds
1969 Duet, flute and viola
1969 Mirror, Mirror, flute, viola, piano
1969 Trio, for brass
1969 Variations for Flute

1970 Cornography, soprano and chamber orchestra
1970 Quintet, for woodwinds
1970 Suite aux Troubadours, soprano and chamber orchestra
1970 Cannons, clarinet and violin
1970 Recitative, English horn and string trio
1970 Interludes, chamber orchestra
1970 Sonata, cello and piano
1971 Mirror of Nature, film
1971 Menage a Trois, alto flute, bass clarinet, E^b saxophone
1972 Five Preludes
1972 C. A. G. E. D. , for strings
1973 Sonata, for orchestra
1973 Aria, soprano and strings
1975 Conversation Piece, viola and vibraphone
1976 From And Antique Land, song cycle--soprano and piano
1977 Equinox, ballet
1978 Tarot, chorus and percussion
1978 A Woman's Journey, theater dance

ANTONIA BRICO

Conductor, Musician, Teacher

The documentary film Antonia: A Portrait of the Woman depicts the life of Dr. Antonia Brico, musician and conductor. Folksinger Judy Collins and Jill Godmilow touched the hearts and minds of millions of people when they produced this award-winning film in 1974. They projected a prime star, but they also deserve credit for the tremendous impact this biographical movie produced. Dr. Brico, the teacher, and Judy Collins, the student--what love, compassion and respect had to exist to produce this film. Dr. Brico, pioneer woman orchestra conductor in America, had been lost in a shadow for some forty years after a brilliant conducting career as a young woman in both Europe and the United States. Brico said, "I had an active artistic life before the filming, but I wanted more than what I was doing; I conducted, but not enough."

On August 3, 1975, after the film had been released, the conductor Brico was reborn: at the age of seventy-three she conducted at Avery Fisher Hall. Stepping on the podium, Brico was greeted with a standing ovation. What had evaded the talented Brico for almost forty years had finally been reached. How sweet the sound of applause must have been to the ears of the conductor. That evening she conducted the Beethoven Second Symphony and the Mozart Haffner Symphony. The performance was outstanding proof that conducting talent is inborn and remains active and pulsating even though denied the prestigious podium for so many years. (Columbia records released the recording debut of Antonia Brico in 1976, as number M 33888. Selections on the recording include Mozart Symphony No. 35 in D Major (Haffner), Overture to the Marriage of Figaro, K. 492, Overture to the Magic Flute, K. 620 and Overture to Don Giovanni, K. 527.

Thousands of young women musicians and artists are in desperate need of a role model. Antonia Brico epitomizes

ANTONIA BRICO
(Photo by Ellen Shub)

superbly that model. Talented women must be able to attain the most prestigious podiums in America and Brico was the first woman in America to pave the way. Dr. Brico had to spend many years of her life struggling financially, but not artistically. When the fame of the podium evaded her, she turned to teaching. Judy Collins was one of her many private piano students. Antonia Brico was born in 1902 in Rotterdam, Holland, and came to the United States in 1907 with her foster parents. At the age of ten she attended an outdoor band concert in her hometown; with the remembrance of those sounds a dream was born. She, too, would make beautiful music by waving a baton like conductor Paul Stemdoff did at that performance. That she was female made absolutely no difference to the ten year old. Only the dream of conducting was important.

Antonia was a determined, sensitive, bright, and emotional youngster who began to develop her talents studying the piano, and eventually studied Bach for fifteen years with the renowned Albert Schweitzer, whom she idolized. The combination of the young Brico and the noted Schweitzer was to meld her mind and heart in a quest for unknown heights and levels of achievements. Brico was, in every sense, a Schweitzer protégée.

Albert Schweitzer, one of the greatest people of the twentieth century, was one of Brico's two great loves in life. Antonia Brico says,

> Albert Schweitzer was the greatest individual to have ever been--his reverence for life was not just humans, but also animals, town, country, and the universe. He did what he wanted to, administering to the sick and the poor, and for that he gave up organ playing which was the most wonderful thing in the world to him. I was present when Columbia Recording Company officials offered him a fantastic amount of money for his hospital if he would make recordings--and I know the happiest times I ever saw him was when he had to practice for these recording sessions.

In 1978 Brico was engaged to conduct in Brussels for a huge benefit concert in honor of Schweitzer. The profits went to the Albert Schweitzer Foundation. Her admiration, love and respect for Schweitzer shall remain for as long as she breathes.

After earning her degree at Berkeley College in California in 1923, Dr. Brico spent six years in Germany studying conducting under the great Karl Mück, who was conductor of the Boston Symphony Orchestra from 1913-1917. These were arduous and demanding years, and Brico learned the art of conducting with complete devotion to the music and the teachings of Mück. She was graduated from the Master School of Conducting at Berlin State Academy of Music. Brico received her first honorary Doctor's Degree from Mills College in 1938. The citation read, "To Antonia Brico for outstanding contributions to the progress of music." In 1978, Dr. Brico will receive her eighth honorary doctorate in honor of her outstanding achievements.

She made her debut in 1930 conducting the Berlin Philharmonic Orchestra. The following is from the New York Times of February 15, 1930:

MISS BRICO TRIUMPHS AS BERLIN CONDUCTOR*

San Francisco Girl Leads the Philharmonic Orchestra in Dvořák Symphony (Wireless to the New York Times)

> Berlin, February 14--Miss Antonia Brico of San Francisco, the first American woman to conduct a concert in Berlin, made a successful debut tonight with the Philharmonic Orchestra which followed her baton most enthusiastically in Dvořák's Symphony in D minor, eliciting thunderous applause. Miss Brico received many floral tributes.
>
> Many members of the American Colony and prominent residents of Berlin were in the audience. Miss Brico, who studied for two years under Professor Pruewer at the musical high school in Berlin on the recommendation of Dr. Karl Mück, hopes to direct concerts in California during the coming summer. She is now a coach at the Municipal Opera here.

The following article was published in the New York Times on January 27, 1931:

LEADS MÜCK'S ORCHESTRA*

> Miss Antonia Brico of California is the First Woman to Direct Group in Hamburg: January 26 (AP). A woman for the first time led Dr. Karl Mück's Philharmonic Orchestra here tonight. The conductor was an American, Miss Antonia Brico of Berkeley, Cal. Last year she created a sensation by being the first woman to conduct the Berlin Philharmonic Orchestra. She has been a pupil of Dr. Mück.
>
> Tonight's program, which pleased the capacity audience, included selections from Mozart, Beethoven and Brahms. Miss Brico took several curtain calls.

Miss Brico returned from Europe to make her American debut after receiving plaudits and accolades from the music critics. In July 1930, Antonia Brico conducted at the Hollywood Bowl Concert before 30,000 people. This was an auspicious beginning for the talented and popular young woman conductor. The career of Brico was a whirlwind of concerts in the early 1930's, and she received the praise of both continents.

The membership of all our major symphonic orchestras were men during this period of Brico's conducting career. "It's never been the men in the orchestras who denied me," Dr. Brico said. It is important to realize that professional musicians respect the ability of the person who waves the baton. This respect was accorded Antonia Brico as a professional musician, not as a lady professional.

Dr. Brico conducted four concerts with the White Plains Pops Orchestra series in the summer of 1933. The setting was the Country Centre of White Plains, N.Y., which had been transformed into a garden of trees, tables, and water fountains reflecting the colored lights that hung from the trees. Over 1,000 people heard this light classical program: Meistersinger Overture by Wagner, Nutcracker Suite by Tchaikovsky, Butterfly Fantasy by Puccini, Londonderry Air, Slavonic Dances by Dvořák, Valse Triste by Sibelius, Liebesfreud by Dreisler, and Les Preludes by Liszt. The orchestra was seated on a platform surrounded by evergreens and statues, setting the scene for a bit of Europe transferred to America.

In January 1933 Antonia Brico made her first New York appearance on the podium at the Metropolitan Opera House as conductor of the Musicians Symphony Orchestra. Membership was composed of unemployed New York and Westchester musicians. Before the third concert, the comments of baritone John Charles Thomas were disastrous when he refused to perform if Dr. Brico conducted this scheduled concert. He was afraid that the talented young conductor would upstage him. In spite of Mr. Thomas and his words, many famous musicians and conductors did believe in Antonia Brico and her ability to conduct. Included in this list were such famous names as Bruno Walter, Arthur Rubinstein, Albert Schweitzer, and Karl Mück.

The following review by Olin Downes appeared in the New York Times on February 8, 1933*:

> Miss Brico's conducting confirmed an early impression of her accomplishments. She accompanied the Strauss songs with sonorities well designed to match the volume of Mme. Schumann's voice. She then conducted two orchestra compositions of completely opposed character, and in each of these, proved her knowledge of her scores, her careful study of every detail and her good technical power over the orchestra. An orchestra of a personnel which is not equal in all of its parts to the best elements of the whole, obeyed her implicitly with a cleanness of attack, balance and care in phrasing, that bespoke the leader's knowledge and control.
>
> Miss Brico has an obvious talent for conducting, and she has laid her groundwork very well. She did not perform Debussy's music as if it were Strauss, but in a manner appropriate to its particular style. While she could not expect a perfect and highly sensitized reading of Fêtes, she did secure one that was clean, with careful gradation of sonority, and that left no detail of the scoring unnoticed. The tempi in Strauss's Don Juan were

> singularly well chosen, if one excepts pages near the conclusion. In these places the conductor was a little precise, so that the music lost a measure of its impetuosity and its lava flow of emotion. This young conductor gives the impression of being meticulous in detail. The brushstrokes are not broad enough. On no occasion was the orchestra given its head. On the other hand, when a concert is given under the circumstances and for the purposes of the Musicians Symphony, the first requisite is care, accuracy, sureness.

In November 1934 a small group of women approached Brico and asked her to conduct for them. She agreed and worked hard to collect and build the orchestra, a difficult task under even the best conditions. To obtain support, Conductor Brico conferred with Mrs. Franklin D. Roosevelt at the White House and won her assistance. She then went to Mayor Fiorello La Guardia of New York City and his wife, who agreed to act as sponsors. This was an important step in the success of the orchestra. In February 1935 Antonia Brico realized one of her dreams when she conducted her own orchestra of 100 musicians in New York's Town Hall concert. The determined women musicians, dressed in black frocks with white Buster Brown collars, performed the music of Handel, Schumann and Tchaikovsky. Elfrieda Mestecbkih was concertmaster.

No salary was paid, but the women shared any profits left, after paying expenses on a pro-rata basis. Most of the musicians made their living in broadcasting or concert work, and were not always able to attend rehearsals on a regular basis. Conductor Brico felt that Muriel Watson, Tympani player, was a genius, "who equals and surpasses many men I have heard."

Brico's talent, confidence, and ability with the baton produced performances that were widely recognized and applauded. She molded the orchestra to the level of professional status within a few months. Dr. Brico said, "I'm opposed to segregation. I formed the women's symphony but when I proved my point, that women were capable of playing every instrument, I then changed the group to a mixed orchestra. I don't believe in groups that are just women conductors, composers or musicians. In life both sexes mix, and in music they should do the same."

Dr. Brico had the famous music critic Olin Downes, then working for the New York Times, as a supporter. He made arrangements for her to meet the acclaimed Finnish composer-musician Sibelius. This was the beginning of Brico's second love in life and she affectionately called him "Papa." Jean Sibelius, national hero of Finland and internationally renowned composer, said of Brico, "A conductor and an artist who understands how to exalt the music and the listeners." Brico later provided the answer to a perplexing question that had baffled music listeners for over twenty years. Why was there not a surge of Sibelius' music printed and played following his death? Brico said, "He had requested of his daughter that she destroy much of his music at his death because he knew he had reached the culmination of his creative genius when he finished writing his Symphony No. 7 in C." During one of her many trips to Finland, she was invited to conduct the Helsinki Symphony in a command performance for Queen Elizabeth of Belgium.

Brico's career as a brilliant young conductor lasted until 1937, when success began evading her. It is impossible that her musical ability had declined, so one must point a finger at the idiosyncrasies of society--non-acceptance of a woman in a traditionally male role, members in the audience feeling compelled to comment on the physical aspect of conducting, professional jealousy, and the absence of women musicians in orchestras. Perhaps Dr. Brico is correct when she says, "I was a novelty at first."

Arthur Judson, who had a monopoly on conductors, and who managed both the New York Philharmonic and the Philadelphia Orchestra, told Brico "she was born fifty years too early." This comment proved to be correct and the brilliant and talented woman conductor found it difficult to accept. The obstacles thrown in her way included the comments made by the doyenne of the Lewisohm Stadium, Mrs. Charles S. Guggenheimer, who strongly felt that it was "The greatest disgrace in the world for a woman to conduct the New York Philharmonic Orchestra." Brico was asked to conduct only because four thousand people signed a petition requesting her. In 1937, Mrs. Guggenheimer's purse was a powerful indication of her strength. Financial backing was then, and still remains today, a necessity to the continuation and propagation of the Arts. As a conductor, Brico had the support of leading men such as Arthur Judson, Dr. Karl Mück, and Arthur Rubinstein. They believed in her ability and talent to stand on the podium. Yet, the "power of the purse" was to influence her destiny.

However, she never allowed anyone to deflect her from her course, even when many notables felt that it was ridiculous for a woman to pursue a conducting career. "If you want to do something, you do it, and don't let a single thing stand in your way." Bless Brico for her determination and courage.

In 1942, Dr. Brico established her home in Denver, Colorado, and conducted the Denver Businessmen's Orchestra. She had directed this orchestra for over thirty years without a contract; this is amazing in the world of professional music circles. This orchestra performs five concerts per year, not nearly enough to satisfy the demands of the gifted conductor. In 1948 she became the permanent conductor of the orchestra and in 1969 the semi-professional group was renamed "Brico Symphony" in her honor. Antonia Brico was to teach and direct the Brico Symphony for some 27 years. These performances were nibbles which left the musical appetite of this giant unsatisfied. During these years she established her reputation as a teacher of voice, piano, and conducting. She was a noted lecturer throughout the United States and kept her mind mentally sharp by continuing to study, practice, and act as a guest conductor in Europe. Dr. Brico conducted many successful concert tours in Mexico, Japan, Germany, Italy, Belgium, and the United States, but the most endearing experience was in Holland when she conducted and received the thunderous applause of her own country people.

The determined Brico always dreamed that she would return again to the podium of major symphony orchestras. Thanks to Judy Collins and her documentary film in 1974, the dreams became reality and the renaissance of the brilliant Brico will be remembered by millions of people.

In the New York Times on Monday, August 4, 1975, Donal Henahan indicated that Brico's return to the podium in New York, after almost forty years, to direct a Mostly Mozart festival was an irresistibly sentimental occasion. She conducted the program following the showing of the film Antonia: A Portrait of a Woman. "Allegro con" Brico conducted Mozart's Haffner Symphony and Beethoven's Symphony No. 2 in a thoroughly professional manner. Donal Henahan felt*

> there were tentative moments in the opening movements in both compositions and that the Beethoven went somewhat too sedately for his listening taste. But the Mozart had rhythmic bite and wonderfully delicate interplay among the sections. The Beethoven was classically proportioned, with regular tempos and enough finely drawn detail to keep one absorbed throughout.

The Brico concert originally scheduled for one presentation was so popular that a second performance was held a few days later.

In August of 1975, Antonia Brico was one of three judges in the International Bach Competition. The twenty-seven men and women were required to play the Goldberg Variations. Specific instructions indicate that it is to be played on the harpsichord with two keyboards. A transcription is required to transfer this music to the single keyboard of the modern piano. The last movement of Barber's Sonata was also performed. This competition was held behind a screen, similar to auditions for many major symphony orchestras in the United States. Keyboard professionals are aware of the strength in the hands that is necessary to perform the Goldberg Variations and Barber's Sonata. The winners of this competition turned out to be a woman in both first and second place. One winner was only seventeen years old. One male judge couldn't believe he had voted for a girl. Brico said of his comment, "I was thoroughly disgusted." It is important to hold auditions and competitions behind screens so that judges, such as the above mentioned one, cannot be biased. Talent is the only criterion to be judged.

Dr. Brico's talents were again in demand, and she was scheduled to conduct the following concerts in 1975: Mozart Festival at the Lincoln Arts Center, The National Symphony Orchestra at the Kennedy Center, The Seattle Symphony Orchestra, The American Symphony Orchestra in New York, and The Hollywood Bowl.

In August of 1975, in observance of International Women's Year, Antonia Brico was saluted at the John F. Kennedy Center for the Performing Arts. This was the first time since 1941 that Brico conducted the National Symphony Orchestra. Dr. Brico opened the program conducting Joyce Barthelson's overture to Feathertop. The composer, then seventy-five years old, was an honored guest at the concert. Perhaps the adage "She who waits will be rewarded" could have some meaning, but the waste of talent for so many years is difficult to accept. Later, in 1978 in White Plains, New York, Brico conducted the premiere of Barthelson's opera The Devil's Disciple, based on a Bernard Shaw writing.

Antonia Brico can conduct at the age of seventy-two because her ability to wield the baton is as unhampered as at the age of twenty-eight. Brico believes in physical fitness and feels that conductors live a long time because they exercise their arms and lungs so much. Since legs are also important for a conductor she "rides a bicycle regularly to keep the lower parts fit." She conducts as an artist, not as a woman. What matters is the concert and the quality of performance. If we close our eyes then only the ears and the mind can perceive the burden of responsibility. She is a dedicated and determined conductor. Whenever Maestra Brico steps on the podium the orchestra unites behind her; musicians respect the ability of the conductor, not the sex of the person.

Thomas Willis, music critic for the Chicago Tribune, wrote the following review on January 13, 1976:

MANY THRONG TO BRICO'S PERFORMANCE*

Antonia Brico: Tenacity to Be Respected

> A friend, who has been in the reviewing business a good deal longer than I, once estimated that no more than one-fourth of the average symphony orchestra audience attended concerts to hear the music. I could not help thinking of the statement Monday night as a capacity benefit crowd thronged into the Auditorium Theatre to hear Antonia Brico conduct her first local concert in 35 years.
>
> During the two years since the Judy Collins-Jill Godmilow documentary attempted to make her the Albert Schweitzer of the women's movement, her ability to attract listeners nationwide has continued to increase. Much of it is no doubt due to the combination of factors Ron Dorfman isolated in the program's Brico biography--guilt, anger, curiosity,

*Reprinted, courtesy of the Chicago Tribune.

and admiration for her determination and tenacity. The film made its points well, and the emotional involvement produced would be expected to carry over into the concert hall.

But is she any good? Was sex discrimination the culprit in the collapse of her career after excellent training here and in Germany? Or was she simply another of those strong starters who lose momentum after the novelty of a new face--or in her case, figure--has lost its appeal? She was discriminated against, no doubt about it. To have made an international conducting career as a female, one would have had to be so good that both orchestras and audiences regarded you as irreplaceable. It has always been that way with oppressed minorities. To succeed you have to try harder than anyone else. And in the arts, there is the matter of talent.

Dr. Antonia Brico maintains an exhausting schedule of lecturing, rehearsing and guest conducting both in this country and abroad. Her recent guest conducting appearance was reviewed by Jerry Klein for the Peoria Star Journal, March 21, 1979:

SYMPHONY'S GUEST BRICO OFFERS ELOQUENT FLUENCY IN LANGUAGE OF MUSIC*

It is said that Antonia Brico speaks six languages, but surely the most fluent, the most eloquent of all is her music.

Last night in a guest conducting role with the Peoria Symphony, she offered a brilliant program beautifully controlled, excitingly played and dominated by a personality so immersed in music that both she and her audiences are transformed by it.

There she came out of the wings, slightly bent, pulling herself onto the podium, a pause, and then spinning magic. She has wisdom now, and experience, and one can sense it in that careful knitting and purling of intricate motifs into themes, phrases and movements to become a magnificent whole fabric.

Her interpretation of the Sibelius Fifth Symphony,

*Reprinted by permission of the author.

a complex, difficult work, was extraordinary.

It seemed as if she were intoxicated with the music, becoming almost ageless, a disembodied participant in the great creative cycle. It breathed, swelled, grew, becoming so full of emotion and power as to be spellbinding, awesome. It was a major achievement, for her and for the orchestra.

But not the only one of the evening. The program opened with the Beethoven Prometheus Overture, Op. 43, done with a clean, driving power.

Then came the Debussy Prelude to the Afternoon of a Faun, lush and full of sunlight and dappled shadows. The woodwinds sounded rich and sensuous, compelling as Pan's pipes in some sunlit meadow, the harp rippling like wavelets, the strings ripe as midsummer wheat.

It was aural, of course, but nonetheless powerfully evocative, calling to mind some Monet landscape, some cool, green garden.

The Benjamin Britten Four Sea Interludes from Peter Grimes, similarly, were shot through with visual suggestions, of tall masted ships, straining canvas and the endless sweep of water and sky. Britten uses the entire orchestra, even to chimes and gongs, painting these seascapes, and the orchestra responded beautifully, playing with the kind of force that could almost be felt.

But is was perhaps in the Sibelius that Brico and the orchestra reached the most formidable expressiveness, performing with control, balance and soaring emotion. It has the trappings of being monumental.

At its conclusion, Dr. Brico wove her way through the orchestra, personally thanking and congratulating principal players and winning a prolonged and affectionate storm of applause. She is called the first lady of music for what are now obvious reasons. It is a language she speaks most persuasively.

The great Antonia Brico says, "Talent is inborn, the genes determine one's ability, but a woman must be five times better than a male if she is to conduct from prestigious podiums; the podiums of major symphony orchestras in the United States remain the last stronghold of male domination in America." Evgenia Svetlana of Russia has for years been respected on the podiums of her country. It is difficult both to accept the recital of subjugation that Antonia Brico endured and to hold back one's feelings and anger at the agitation illustrated by society. Certainly, Dr. Brico suffered years of frustration and torment, and the world of music suffered, too, because she was denied the podium where she could best share her ability and talent. It is sad and frightening to realize that societal attitudes almost destroyed one of America's "Leading Ladies."

RADIE BRITAIN

Composer, Writer, Teacher

Radie Britain, creative genius of the twentieth century, has received over fifty national and international awards for her composing. She is also a prolific writer whose most recent book, Composer's Corner, has been acclaimed throughout the world.

Britain's ability to create musical beauty in over one-hundred and fifty classical compositions is enhanced by her power to eloquently communicate with the written word. Miss Britain writes that a person must "escape the evils of conformity in order to create." For her the time is best passed sitting at one of her two Steinway pianos, which have served as the catalysts to her freedom since she was a child in Texas.

Britain feels,

> Going into the cathedral of silence, we are able to eliminate the static in our lives in order to discover inspired melodies. We should not work with anxiety, but with expectancy.

Radie Britain was born on a ranch near Amarillo, Texas, in 1903. Her parents pioneered many sections of land as cattle ranchers. They moved to the college town of Clarendon, Texas, when she was a young child. Her mother was to influence her talented child through the love of the arts, the importance of education and the encouragement of Radie's fullest potential as an individual. At the age of seven, she began the study of piano by attending Clarendon College Conservatory of Music. Her teachers were from Leipzig and Dresden, Germany.

Miss Britain's parents, Katie L. and Edgar Charles Britain, provided her with the very best musical training

RADIE BRITAIN
(Photo by Mauricé--Chicago)

possible in both America and Europe. Their remarkable foresight and encouragement prepared the talented girl to fully explore and develop in the world of creative expression. She diligently pursued her demanding studies and has shared her creative ability with music and words.

Radie Britain's father never wanted her to leave the state of Texas. "He adored me and I worshipped him," said Miss Britain. "He loved Texas and the great outdoors. As I rode my horse, my arms would float with the reins and I would dream I was conducting. I also dreamed that I would bring honor and fame to my parents' name." Radie Britain did accomplish this, but through composing and writing rather than by conducting.

Radie Britain comments on her native state of Texas: "I enjoyed the pioneer life and it has been reflected in my composing." One need only to listen to her orchestral compositions Canyon, Drouth, Red Clay, Paint Horse and Saddle, Chicken in the Rough, and Cactus Rhapsody to immediately recognize this influence.

Most parents during this time would never permit their daughters to travel alone and reside in a large city, but Britain's father felt she would accomplish more if she were alone. His theory proved correct. She enrolled in the American Conservatory and studied with two inspirational teachers, Heniot Levy and Frank Van Dusen. She studied piano, organ, and composition, and graduated with honors. During the first semester her piano teacher Heniot Levy never complimented her, but at Christmas time he said, "If you keep working hard you will receive your teaching certificate at the end of the school year." Britain could hardly believe it, because she had suffered such agony by the silent treatment she had received.

Following graduation Radie Britain knew that if she ever wanted to compose she would have to go to Europe to study. Her father said, "No daughter of mine will ever cross that ocean." Each time she brought home a certificate her father thought she had finished studying. She started to teach piano privately and saved her money. She also continued to perform and study privately. Finally her father realized that she was determined to go to Europe and he relented.

She first studied in Berlin but that was a disaster, neither of her teachers spoke English. Following this episode she went to Munich to hear a friend's debut and was introduced to Dr. Albert Noelte. He promised to assist her with her compositions if she would move to Munich. She did, and following the first lesson he said, "You have talent. I'm going to pass on to you all the knowledge I have." Radie Britain is certain that her creative ability would never have been uncovered if she had not met Dr. Albert Noelte. She later did advanced piano work with Joseph Pembauer and Alice Ripper.

Richard Strauss, then conductor of the Munich Opera Company, was a close friend of Noelte as were many other important musicians that were introduced to Radie. As music critic, Dr. Noelte was able to supply tickets for any concert that Radie desired to hear. This was a marvelous experience for this young aspiring composer. She enrolled in the master classes of Leopold Gadowsky and studied organ with Pietro Yon and Marcel Dupre.

Miss Britain confided, "Dr. Noelte fell in love with me--but I wasn't in love with him. However, it did make him more interested in my compositions and he helped me secure my first music published."

Her debut as a composer was made in Munich, Germany with the baritone Eric Wildhagen, of the Munich Opera Company and Miss Britain as the accompanist. Presented at that performance in the late 1920's were her songs Had I a Cave (Robert Burns), published by Otto Halbrieter; Open the Door (Robert Burns), published by Robert B. Brown Music Company; Withered Flowers (Friedl Schreyvogal), published by Composers Press; and Immortality, unpublished. She received raving press reviews from seven German newspapers including the following brief excerpts:

> Munich Post by Dr. H. Nuessle. The songs are proof of a highly cultured, refined musician and sensitive emotional conception, in the harmonic treatment of modern modernity, but here also showing fascinating personal traits.
>
> Munich, Neueste Nachrichten. Be it said beforehand that these songs met with unusual success. They show all signs of an equally noble and refined talent in their strongly expressive melodic line, which in connection with an uncommonly rich harmonic background really deepened the atmosphere and the emotional contents of the poems.
>
> Seebote, Germany. An artistic climax was reached with the first performance of four songs by the genially gifted American composer, Radie Britain. From each of these songs speaks an artistic soul of profound tenderness and high culture, an artist, whose extremely sensitive, melodic and uncommonly interesting harmonic mode of expression does, in a masterly way, justice to the most variegated phrases of the tastefully chosen poems.

Radie Britain studied with Albert Noelte for a period of two years. When she returned to the United States following the death of her younger sister, Noelte told her, "If you cannot return, I will come to America and see that you complete your studies." Noelte did come to America as an instructor of composition and counterpoint at Northwestern University. Britain was then instructor of harmony and counterpoint at the Chicago Conservatory.

Noelte realized it would take Radie Britain several years to master the necessary materials to become an outstanding composer. When she composed Saturnale for orchestra in 1933 the teacher-student relationship with Noelte became estranged. He heard the Chicago Symphony Orchestra rehearsing her new composition and threw up his hands and said, "That isn't the way I trained you, you're on your own, you don't need me." Miss Britain felt it was time to part because they were beginning to disagree, and she found a need to compose in her own idiom. These artistic personalities had, as is common, conflicts in personal tastes. Lives are lived in a series of platitudes, and this was just one part of a creative adventure for both of these outstanding musicians.

Miss Britain feels that women have traditionally had to work harder than men to achieve the same level of success. Her mother named her Radie because she felt it was a strong name and she wished her to be something special in life. Miss Britain said, "I never enjoyed my name until I started to create. Men always thought Radie was a man's name--so as long as I'm not seen, many people think my compositions are written by a man."

When Miss Britain's orchestral composition Heroic Poem was premiered by the Rochester Symphony Orchestra in 1932, she received an invitation to attend the performance from the conductor Howard Hanson addressed to Mr. Radie Britain. She refused this invitation, but did not disclose that she was a woman and at that time was some eight months pregnant. She had the opportunity to meet Howard Hanson some years later, and he was absolutely amazed that she was a woman. Heroic Poem received the International Award sponsored by the Hollywood Bowl in 1930 and in 1945 Britain was the first woman to receive the prestigious Juilliard National Prize in recognition of this composition. (The American Music Center is the distributor of Heroic Poem.)

Miss Britain wrote the following notes to accompany the score for Heroic Poem:

> This piece, dedicated to the memory of a heroic feat, does not desire to be classed as a "Symphonic Poem" in the generally accepted sense of this term. It does not attempt to picture, or to strictly follow, the various mechanical and realistic phases of this heroic adventure although, on the other hand, it does not entirely avoid allusion to such realistic phenomena as are characteristic of and inseparable from the nature of this adventure and the technical means of its realization.
>
> The composer's main object, however, was to try to express in sound the emotional phases of an adventure that might be called a prototype of modern romance: to touch upon its human aspects and its ethical meaning, not only in the relation to the individual, but to humanity in general. To the individual, the venturing hero, refer to the opening phrases; the sinister aspect of a bold inspiration at its first manifestation. To his human environments, his character and conquering spirit, refer certain lyrical as well as martial and ethical themes. According to the nature of the venture, the clash of motoric forces and that of an indomitable spirit with the threatening elements presented themselves for musical consideration as well as plausible uncertainty of the outcome, the increasing confidence of the final victory, and triumphant victory itself, and as emotion in its purest and most intense form reverts to the primitive, the composer thought it not amiss to make fragmentary use of the anthems of the two nations, thus symbolizing the appeal from soil to soil; an appeal that found its joyous echo in all humanity. And in the midst of the turbulent rejoicing stands the lone figure of the hero whose daring had materialized the dream of aeons.

Heroic Poem is dedicated to Charles Lindbergh's flight to Paris and was written in Chicago in 1929. In addition to the Rochester Symphony Orchestra's premiere performance conducted by Howard Hanson it has been performed by the Chicago Philharmonic conducted by Richard Czevwonsky, the Chicago Women's Symphony conducted by Ebba Sundstrum, and the Atlanta Symphony Orchestra conducted by Henry Sopkin.

Prelude to a Drama has been performed more than any of Britain's other orchestral compositions. The piece is six minutes in duration and flows with continuous rich and robust melodies and is filled with strong contrapuntal voices that weave in and out with passion and nobility. The composition was written in 1928, and is published by Seasaw Music Company. Scored for woodwinds, brass, tympani, percussion and strings, it was performed by the Chicago Symphony Orchestra in 1938, conducted by Dr. Frederick Stock. In 1950 the Los Angeles Philharmonic Orchestra conducted by Alfred Wallenstein presented the composition as did the following orchestras: Atlanta Symphony Orchestra in 1952, Henry Sopkin, conductor; a Cairo, Egypt Broadcast in 1955 by the United States Air Force Symphony of Washington, D. C., Colonel George Howard, conductor; and the Moscow Symphony Orchestra in 1961 with Konstantin Ivanov conducting.

In a rehearsal with the Illinois Symphony, Albert Goldberg, conductor, suddenly thrust the baton in Miss Britain's hand and said, "You know the correct tempos, conduct it." She took the baton with nervous anticipation; "we finished together." Britain realized that her musicianship had come to her rescue.

Herman Devries writing for the Chicago Examiner in 1938* offered the following review:

> Radie Britain's Prelude To A Drama voices the divine in music form, and under Frederick Stock's baton the work made an even deeper impression than upon the first hearing when it was premiered with the Illinois Symphony under the direction of Albert Goldberg. Few women composers have been so honored by our leading orchestras, and Stock and the Orchestral Association have done wisely in bringing to the public's notice a work of such great merit as to deserve a place in the regular repertory.
>
> Recalled several times at the conclusion of the work, Miss Britain can be sure of her success with the audience, orchestra and director.

The talented Britain was one of the first recognized

*This quote and the one below reprinted courtesy of the Chicago Tribune.

women composers in American twentieth-century music. She has composed over one-hundred and fifty compositions for orchestra, chamber ensembles, stage works, choral, piano, violin, harp and voice.

She received two invitations and spent two seasons at the MacDowell Colony in Peterboro, New Hampshire. It was during these summers at MacDowell that the young Miss Britain was to be influenced by Edward A. Filene of Boston. He and his secretary would often drive to Peterboro and invite Radie to spend weekends in Boston. Britain said,

> He was very active in politics and would practice his speeches and discuss world affairs. It meant a great deal to me to listen to him during my formative years and these visits helped build my character and confidence. I learned from him to always carry a pad and pencil or leave one in every room so when I had an idea I could write it down. Filene taught me not to try to carry every thought in my mind but to write it down and when I needed the idea I could refer to my paper. This has been helpful to me for many years.

During this period she composed Southern Symphony and Light. Southern Symphony was premiered by the Illinois Symphony Orchestra in 1940, conducted by Izler Solomon. The performance was reviewed by Herman Devries for the Chicago Examiner:

> In Radie Britain's Southern Symphony Izler Solomon picked a winner. The piece is generously dotted with Southern melodies, orchestrated in a manner that enhanced tenfold the value of their simplicity in an instrumentation alive and palpitating with the ardor of Miss Britain's Texas ancestry.

In 1935 her composition Light, dedicated to Thomas Edison, won the First National Prize sponsored by the Boston Women's Symphony Orchestra and was premiered by the Chicago Women's Symphony in 1938 conducted by Gladys Welge. The women symphony orchestras founded in the early part of the twentieth century were the result of women instrumentalists not being permitted to audition for the class A orchestras. (Today all major orchestras do permit women to audition, with these auditions usually held behind closed curtains, so the results are based solely on ability. As a result of this new method of audition, there are women in all major symphony orchestras in the United States. New Federal Guidelines likewise played a major role in the acceptance of professional women musicians.)

In 1935 Britain composed Prison (Lament), originally written for a student who played in a Russian balalaika orchestra. Later it was written for string quartet and orchestrated for chamber orchestra. Following a performance of the piece for violin and piano in Chicago, there was a bombastic shout of "Bravo! Bravo!" The same shouts were heard following the performance of Light and the enthused man ran backstage to meet the composer. He was the great sculptor Edgardo Simone, who told Britain, "the only other piece I liked as much as Light was Prison because he writes from the heart." Britain responded "I wrote Prison also." He enthusiastically answered, "You are a genius."

Simone and Britain were married for ten years until his untimely death. Their theme song was based around Prison and during their marriage, Radie Britain began to write a book on their great love life together, which exploded with temperament. Following his death she found a musical will he had placed in a folder on one of her Steinway pianos, but the manuscript was left unfinished for several years.

In 1978 Britain revised the manuscript she had started some years before, and completed it. The book, which she titled Bravo!, was being considered for a movie when I met her in 1979. It is a great love story of two talented and creative people. Said Britain, "We are all in prison as we struggle constantly to free ourselves."

Prison was performed at the White House in 1936 and it is believed that Miss Britain was the first classical American woman composer so honored. The following is an outline of some of Radie Britain's orchestral compositions and their premieres:

1) Izler Solomon, conductor of the Illinois Symphony Orchestra, premiered Rhapsody for Piano and Orchestra, Southern Symphony, and Drouth in the 1930's. In 1960, Drouth was performed by the Madrid Symphony Orchestra conducted by Vincenti Spiteri.

2) Dr. Howard Hanson, conductor of the Rochester Symphony Orchestra, premiered Canyon and Suite for

Strings (which received the First National Prize sponsored by Sigma Alpha Iota Musical Sorority in 1945).

3) Ruth Haroldson, conductor of the Whittier Symphony Orchestra, premiered Pastorale and San Luis Rey in the 1940's.

4) George Bledsoe and A. Clyde Roller, conductors of the Amarillo Symphony Orchestra, premiered Phantasy for Oboe and Orchestra and Cowboy Rhapsody in the 1950's.

5) Colonel George Howard, Major Arnold D. Gabriel and captain John F. Yesulaites, conductors of the United States Air Force Symphony, premiered Cactus Rhapsody, Saturnale, Angel Chimes, and Minha Terra in the 1960's.

6) Her compositions have been programmed not only in America's leading symphony orchestras but also in Spain, France, Russia, and Egypt.

Miss Britain composed Cosmic Mist Symphony in 1962 in three movements: In the Beginning, Nebula, and Nuclear Fission. For this work, she received the First National Prize of five-hundred dollars sponsored by the National League of American Pen Women in Washington, D.C. In 1964 it was selected for the symposium sponsored by the Rockefeller Foundation and performed by the Houston Symphony Orchestra, conducted by A. Clyde Roller.

When Radie Britain wrote her first orchestral composition in 1927 little did she realize what strange happenings would occur. Symphonic Intermezzo received its world premiere by the Women's Symphony Orchestra in Chicago, conducted by Ethel Leginska. It was repeated by the Boston Women's Symphony Orchestra.

When Ethel Leginska took her orchestra on tour she told Radie Britain that she would program her composition if she would tour with the orchestra and play in the percussion section. When Britain insisted that she had never played percussion instruments, Leginska said, "You write for those instruments, you should be able to play them." So Britain, hurriedly, took a few percussion lessons with a member of the Chicago Symphony Orchestra and went on tour with Leginska. Britain remarked, "If I had made a wrong entrance with my bombastic drum beat I'm sure, with Leginska's erratic temperament, she would have hurled her baton, instantaneously, at me." This tour was to conclude Britain's career as a percussionist!

Miss Britain has composed nine pieces for chamber orchestra. They include Chipmunks scored for woodwind, harp and percussion; Phantasy for oboe, harp and piano; Cactus Rhapsody for oboe, clarient and piano; and Portrait of Thomas Jefferson for string quartet. Also, she has written a string quartet in three movements. Miss Britain has received five First National Awards sponsored by the National League of Pen Women for her chamber works between the years 1936 and 1964. These works are excellent examples of her ability to mold beautiful vocal and instrumental sound into melodies and harmonies of lasting value.

Her ability to compose for choruses is enormous, with almost thirty pieces written for mixed chorus, women's voices, men's voices and scored for orchestral, piano and chamber group accompaniment. Nisan, composed for woman's voices from a text written by Kate Hammond and accompanied by strings and piano, received its world premiere in Detroit, Michigan, in 1963 conducted by Dr. Harry Seitz. It won First International Prize sponsored by Delta Omicron Fraternity. The work received a standing ovation and is published by Robert B. Brown Music Company.

Britain wrote a three-act opera with the text by the late Rupert Hughes, whom she had met at an ASCAP dinner. He desired to hear her music. "We made a date for eight o'clock the following evening. When he came, I told him I was just finishing dinner and offered him desert. He said, 'My darling, I thought you invited me for dinner.' It produced such a humorous situation between us--but a strong friendship developed. We spent many hours together, first having dinner at the Hollywood Brown Derby, and then working until midnight on the music and libretto for the opera, Carillon." Hughes felt that Britain was the one composer, of all the Americans, who could best write the music for the work. Miss Britain continued, "Working with Rupert Hughes was a great inspiration for me. He was a brilliant writer, music critic and movie producer. Following this opera we collaborated on several other works."

Her ten stage works include operettas, ballets, musical dramas and a chamber opera. In 1933, she orchestrated the ballet Wheel of Life that was performed in Chicago at the Goodman Theater by Diana Huebert and Cast. She received a commission from Marygrove College of Detroit, Michigan, to compose the music for Lady in the Dark from Shakespearean Sonnets in 1962. Saint Mary's College of Omaha, Nebraska, commissioned her in 1964 to write the music for the one hour performance of Western Testament written and directed by Sara Lee Stadelmen. This stage work received three major performances and television presentation in Omaha, Nebraska. Her chamber opera Kuthara, in three acts based on a text by Lester Luther, was first performed in Santa Barbara, California, in 1961 and was sponsored by the National Society of Arts and Letters.

Radie Britain's daughter, Lerae, received her Master's degree from the University of Southern California and teaches anthropology in Hawaii. She wrote the text in 1965 for The Builders and in 1963 for Awake to Life which her mother scored for mixed chorus. Awake to Life was premiered by the Southern California Mormon Choir, conducted by Frederick Davis. They collaborated on a book, Hawaiian Pianoramo. Lerae's historic writing on the Polynesian culture was very beneficial to her mother's search for authentic chants to the gods which culminated in a preservation of the Authentic Polynesian songs and dances in piano form.

Composer Britain's music is published by Neil Kjos Company; Walter T. Foster; Willis Music Company; Calvi Music Company; Ricordi and Sons of Brazil; Robert B. Brown Music Company; Heroic Music Publication; Seesaw Music Corporation; and Harold Branch Music Company of New York. A composer can best share her music through publications and recordings, for indeed, without these possibilities pitifully few people could share the musical genius of this outstanding twentieth-century woman, a recipient of ten consecutive ASCAP awards.

In 1975 her biographical material and forty manuscripts of her work were placed in the music library of the University of Wyoming, Laramie. Many of her scores are in the Library of Congress and in the Archives of Hans Moldenhouer in Spokane, Washington. The Fleisher Library (founded by Edward A. Fleisher as a hobby to collect manuscripts) in Philadelphia, Pennsylvania, has the entire orchestral collection of Radie Britain's compositions. This library makes the music available to conductors for performances. Fleisher hired copyists to write out all the parts to scores and they are kept in steel boxes. Said Britain, "It is marvelous to have the scores preserved for posterity."

Composer Britain has shared her intellectually stimulating life and her world travels with her late husband, the noted sculptor Edgardo Simone, and with her supportive husband, Ted Morton, one of the pioneers of aviation, who flew a Jenny in the early days. He was instrumental in opening many fine airports in the Middle West. The Morton Air Academy received a government contract, training many pilots during World War II.

No individual could possibly express with words the depth of feeling and expression that Radie Britain has created over a period of years with her writings. The reader can best appreciate her talent by reading A Mother's Message to Her Daughter.

> It is not the duration but the quality of life that is important. Remember, we are masters of our own fate and, hopefully, every experience guides us toward perfection.
>
> If we listen to our inner computer that is tuned into the Great Computer, our lives will reflect the Light of Love and we can erase the sharp edges of our personality. We must discard the chip on our shoulder against our fellowman for it only weighs us down. Rays of goodness should be so strong that they pierce directly through those who cross our path.
>
> God gave living space for everyone so avoid taking negative and destructive pictures. Look into life's mirror and see if the reflection measures up to the highest expectations of our treasured dreams.
>
> We are cast in God's image. We must check our road map for guidance toward perfection. Lift the veil and observe the inner men. The perfect man in everyone, for God's pattern is perfect. If we attempt to re-shuffle His plan it will be difficult to process and reshape the perfect Substance of our lives.
>
> As we penetrate into the over-all design of life we are able to relinquish pettiness, snobbishness and selfishness, probably all characteristics held over from inherited racial prejudices.
>
> We must learn to blot our thoughts that are unworthy to enter into our castle. Light must shine

upon our soul to relieve it of impurities.

We are children of God, treading on the path that we have created. We have the opportunity to fill it with flowers of loveliness, music of harmony, painting a picture of eternal beauty which will not evaporate when the ocean waves of life sweep over our character. We must be so firm and strong that we are still standing tall as life's forceful current rolls out to sea again.

Learn to view the life from the mountaintop. Be your own severe judge, for you are creating a human being which will finally be presented to your Creator. Hopefully, as He holds you close, He will whisper, "Well done, my good and faithful one. You have designed and produced a beautiful and creative Force of Eternal Love."

Composer-writer Radie Britain is a private teacher of piano and composition who shares her musical talents as performer and her creative ability as a composer with her many students. She finds happiness in igniting a spark of curiosity in her students, for she knows that inquisitiveness opens the door to creative possibilities. Her pupils have been recipients of many awards. This is a tribute to Miss Britain's ability and teaching skills. She is a member of the American Society of Composers, Authors and Publishers, National League of American Pen Women, and is presently the National Chairwoman of the Composers Division, life member of the Musicians Union, Local 47, Los Angeles Music Teachers Association, National Association for American Composers and Conductors of Washington, D. C. and Los Angeles Chapters, and a life member of Texas Composers, Director of National Society of Arts and Letters of Santa Barbara, California.

Miss Britain is an honorary member of Sigma Alpha Iota, Schubert Club of Los Angeles, Texas Federation of Music Clubs, Texas Teachers Association, Philharmonic Club of Amarillo, Texas, the Etude Club of Los Angeles, and the Los Angeles Women's Press Club.

The Honorary Doctor of Music Degree was conferred on Miss Britain by the Musical Arts Conservatory of Amarillo, Texas; the Award of Merit by the National League of American Pen Women of Washington, D. C.; in 1979 she was honored by the Mary Carr Moore Manuscript Club with a musical trophy inscribed "Great American Woman Composer," also the Award of Merit by the National Band Association and the National Society of Arts & Letters of the Santa Barbara, California Chapter.

Composer-author Radie Britain reflects a Pandora's box of creative ingenuity that is forever overflowing, bubbling and bursting with new and exciting mediums of expression. She is an idol to many aspiring young women and men who have the talent, dedication and determination to carve a niche in the world of the arts.

She pioneered for acceptance of women as serious classical composers and has paved the road and made it a smoother path for women composers to follow. What new heights of artistic expression she will attain remains to be seen. One only knows that so long as Radie Britain breathes, Radie Britain will create, and those creations will be shared with humanity.

In describing her composing she says,

> I'm a very spiritual person. I believe the energy and rhythm of life is around us and through us. I am able to block out all things of this world and meditate. The music flows through me and I just write as fast as I can. I will hear a melody--those voices coming from the external sphere, realizing there is a power greater than me coming through. I'm very humble but it is up to me to be technically qualified to put these melodies on paper. There is no end to what you can learn--for life is so short.

Only Britain's orchestral compositions are listed below. They are available through the Fleisher Library in Philadelphia or Neil Kjos Company, Walter T. Foster, Willis Music Company, Calvi Music Company, Ricordi and Sons of Brazil, Robert B. Brown Music Company, Heroic Music Publication, Seesaw Music Corporation and Harold Branch Music Company.

Partial List of Compositions

1928 Symphonic Intermezzo
1928 Prelude to a Drama
1929 Heroic Poem
1933 Rhapsody for Piano and Orchestra
1934 Nocturn for Small Orchestra

1935 Infant Suite for Small Orchestra
1935 Southern Symphony
1939 Pastorale
1939 Drouth
1939 Canyon
1939 Saturnale
1939 Ontonagon Sketches
1940 Suite for Strings
1940 Prison (Lament) Small Orchestra
1941 San Luis Rey
1941 Saint Francis of Assisi
1942 Phantasy for Oboe and Orchestra
1942 We Believe
1945 Jewels of Lake Tahoe
1946 Red Clay
1946 Serenata Sorrentina
1947 Paint Horse and Saddle
1951 Chicken in the Rough
1953 Cactus Rhapsody
1954 Angel Chimes
1955 Radiation
1956 Cowboy Rhapsody
1958 This Is the Place
1958 Minha Terra
1962 Cosmic Symphony
1963 Little Per Cent
1963 Kambu
1965 Brothers of the Clouds

In addition, Radie Britain has composed 9 pieces of chamber music, 11 stage works, 30 choral works, 32 piano pieces, 6 pieces for two pianos, 7 pieces for violin, 3 pieces for harp, and 41 songs.

RUTH CRAWFORD (SEEGER), 1901-1953

Composer, United States Folklorist

Ruth Crawford was born in East Liverpool, Ohio, the daughter of Anglo-Saxon parents, whose father was a Methodist minister. She studied piano with Valborg Collett and Bertha Foster. After teaching piano at the School of Musical Art in Jacksonville, Florida, from 1918 to 1921, she went to Chicago where she studied harmony, counterpoint, composition, and orchestration with Adolf Weidig and John Palmer at the American Conservatory, and piano with Heniot Levy, Louise Robyn, and Djane Lavoie-Herz.

In 1930 she was the first American woman composer ever to win a Guggenheim Fellowship, which enabled her to study in Paris and Berlin. She had already been judged one of America's most promising classical composers, but failed to produce a long symphonic composition during that year, and her fellowship was not renewed. (This requirement is more flexible today.)

She was a contemporary of such avant-garde composers as Alban Berg and Béla Bartók. She had developed her style to include such modern techniques as tone clusters, serialism, heterophony and diverse metrical patterns. Ruth Crawford's techniques were advanced for her time, and the compositions are considered highly stylistic even after five decades. One of the two works chosen to represent the United States at the Festival of the International Society for Contemporary Music in Amsterdam in 1933 was Crawford's Three Songs, for contralto, oboe, piano, and percussion, with orchestral ostinato.

Ruth Crawford spent a summer at the famous MacDowell colony in Peterborough, New Hampshire, and a year in New York continuing to develop her style. The MacDowell colony was founded and perpetuated by Edward MacDowell's widow as a living memorial to her composer

RUTH CRAWFORD SEEGER
(Photo used by permission of Organization of American States)

husband. It is a year-round working retreat for artists. The fellowships are small but they fulfill a function of providing a workable living situation for creative work. The colony provides a room, studio, and meals for each artist in residence. Breakfast and dinner are served in a dining hall, but lunch is delivered so that the flow of creativity will not be interrupted. Those who can afford it pay a small stipend.

She married Charles Seeger, folk musicologist and Chief of the Music Division of the Pan American Union, in 1931. The Seeger family had seven children: three from Charles Seeger's first marriage, including composer-folksinger Pete Seeger, and four children born of the Crawford-Seeger marriage--Peggy, Michael (both folksingers), Barbara, and Penelope.

Most of her compositions were written in the early 1930's and signed Ruth Crawford. Just before her death in 1953, she began composing in quantity under the name Ruth Crawford Seeger. That her compositions have survived in the repertory for almost fifty years is a result of her ingenious modernistic style.

Ruth Crawford Seeger's contributions to the field of folk anthology were extensive and world renowned. She made musical arrangements for her friend Carl Sandburg's book The American Song Bag. She was music editor of Our Singing Country by John A. and Alan Lomax. For this book, she transcribed over 200 songs recorded in field research on gramophone recordings. Ruth Crawford Seeger arranged three books of folksongs for children: Folk Songs for Children, Animal Folksongs for Children, and American Folksongs for Christmas, all published in the 1940's and 1950's by Doubleday and still popular today. Her book Animal Folksongs for Children presents forty-three songs; thirty-two of them were fresh notation from field recordings in the Archive of American Folksongs in the Library of Congress in Washington. The Seeger children acted as a testing source for many of the songs their mother edited and published. Seeger also used her material in the Silver Spring Cooperative Nursery School in Maryland.

Ruth Crawford Seeger felt that people should improvise on the words of folksongs, but that traditional words should also be kept alive. In her words "strive to maintain a balance between two outstanding values--the vigorous beauty of the traditional text, and an inherent fluidity and creative aliveness which invites improvisation as a natural development in the life of a song."

She was co-editor with Charles Seeger of Folksongs U.S.A. by John and Alan Lomax (published by Duell, Sloane, and Pearce of New York) and music editor of Treasury of Western Folklore (published by Crown, Inc. 1951).

During her lifetime she made over six thousand transcriptions of American folksongs from field recordings in the Library of Congress. She composed over three hundred piano accompaniments for these folksongs, and some were used in the four folk music books she edited.

Ruth Crawford Seeger was a noted national authority on the use of Anglo-American folk music in the educational process of early childhood teaching. She often lectured and demonstrated her creative skills and her extensive resourcefulness before gatherings of professional educators.

Ruth Crawford and Mrs. Henry Harris Aubrey Beach are two of the women composers whose music was recorded as part of an Anthology of American Music in 1976. Crawford's composition Three Songs ("Rat Riddles," "Prayers of Steel," "In Tall Grass," with text by Carl Sandburg written in 1932), was recorded in 1978 by members of the Speculum Musicae with Paul Dunkel as conductor, and Beverly Morgan, mezzo-soprano. It represents one of her longest and finest contributions to modernistic music. Mrs. Beach's Sonata for Piano and Violin in A minor Op. 34, was recorded by Joseph Silverstein, violin, and Gilbert Kalish, piano.

All of the Three Songs are based on heterophony. The role of rhythm is larger than that found in traditional compositions and because of the absence of harmonic modulation it plays an important part in the delineation of form. In "Rat Riddles," the starkness of the voice is accompanied by piano and oboe chasing each other around to percussion background and the counterpoint is extremely complex. "In Tall Grass" is somewhat similar, especially the instrumentation, but to realize the full extent of tonal possibilities, this needs repeated listenings--the dissonance reflects true tonal beauty. One can only try to imagine the multiplicity of the difficulty of notating this composition, especially in the 1930's. Ruth Crawford was a true pioneer in the modern compositional approach as employed in Three Songs.

The structure of these songs is extremely complex and was analyzed by Charles Seeger in his essay on Crawford in Henry Cowell's anthology, American Composers on American Music (published in 1933 by Stanford University Press and reprinted in 1962 by Frederick Unger), an excerpt of which follows*:

> The style of her work before 1930 is basically homophonic, not too noticeably of the Scriabin School, but embroidered with sudden whirls and whip-snaps of thirty-second notes that give a distinct and characteristic vitality to what is often a languid moodiness in the basic chordal structure. These vicious little stabs of dissonance remind one of the lions' tails in the movies of the African veldt. As an integral part of a more mature technique, the device becomes handled most successfully in the ironic setting of "Rat Riddles" (Three Songs, 1930-32), where the piano and the oboe chase each other around in the most surprising arabesques to a percussion accompaniment, the two instruments and the voice and percussion giving the impression--such is the independence of parts--of a whole small orchestra, busily engaged in a contrapuntal tutti. Upon the gay irregularity of the fabric of these instruments, as concertanti, has been superimposed a slow and solemn orchestral ostinato of a purely percussive character, whose regular tread makes a very unusual effect--a counterpoint between two groups, one in florid counterpoint, the other independently homophonic.
>
> The third song, "In Tall Grass," is executed along similar lines--the same instruments concertanti in much the same texture but the ostinati divided into two groups, strings and wind, giving a repetition, not of a tonal, but of a dynamic pattern, the strings a faster, the wind a slower one. All three of these songs are comparatively heterophonic by complete heterophony. We understand a polyphony in which there is no relation between the parts except mere proximity in time-space, beginning and ending, within hearing of each other, at more or less the same time: each should have its own tonal and rhythmic system, and these should be mutually exclusive, while the

*Reprinted here by permission of the publisher.

forms should be utterly diverse. Heterophony may be accidental, as, for instance, a radio-reception of Beethoven's Eroica intruded upon by a phonograph record of a Javanese gamelan. But from an artistic point of view, a high degree of organization is necessary (1) to assure perfect non-coincidence and (2) to make the undertaking as a whole worth while.

The basic principle ("together-soundingness" in which "separate-soundingness" predominates) can be applied in a modified way, as in these songs, of which the second one, "Prayers of Steel," is the most heterophonic. Tonally, all the parts (except the percussion) use the duodecuple gamut, but with practically no unisons, or, indeed, any apparent chordal structures between them. Rhythmically, there is regular, planned coincidence of beat and accent, based upon persistent repetitions of five diverse metrical patterns, the basic polymetrical (rhythmic-chordal) complex, rigid and severe.

This four-part structure is presented three times by the concertanti, the third containing an extension of one measure. After a measure's rest, the whole is given da capo, making twenty-eight measures in all. The fifth part is presented by the ostinati in double octaves and has, instead of a repetitive, a cumulative pattern, given four times in the total of twenty-eight measures, but in four different versions:

The initial tone of each gruppetto presents, transposed at a major third and in metrical augmentation, the first phrase of the oboe part. This oboe part is built upon an initial "set" of seven tones. In the first two-measure phrase, this is presented five times, the accented tones which mark off the five sets being, in consecutive order, the first five tones of the initial set, the remaining tones in each set following in their original order:

The second two-measure phrase has the same scheme except that the whole business is transposed upon the second tone of the initial set. The third, fourth, fifth, and sixth two-measure phrases are similarly constructed, and each is transposed upon the third, fourth, fifth, and sixth tones, respectively, of the initial set. Less than a dozen liberties (shifting and substitution of tones), taken to avoid the "hitting of unisons" between parts, are the only departures from this outline. The voice part is the

> only rhythmically free part. Tonally, it is centered rigidly upon G sharp.

On April 24, 1974, in a concert in Juilliard's Twentieth-Century Music Series conducted by Richard Dufallo, Crawford's Three Songs was programmed. One music critic, who considered Crawford a remarkable composer with great future potential, felt the composition was too complex, too diffused and too long for this non-professional group to perform. The performance offered a contemporary composition that is unfamiliar to a critic when reflected in a review. So many critics tend to "turn off their ears" when the music is new and different. This has been true of critical reviews for over one hundred years. The composition has many intellectual subtleties and complexities, as indicated in Charles Seeger's analysis.

In February of 1975, under the auspices of the Performers' Committee for Twentieth Century Music, an entire program of Crawford's music was performed. Her genius was conveyed in the retrospective concert that included such masterpieces as String Quartet (1931), Three Songs to texts by Carl Sandburg (1932), Suite for Wind Quintet (1952), and Orchestral Composition (1941). These works range from abstract structuralism to folk idioms, and have coloristic timbres. Fragments of these compositions remind the listener of Berg and Bartók.

John Rockwell wrote the following comments on February 21, 1975, in the New York Times*:

> Ruth Crawford Seeger has long held an honorable position in the history of modern American music, particularly for the extraordinarily evocative slow movement of her String Quartet. The Seeger program conveyed her genius. Here is a composer we will be hearing much of during the bicentenary celebrations, but who should survive in the repertory long after that.

The Cabrillo Music Festival at Aptos, California, in August 1974 programmed several women composers. The festival has been noted for many years as an adventure in contemporary compositions. Ruth Crawford Seeger's "Andante" from her String Quartet was the most impressive of all music performed, according to Mr. Commanday, music editor of the San Francisco Chronicle. The composition was written almost thirty-five years earlier and still retains its rightful place of honor on the lists of outstanding contemporary works.

In 1975, the New York Philharmonic Orchestra conducted by Sarah Caldwell, in the Celebration of Women Composers Concert, played a program of three generations of women composers, including Crawford's prophetic String Quartet. Because of the insufficient time to rehearse and missing parts, only the third movement was heard. The orchestra's performance again proved that the caliber of the composition will remain in the repertory of many performing groups. Because of the shifting dynamic balances in the chord structure, and the urgent crescendos of the sonorities, it is an excellent example of contrapuntal dynamics. It is fast becoming an American classic, because it fully displays the creative integrity and the technical resourcefulness of a gifted composer.

The year 1975 was acclaimed International Women's Year and more was accomplished in promotion and public recognition of women in twelve short months than had been accomplished in the past century. There have been many women composers since Saint Cecilia in the third century; although women composed for hundreds of years, the societal structure prevented public presentation of their work. Imagine the amount of talent that was never shared with the world.

In February of 1976, the United States National General Assembly adopted a resolution designating 1975-1985 as the Decade of Women. The foundation that was developed in 1975 will be expanded, and the efforts will be increased, providing women the opportunity to develop and express their talents.

Ruth Crawford's String Quartet is the most performed and best known work, of the serious music, she composed during her short life. Mr. Andrew Porter, writing for The New Yorker on February 10, 1973, best relays the creative power of the composer and frankly and honestly reveals his lack of knowledge, before this time, of her compositions. One must admire Andrew Porter for his integrity:

MODERN PLEASURES*

Ruth Crawford (1901-53) was but a name to me--mainly for her work on American folk song--until, last Monday, in Carnegie Recital Hall, the Composers String Quartet played her String Quartet of 1931. The piece crops up in accounts of contemporary American music, where it is described as uncommonly advanced for its date. It certainly is. Study in Berlin and Paris had preceded the composition, but influences are harder to discern than pointers to the future. Some of Elliott Carter's rhythmic procedures are foreshadowed in the first movement, and while the softly shifting cluster-chords of the slow movement may owe something to Berg's Lyric Suite, closer parallels can be found in Ligeti and Lutoslawski compositions of recent years. In the first movement, melodies that are subtly varied either by free repetition or by free inversion progress in different metres, often against fixed points of reference in the form of long-held notes. In the scherzo, the instruments seem to be nudging one another forward in merry, friendly play. The slow movement moves mysteriously to a fierce climax, then sinks to silence. In the finale, the first violin is a wild beast to whom the other instruments whisper rapidly in octaves; he becomes ever less violent, less abrupt, more lyrical in his utterances, while the others do exactly the opposite, until midpoint is reached. After a pause there, everything is spun out in reverse, a semitone higher. The first violin begins the movement with an exclamation of a single note, then one of two notes, one of three, and so on, while the others respond with a phrase of twenty notes, then one of nineteen, progressively reducing until their single note marks the turning point of the palindrome. It is highly schematic, but the effect is not one of mere contrivance. Before the eye has worked out the ground plan of the movement (a score is published by Merion Music), the ear has already welcomed a quirky, shapely, and

*From A Musical Season by Andrew Porter; copyright ©1974 by Andrew Porter; originally appeared in The New Yorker. Reprinted by permission of Viking Penguin, Inc.

> fascinating stretch of music. Ruth Crawford's quartet is a good example of the string quartet's aptness as a medium for testing new procedures, which I wrote about last week. In 1931 it was an audacious piece, and all completely assured in execution. All four movements can still be enjoyed. (A recording by the Amati Quartet is available on special order from Columbia; a new recording, by the Composers Quartet, who played it very well, is due from Nonesuch.) The recital continued with David Del Tredici's I Hear an Army, for soprano and string quartet, a work of imaginative and picturesque incident (though Catherine Rowe, the singer, lacked beauty of tone), and ended with Carter's First Quartet; rightly, the evening took its part in a series titled The Pleasures of Modern Music.

In 1952, Ruth Crawford Seeger again began to compose in earnest, including her much performed Suite for Wind Quartet. She completed several compositions during this period.

Cancer suddenly and silently deprived the musical world of her talents on November 18, 1953, when she died at the age of fifty-two. No longer could she share new talents or publish new books on folk music. Her final book, Let's Build a Railroad, was published several months after her death by American Book Company. In a few short years, she shared her wealth of musical knowledge and talents with millions of people throughout the world. One can only surmise what heights of attainment might have been produced by Ruth Crawford Seeger, had death not claimed her.

Recordings

String Quartet, Nonesuch Label (number 71280) and Columbia Records (Cms-6142).

Study in Mixed Accents; Nine Preludes for Piano, Block Composers Recording Inc. (number S-247).

Suite for Wind Quintet, Block Composers Recording Inc. (number S-249) and Nonesuch (H 71280).

Three Songs (after Sandburg), New World Label (number 285).

Two Movements for Chamber Orchestra, Delos Label (number 25405).

Partial List of Compositions
(Principal publisher: New Music Edition)

1925 Five Preludes, for piano
1926 Sonata, for violin and piano
1926 Suite, for small orchestra
1927 Suite, for five wind instruments and piano
1928 Four Preludes, for piano
1929 Five Songs, for contralto and piano (Sandburg)
1929 Suite, for four strings and piano
1930 Four Diaphonic Suites
1. For two celli
2. For two clarinets
3. For solo flute
4. For cello and oboe

1930 Three Chants, for women's chorus
1931 Piano Study in Mixed Accents
1931 String Quartet
1932 Three Songs, for contralto, oboe, percussion, and piano, with or without orchestral ostinato (Sandburg)
"Rat Riddles"
"Prayers of Steel"
"In Tall Grass"
1941 Composition for Orchestra
1952 Suite for Wind Quintet

EMMA LOU DIEMER

Composer, Performing Artist, Professor

Dr. Emma Lou Diemer ranks with the musical giants of the twentieth century--her reputation has been solidly established on her tripodal accomplishments. Her creativity flourishes as a gifted composer of over one hundred and fifty compositions (with more than ninety of them published); as a distinguished performer and concert artist on organ, harpsichord, and piano; and as professor of composition sharing her talent and unique teaching skills with undergraduate students.

Diemer has impressive educational credentials and career pedigree. She earned her Bachelor of Music Degree and her Master of Music Degree from Yale University in New Haven, Connecticut, where she studied with Richard Donovan and Paul Hindemith. During the summers of 1954-55 she studied composition at the Berkshire Music Center at Tanglewood in Lenox, Massachusetts, with its internationally known faculty. The composers-in-residence during the summer season usually change each year in order to develop new ideas and expand the compositional abilities of gifted young composers and she had the opportunity to study with both Roger Sessions and Ernest Toch. She completed her formal education at Eastman School of Music with Bernard Rogers and Howard Hanson in composition and with David Craighead on organ. The Doctor of Philosophy Degree, in composition, was conferred on her in 1960.

She has studied with many noted composers of the twentieth century. Since composing cannot be taught as pure subject matter, talented composers share and encourage young gifted students to develop their natural abilities. That Diemer is talented and had the opportunity and encouragement necessary to create helped pave the road to a brilliant and productive career in composing and performing.

Emma Lou Diemer was born in Kansas City, Missouri, in 1927. She was the daughter of Myrtle Casebolt and George Willis Diemer. Her first compositional efforts were at the age of seven when she created little pieces for piano, long before she was able to notate. By the age of thirteen the gifted young girl was well on her way to creating several full-scale piano concertos and other works for the keyboard. It was during this time that she was first engaged as a church organist, a commitment she still maintains, in addition to numerous other demands on her talent. Of her childhood, Diemer says,

> There was no time in my life that I didn't love music and playing the piano. During high school I would write music in the morning, before going to classes, because the house was quiet and I was alone. In the beginning composing was a romantic vision, I was trying to decide whether to be a concert pianist or to do something different. I was influenced by the music of Frederic Chopin, Claude Debussy and especially the big sound of George Gershwin. Every Sunday afternoon I would listen to the broadcast of the New York Philharmonic Orchestra and reflect on the compositions I heard. When I decided to become a composer, I knew there were great men composers and naturally I would become a woman composer.

When she first composed, her work was basically imitative. Diemer sent one of her compositions she wrote as a teenager, to a friend who was a fine pianist. "I was angered when he wrote back and criticized my music and thought the composition was immature. My music has always been very personal to me."

While still in high school she studied composition privately with Gardner Read, who was visiting professor at Kansas City Conservatory. Dr. Diemer explains "During that time I decided to write music that avoided tonality, although I was not familiar with twelve tone music. So, I wrote my first piece and didn't repeat notes and it sounded very dissonant."

She was nominated as a Fulbright Scholar, for the academic year 1952-53, to study composition and piano at the Royal Conservatory in Brussels, Belgium. The opportunity to spend the year abroad brought her in contact with

EMMA LOU DIEMER
(Photo by Maury Mills)

the active concert life of Brussels, with trips to other capitals adding enrichment. She performed as a pianist and composer at the American Embassy and accompanied singers in several programs. Her professors, André Dumortier and Jean Absil, were impressed with her achievements and had lavish praise for her work.

Under the auspices of the Ford Foundation and the National Music Council, Diemer was appointed Composer-in-Residence for the Arlington, Virginia, secondary schools from 1959 to 1961. She was the first woman so honored. During her two-year residency in the Arlington schools she composed prodigiously, and twenty-two compositions were published. Some of these include Youth Overture and Symphonie Antique, for orchestra, and Suite Brass Menagerie, for band (all published by Belwin-Mills); O Come, Let Us Sing Unto the Lord, for mixed chorus and piano or organ, published by Carl Fischer; Three Madrigals, published by

Boosey and Hawkes; and Fragments from the Mass and Four Carols, for women's voices, published respectively by E. B. Marks and Elkan-Vogel.

During 1964-65 she was a composer-consultant under the Contemporary Music Project of the Music Educators National Conference in the Baltimore, Maryland, public schools. Lawrence Sears, contributing critic for The Evening Star, Washington, D. C., wrote on November 17, 1965, following the performance of her Festival Overture by the University of Maryland Symphony Orchestra*:

> Emma Lou Diemer is emerging as one of our leading young composers, and certainly our most published and performed among the ladies. Her Festival Overture dates from 1961 when she was writing for Arlington public schools under a Ford Grant. It is bursting with contained excitement. The orchestra let it all come out and reveled in the great sonorities they created.

During this period of her career Emma Lou Diemer became recognized as a noted organist as well as a composer for the instrument. Reviews were extensive and only a sampling will be offered.

Paul Hume wrote for The Washington Post in 1961, following the close of the Festival of Organ Music of the local chapter of the American Guild of Organists**:

> Miss Diemer is a greatly gifted young lady in many directions. For her final offering, the organist chose Fantasie which she wrote in 1958. It opens with a conventional toccata-like passage, free in form, and covering both manual and pedal boards at high speed. If it has echoes of the modern French style in it, it is neverless more a piece of American writing, and superbly idiomatic.
>
> Neither the toccata, nor a subsequent moderato passage suggested the wonderfully novel subject on which the closing fugue was built. Tricky, and full of pitfalls for the unwary, it is a brilliant piece and it was played with all the dash and punch it deserved.

*Reprinted by permission of the author.
**Reprinted by permission of the publisher.

Wendell Margrave, contributing editor for The Evening Star (Washington), reviewed the dedication recital on the new Reuter organ of the Luthern Church of the Reformation on Capitol Hill on October 25, 1965, performed by Dr. Diemer*:

> Miss Diemer closed her program with her own Toccata, the most exciting music I have ever heard from her pen, and one of the best modern works for organ. It is soon to be published by the Oxford University Press.

Dr. Diemer has composed a steady stream of works, mostly for choral groups, orchestras, bands, solo instruments, and chamber groups, but including some electronic pieces as well.

One of the many compositions written early in her career was a flute concerto premiered by Mark Thomas and the Omaha Symphony conducted by Joseph Levine, the first time this orchestra had ever premiered a major symphonic work. Mr. Martin W. Bush reviewed the concert for the Omaha World-Herald on February 18, 1964**:

> ... The first was that our orchestra never before had been privileged to offer a world premiere of a major work. Never before had a flute concerto been played in our symphonic history. Never before had a major symphonic work by a distaff member of the distinguished composers' sanctuary been offered--and an American at that.
>
> I had neither seen the score nor heard a rehearsal of Dr. Emma Lou Diemer's Flute Concerto as played by Mark Thomas. Thus a report of its playing necessarily is from the hip. But it seemed to be of excellent craftsmanship, there was profile to its thematic material, harmonic treatment was reasonably safe and sound for this day, and as a whole it "came off" most effectively.
>
> Orchestration was so adroit and Mr. Levine's accompaniment so splendidly wrought as to allow Mr. Thomas' virtuosity, of which he has an abundance, to shine stunningly. Assuredly one wishes Dr. Diemer's work a fervent bon voyage as it embarks on the rough seas of musical public opinion.

---

*Reprinted by permission of the author.

**Reprinted by permission of the publisher.

Diemer was commissioned by the Fairfax County (Virginia) Symphony Orchestra to compose the Fairfax Festival Overture. This was an opportunity to write a colorful work for large orchestra. Her first inclination was to make it a piano concerto, but the conductor of the orchestra wished a more orchestra-centered composition. Diemer says of the piece, "The prominence of the piano remains, but it does not overshadow the orchestral writing."

News of Music published in The Washington Evening Star by Lawrence Sears, contributing critic, in February 1969:

> The Fairfax County Symphony Orchestra celebrated its 10th anniversary last evening by giving itself a present. Their concert opened with a newly commissioned Fairfax Festival Overture by Emma Lou Diemer.
>
> Miss Diemer's Overture was the big news of the evening, and the excitement of the music fairly leaps out at you. Her work first came to my attention in 1959 when she was appointed Composer-in-Residence in the Arlington County Schools on a Ford grant. I believe she is the only woman composer to be so honored, and her list of published works shows the acceptance her work has gained. I recall her Youth Orchestra and the Symphony Antique with pleasure.
>
> Her new Fairfax Festival Overture is scored for large forces, with emphasis on winds and brass. It also includes an important piano part, which she played. Miss Diemer has retained her facility with themes and acquired a more pungent harmonic style over the years. The performance was a mile-stone for the players and a challenge they obviously enjoyed. *

Generally speaking, twentieth-century composers seek tonal adventures as they explore new artistic concepts and yet, they merely reflect the quest for independence of musical thought that has forever been a part of the history of music. The musical pendulum swings between two extremes--from conservative to daring and innovative.

A steady growth and development has taken place in Dr. Diemer's work. Considering her total output, produced over a period of thirty years, Dr. Diemer observes that

---

*Reprinted by permission of the author.

there have been some obvious and deliberate changes of style, ranging from neo-classical to neo-romantic to pseudo-avant-garde. One quality has been generally uppermost in her creative endeavors, that of communication through an immediacy of expression, and an avoidance of undue complexity and tedious erudition. She says, "I find it easy to be complex and difficult, it is much harder to be lucid and technically within reach. I place much greater value on the latter of the two qualities." As to whether or not she is "always composing": "Perhaps I subconsciously have compositional ideas, but I am not greatly aware of them. For many years I composed using the piano and even now I will often go the piano while writing a piece of music and play it to be sure it is what I want." She continues,

> Writing for non-professional musical groups is a good discipline for the composer. The music must not be too out of reach technically, and I believe it should have almost immediate appeal. It is this feeling of spontaneity that I like to attain in writing--the style not too removed from the past, but not too enmeshed in it, lest I myself become bored. The ability to write in both rather simple and rather complex styles for different works makes composing both a pleasure and a challenge. I must admit, I take more satisfaction in producing a work which combines spontaneity with intellectual fervor--unfortunately, the works written in this genre (organ pieces, the piano etudes, flute concerto, etc.) are, it seems, infrequently played.

The South Carolina Music Educators Association commissioned Diemer's Three Anniversary Choruses (I Will Sing of Mercy and Judgment, Ode, Sing Aloud Unto God), performed by the South Carolina All-State Chorus accompanied by the All-State Orchestra with Dwight Gustafson, conductor, in 1970. The music is published by Carl Fischer. Dr. Diemer's program notes for the concert clearly explain her intent:

> The Three Anniversary Choruses were written in the spring of 1969 following the commission from the South Carolina Tri-centennial Commission to write a fifteen-minute work for chorus and orchestra. The text was chosen from the Psalms and from two writers of South Carolina, Archibald Rutledge and Henry Timrod. The words for the first chorus are from Psalm 101, and sing of the

psalmist's determination to make himself more worthy, and to free his country and city from those influences that he considers destructive. In the second chorus, in which lines of Henry Timrod and Archibald Rutledge are interwoven, the Ode expresses the fading of glory and fortune, but an abiding expression of faith in the power of love. The third chorus, from Psalm 81, is a call for joyful celebration and grateful praise for the deliverance of the people from trouble.

In the work, the chorus and orchestra are equal in importance, with the chorus rarely singing unaccompanied. The classical fast-slow-fast organization of the tempos of the three movements of the work is echoed in the fairly symmetrical plan of each chorus: the first using a thematic "rondo" plan of A-B-A-C-A-D-A, the second a free A-B-C-D-C-A design, and the third an A-B-C-A-B-C-A (coda) arrangement of sections. The letters indicate contrasts of thematic ideas, often with changes also of "tonality," texture, dynamics, orchestration, and sometimes tempo.

It was the composer's hope to write a work accessible to both participants and listeners, and at the same time worthy of the importance of the Tricentennial celebration.

Emma Lou Diemer's compositions have been extensive, especially in the area of choral and church music. A fine example of her choral writing would be Laughing Song, scored for soprano, alto, tenor and bass with piano duet (published by Shawnee Press). J. Tucker Cook, faculty member at Washington and Lee University, Lexington, Virginia, reviewed Secular Choral Octavo Music for Notes (vol. 32, no. 1), September, 1975*:

Laughing Song

The majority of the new works listed below use what may well have become a common musical language in choral music: while traditional harmonic values of dissonance resolution and a certain hierarchy of chordal and tonal importance exists, freely used dissonant combinations predominate. "Bar-line"

*Reprinted by permission of the author.

rhythms are generally absent, creating an admirable suppleness of movement, and recognizable lyric melody is common. While atonal and intervallically organized choral works are being written as well, it is this former manner that appears most often. Since the Bicentennial Year approaches, it is nice to say that all the works below are by American composers. But nothing can celebrate the growth of American music more than the fine choral organizations that have been developed in secondary schools throughout the country. The works by the first four composers that follow were all written for or commissioned by, junior high or high school groups. (The first four composers on the list: Emma Lou Diemer, Tom Fettke, Sydney Hodkinson and Donald Jenni). Given the imagination and good quality of music these display, as well as their diversity of compositional style, it seems to me they are far more representative of the musical life of the United States than the numbing mediocrity of most of the music appearing specially for the Bicentennial.

Emma Lou Diemer has always handled the chorus well in her own distinctive manner, and Laughing Song is no exception. The frequent use of chords in which the second, fourth and fifth are prominent and the third absent creates a bright, expressive choral sonority. A good feeling for rhythm, which is vigorous and biting, aids the overall sound as well. The text is by William Blake, "When the green woods laugh," from Songs of Innocence, and the work has its share of "ha, ha, ha's." While the score indicates that the secondo of the accompaniment may be used alone, it is evident that the primo part adds greatly to the expressive intent of the composer. There is a fairly extended acappella section in which both soprano and tenor divide, and though the ranges are not severe, the work ends with some sopranos singing a high B♭ for quite a while. There is a marvelous energy to this place, and though it is not an easy one, the time spent on learning it would be well-repaid.

Dr. Emma Lou Diemer is a quiet, unassuming and talented composer who has written in most compositional media. Her contributions in choral, chamber ensemble, and church music have been extensive and she has been the recipient of numerous awards and letters of commendation. Donald G. Hinshaw, the president of Hinshaw Music, Inc. of Chapel Hill, North Carolina, as well as an author, composer and music editor, reflects in his article "Contemporary Composers," published in the Journal of Church Music, about Emma Lou Diemer's contributions to twentieth century music*:

> She has had works performed by major choruses and orchestras throughout the country and has received innumerable commissions for her compositions.
>
> However, in my opinion, the unique contribution of Emma Lou Diemer which distinguishes her from other American composers of such stature, is her abiding concern for church music. Throughout her career she has been a practicing church musician in both large and small churches and has developed a sincere sensitivity for their needs and problems. She feels that music for the church should present the finest qualities of a composer, and be served by the finest composers.
>
> To write in a simpler, practical style, and to make her music singable and playable by "average" musicians without compromising her own aesthetic requirements is a continuing challenge to Emma Lou. There are many people writing music these days--some of it imaginative but impractical, some of it practical but unimaginative. Too much church music is turned out by an assembly-line technique. Granted, much of this is practical, but this is not enough. What is needed is the artistic imagination, skill and concern of truly gifted composers to create new music for the church.
>
> To achieve some of her goals, Emma Lou has tried to introduce contemporary musical language in the form of rhythmic subtleties, harmonic and melodic structures that would acquaint musicians with the serious music of our time. At the same time she attempts to absorb into her style only those elements which are compatible with tradition and which serve her purpose of personal expression and communication rather than experimentation. For example, she makes considerable use of modal, diatonic writing; chords built on thirds, fourths,

*Reprinted by permission of the author and publisher.

> and fifths; ostinato rhythms and syncopations. There is often a great deal of unison or doubling of voice parts or canonic treatments. She attempts to keep vocal parts fairly easy and to enliven the rhythmic and harmonic texture by the use of a vivid, more difficult accompaniment.
>
> Emma Lou may be quiet, but she has given us some of the most powerful and skillfully crafted church music for which we must be greatly indebted.

Dr. Diemer has prodigiously shared her talents as a composer and concert artist in numerous performances and has been acclaimed by music critics in both artistic fields. An excellent example of her skills as a performer-composer was a Concert of Keyboard Compositions by Women Composers which she presented on the organ, piano and harpsichord in 1976.

The program not only was performed by the gifted Diemer but was entirely researched by her. She provided extensive program notes on the composers and their works. A review of the exciting concert was written by Ardis O. Higgins for Santa Barbara News-Press (California) on April 30, 1976:

DIEMER KEYBOARD CONCERT
A RARE MUSICAL OFFERING*

> When music composed by women is given priority for a whole concert, it is a rare event. When added to that is a superb performance by one of those recognized composers playing the entire program on a variety of keyboard instruments, it is rare indeed.
>
> Declarations for Organ which opened the program was composed in 1973 for the Flentrop Organ in Lotte Lehmann Hall, geared to its mechanical action which she explored through registration techniques. Pitch, sound, and intensity were changed by moving stops in or out while holding chords. Pushing the stop in creates a falling in pitch, while pulling a stop out raises pitch. The Declarations were based on a tone row pattern in four parts of three notes each.

*Reprinted by permission of the publisher.

> While Dr. Diemer changed her organ shoes backstage she played the next number, Pianoharpsichord-organ, on tape. In 1974 she won a Creative Arts grant to work on this composition. After making a counting track, she performed each instrument individually, recording it on the tape.
>
> The organ section was played on a local church organ; the piano portion, at home; and the harpsichord on the instrument in Lehmann Hall. She then "mixed" the three tracks of seven minutes each (eliminating the counting track) and created one total combination on tape. Speakers were placed on stage relative to the position of the instruments. The techniques used in composition included use of tympani sticks on piano strings and the strumming of the strings with the fingers. On the harpsichord she created large sound clusters by use of the whole arm movement on the keyboard. The "mixer" used to make the final tape was secured for the Music Department by a General Research Grant from the University awarded Dr. Diemer.

For centuries composers have broken old traditions and developed new horizons of sound possibilities, were this not true we would still be listening to chants and drums. We live in the jet-age of sophisticated electronic devices--should our arts not reflect this? Diemer's Patchworks, performed on a thirty-two stage sequencer and keyboard synthesizer with overlays of four to sixteen tracks of sound inventions, was composed in Santa Barbara, California, in 1977. According to Dr. Diemer, in Patchworks she set about to create a lively and sometimes amusing work. The elements of rhythm and timbre were almost exclusively those pursued. An improvisational technique was used to create each of the tracks: a "patch" was set up on the sequencer-synthesizer and then used for improvisation, changes being made in the "patch" as the piece progressed. Contrasting "patches" were chosen and added accumulatively to the original "patch."

The piece was performed at the Contemporary Music Festival and reviewed by Richard Ames for the Santa Barbara News-Press on January 27, 1978; the following is an excerpt from the paper*:

---

*Reprinted by permission of the publisher.

The brief program opened with Emma Lou Diemer's Patchworks, a light-hearted series of studies in timbre and rhythm improvised on a 32-stage sequencer and keyboard synthesizer with overlays of 4 to 16 tracks of sound inventions. The first was a sequence of jazzy syncopated riffs, the second a rhapsody of water sounds, the third a sharply percussive scherzo, the last a blending of all the elements, in the composer's words "building to a climax and ending quickly and harmlessly."

The work is an attractive mélange of electronic sounds which resemble in their masses Ravel-like distortions of harmonies. Everything is light and airy with witty dislocations creating amusing absurdities. Most of the effects recreate, with a slight twist, the experiences of conventional orchestration, but the slightly different resonances and overtones provide a surreal clarity.

Toccata for Flute Chorus was commissioned and recorded by The Armstrong Flute Ensemble in 1968. It is available on Golden Crest label (CR number 4088) and the four artists on the disc are Britton Johnson, Walfrid Kujala, Harry Moskovitz, and Mark Thomas. Diemer scores the piece for piccolo, E♭ flute, alto and bass flute. One reviewer considered and commented on the Toccata for Flute Chorus as the most effective showpiece on the record, the sounds of the lower flutes as a thing of beauty to the listener.

Dr. Diemer comments on the piece: "There is some suggestion of pitch serialization in this work, but it is basically freely atonal, linear, quite contrapuntal in style, with the four flutes taking part in the music on an equal basis. The work is in a large ternary design, and written for good musicians."

Emma Lou Diemer's compositions reflect the infinite possibilities of both instrumental and vocal sounds. She is an adventurer and her compositions clearly indicate that her talent is illimitable. She is a leader among her contemporaries. She has a long list of awards and commissions including an Arthur Benjamin Award for orchestral music, Creative Art Grants from the universities of Maryland and California, an ASCAP Standard Award every year since 1962, a National Federation of Music Clubs award, a previously mentioned Fulbright Scholarship and Ford Foundation Composers Grant, and others.

Dr. Diemer was honored by the Yale University School of Music Alumni Association, as the recipient of a Certificate of Merit, in the fall of 1977. The citation read:

> Emma Lou Diemer, you have made a distinguished place for yourself in academia and in the field of musical composition since your graduation from the School of Music in 1950.
>
> Under the tutelage of renowned composers including Paul Hindemith, Howard Hanson, Roger Sessions, and Ernst Toch you have gone on to compose well over one hundred published works for all types of vocal and instrumental ensembles. Your compositions reflect a sensitivity to a varied number of musical textures, bringing critics to view your works as "music of tolling beauty" embodying "monumental energy and creativity."
>
> Your verve and talent have permitted you to be successful not only as a composer, but also as a performer and teacher. You were one of the first recipients of a unique Ford Foundation grant naming you composer-in-residence for the secondary school system of Arlington, Virginia. Your career as an organ and piano artist has flourished while you held faculty positions at the University of Maryland, and presently at the University of California, Santa Barbara.
>
> You have been commissioned to write compositions for all levels of performing groups, from children's choruses to symphony orchestras, reflecting the breadth of your creativity and musical direction. For your dedication to the highest standards of music and teaching, the Yale School of Music Alumni Association is proud to award you its Certificate of Merit.

Dr. Diemer has received commissions from the Kindler Foundation, Maryland State Teachers Association, Fairfax County (Va.) Symphony Orchestra, Wayne State University, Armstrong Flute Company, South Carolina Tricentennial Commission, North Texas State University, Lutheran Church in America, Dallas Civic Chorus, Hood College, Sacramento Chorale, Dickinson State College, Mu Phi Epsilon, Meredith College and others. In 1973 Dr. Diemer was the only woman reviewed in the Music Journal's Gallery of Living Composers. In 1977 she joined the roster of distinguished American composers commissioned by Mu Phi Epsilon to write compositions for premiere--the same year she was a contributor to the supplementary publications for the new Lutheran Book of Worship.

The arts can only flourish when talented composers share with younger generations their insight and reflections. That Emma Lou Diemer is in the position to help young composers establish their talent and develop their potential is of essence in the continual development of the musical arts. Dr. Diemer has been a member of the faculty of the University of Maryland where she taught theory and composition for five years, and presently holds senior rank as professor of theory and composition at the University of California at Santa Barbara.

The new dimensions and musical adrenalin that has resulted from Diemer's talent is obvious. Dr. Diemer's pioneering will help pave the road for women composers in a demanding artistic profession. She has been inexhaustible in her efforts to genuinely contribute to the field of contemporary musical composition and is a valuable and respected member of the music community. Her music demands not only respect of technical ability and musicianship, but because of a strong personal imprint as well.

Recordings

Toccata for Flute Chorus (Golden Crest number CR 4088), The Armstrong Flute Ensemble, 1968, 220 Broadway, Huntington Station, N. Y. , 11746.

Choral Music of Emma Lou Diemer, University Chorale, West Texas State University, Schola Madrigalis, Brass, Organ, Piano, Percussion. Dr. Hugh Sanders, Conductor. Golden Crest Records, number ATH-5063.

The music of Emma Lou Diemer is published by Belwin-Mills, Elkan-Vogel, Boosey and Hawkes, Southern Music Company, Carl Fischer, Oxford University Press, Seesaw Music Corporation, New Scribner Music Library, the Build of Carillonneurs in North America, and other publishers.

The following is a partial list of Emma Lou Diemer's compositions:

1948 Suite, for flute and piano
1954 Quartet, for piano, violin, viola and cello

1954 Serenade, for flute and piano
1955 Toccata, for marimba
1957 Honor to Thee, mixed chorus, piano or organ
1958 Fantasie, organ
1958 Concerto for Harpsichord
1959 Youth Overture, orchestra
1960 Symphonie Antique, orchestra
1960 Brass Menagerie, suite for band
1960 Woodwind Quintet No. I
1960 O Come, Let Us Sing Unto the Lord, mixed chorus, piano or organ
1960 Three Madrigals, mixed chorus and piano
1960 At a Solemn Musick, mixed chorus a cappella
1960 Fragments from the Mass, women's chorus
1960 Four Carols, SSA women's voices
1961 Festival Overture, orchestra
1961 Now the Spring Has Come Again, mixed chorus, piano
1962 Sextet, for woodwind quintet and piano
1963 Three Mystic Songs, for soprano and baritone
1963 Concerto for Flute
1964 Toccata, for organ
1965 Four Chinese Love-Poems, for soprano and harp or piano
1965 Seven Etudes, for piano
1967 Verses from the Rubaiyat, mixed chorus a cappella
1967 Dance, Dance My Heart, mixed chorus, organ, percussion
1968 Toccata, for flute chorus
1968 For Ye Shall Go Out With Joy, mixed chorus, piano or organ
1969 Toccata and Fugue, organ
1970 O to Make the Most Jubilant Song, mixed chorus, piano or organ
1970 Celebration--Seven Hymn Settings, organ
1970 Anniversary Choruses, chorus and orchestra
1971 Sound Pictures, piano
1972 Music for Woodwind Quartet
1972 Declarations, organ
1972 Four on a Row, piano
1972 Three Pieces for Carillon
1972 Madrigals Three, mixed chorus, piano
1972-3 A Miscellany of Love Songs, for voice and piano
1973 Psalm 134, mixed chorus a cappella
1973 Trio for flute, oboe, harpsichord, and tape
1974 Sing, O Heavens, mixed chorus a cappella
1974 Praise to the Lord, mixed chorus, organ, brass, timpani

1974 Pianoharpsichordorgan, chamber ensemble
1974 Quartet, for flute, viola, cello, harpsichord, and tape
1976 California Madrigals, mixed chorus and piano
1976 Four Poems by Alice Meynell, for soprano and chamber ensemble
1976 Movement, for flute, oboe, clarinet, and piano
1977 Patchworks, for electronic tape

Plus about ninety other compositions, 1956-77.

MARGARET HILLIS

Conductor, Musician

Margaret Hillis' conducting reflects her dedication and discipline for the art she loves. Dr. Hillis possesses superior credentials, inexhaustible energy, and a determination for excellence that is indomitable. Like all dedicated, successful people, Hillis prodigiously pursued her career with a confirmed belief in her ability and a positive self-image. That she had her share of detractors is expected. She is an articulate, intelligent, and charming individual whose personal philosophy is based on dedication and perfection.

Margaret Hillis was born on October 1, 1921, the daughter of Bernice (Haynes) Hillis and Glen Hillis, in Kokomo, Indiana. Her grandfather, Elwood Haynes, was one of the early inventors of the horseless carriage. Her parents were financially successful and provided her a varied musical background including lessons, concerts and travel. Miss Hillis can recall, "traveling with my mother for periods of two weeks at a time and hearing as many as sixteen concerts, plays, and operas." Her exposure to the arts included piano lessons and playing French horn, clarinet, tuba, saxophone, and the string bass; an impressive list of instruments for any one individual to play proficiently. Besides playing the instruments, Margaret "lugged" the tuba when marching with the local high school band, unusual for a woman then, and even now. She was student director of her high school band and orchestra.

Her grandmother Haynes had a pipe organ in her living room, the pipes were in the basement, and there was grill-work over that end of the floor, her mother often told the story of "Margaret at the age of eight months crawling just as fast as she could to get to the grill-work, when the organ was played, and with any object at hand keeping time by beating on the grill work." Some many years later composer-

MARGARET HILLIS
(Photo by Terry's Photography)

critic Virgil Thomson described Miss Hillis "as a first-class musical temperament, powerful, relentless, thorough."

As a little girl, she knew she wanted to conduct an orchestra. The first large ensemble she saw was the Sousa Band, and she just knew that someday she would be a conductor. She never realized at that age that girls did not conduct orchestras and bands. There was a period of time during her teens when she considered making golf her career. She was Junior State Champion and with her ability to concentrate and her tremendous golf swing (she could drive her tee shot a distance of 225-250 yards), she in all probability would have been a successful touring pro.

Music was the victor, and she enrolled at Indiana University. Following the completion of her junior year, because of the outbreak of World War II, she took a leave of absence. Thousands of college students redirected their energies and joined the armed forces and other organizations. She wanted to do something to support the country, so she learned to fly and had all the qualifications to receive her commercial license when the requirements were changed and a person had to have 20/20 vision without glasses, and Hillis could not pass this test. She received flight instructor's rating and taught as a civilian for the United States Navy. This was the introduction the young Navy men had to the airplane, and she worked with the flight trainees twelve hours a day, seven days a week. Hillis did this for two years until the program was phased out.

She returned to college crediting her time spent with the service as the best lesson of all--it taught discipline, and she had considerably more power of concentration. She buried herself working as a composition major and loved every minute of the work. She received a Bachelor of Arts degree in 1947.

Miss Hillis wanted to go into orchestral conducting and was advised not to even consider this profession because no woman could make it. One of her professors, Bernhard Heiden, recognized her talent for conducting and suggested that she go into the field through the back-door by studying choral conducting. She was accepted at Juilliard School of Music, studied under Robert Shaw and Julius Herford, and received her Master's Degree in choral conducting in 1949.

Dr. Hillis had her start as a choral director in 1950

with the Tanglewood Alumni Chorus and presented a full series of concerts in New York. She was Robert Shaw's assistant for two years and accumulated valuable vocal rehearsal and performance experience.

In 1950 she founded her own performing group, the American Concert Choir and American Concert Orchestra, and began a long series of concerts and recordings that constituted a brilliant chapter in the history of American choral singing. In 1958 the U.S. State Department invited Miss Hillis and the American Concert Choir to represent the United States at the Brussels World Fair. Miss Hillis and her American Concert Choir and Orchestra received international acclaim during the 1950's, performing the compositions of such giants as Bach, Gluck, Haydn, Poulenc, Schoenberg and Stravinsky. Reviews included comments such as "exactitude of musical detail," "cultural value cannot be over-estimated," and "authenticity of style unique."

Betsy Jolas, leading French contemporary composer and at one time editor of Ecouter aujourd'hui (the periodical of the French Radio-Television Network), has highly praised the work of Miss Hillis and the recordings made during this period. "I admire her and can distinctly remember her record of Stravinsky works which I thought were excellent, and I played it over the radio often."

During this time, Miss Hillis and her American Concert Orchestra did a series of television programs that warmed the hearts of music lovers, and her already large following of devoted listeners was expanded. The series of programs was in New York over stations Columbia, National, and American Broadcasting Companies.

Maestra Hillis is the most respected choral conductor in America today. In October 1976 Musical America chose her as "Musician of the Month" with an impressive review written by Karen Monson. In 1957 her picture appeared on the cover of this magazine with a review of her accomplishments. In 1974 Opera magazine devoted to her a lengthy article, "The Chorus Lady," written by George McElroy and Jane W. Stedman. She has been reviewed many times during her professional career by both leading newspapers and magazines.

In 1977 she held four podium jobs that would have been impossible for a less dedicated person. However, Hillis is nurtured to perfection by the demands on her talent. She conducts the Chicago Symphony Chorus and the Elgin (Illinois) Symphony Orchestra, is a resident conductor of the Civic Orchestra of Chicago (training orchestra of the Chicago Symphony), and had chaired the Department of Choral Activities at Northwestern University until August of 1977 when she resigned that position. Hillis is a superb model for young aspiring women and men in the United States. She is in the position to influence young talent and to promote their cause: "There are times that I wish I were twins or quadruplets because I love to teach, not full time, but I love to work with young people, and I feel I have an obligation to pass along as much knowledge as I can to them." Gifted singers are encouraged to seek out new musical opportunities and experiences by Hillis. It has often been said that every great artist must bear the responsibility of perpetuating his/her art by teaching it to a new generation, and Margaret Hillis continually fulfills that responsibility.

Dr. Hillis' background was mainly instrumental, except for conducting a Sigma Alpha Iota chorus as an undergraduate at Indiana University in a piece by Randall Thompson. In high school she was assistant director of the band and orchestra. To conduct an instrumental ensemble is the height of excellence; until one experiences choral conducting, one cannot realize the monumental possibilities that exist here. The opportunity for a woman to conduct a professional orchestra in the 1950's was almost nil. Bitter as it was to accept, Hillis followed the only possible path to the podium, the route of choral music.

Headlines in The New York Times of April 27, 1957, read, "Miss Hillis leads St. John Passion concert choir, ends season with performance of Bach masterpiece." A review by Edward Downes follows*:

> A large and dedicated audience gathered at Alice Tully Hall last night to hear an equally dedicated group of artists under the direction of Margaret Hillis perform Bach's great Passion According to St. John.
>
> The listeners obviously were grateful for the opportunity to hear this passion music, which is often

*© 1957 by The New York Times Company. Reprinted by permission.

> passed up in favor of the same composer's overwhelming St. Matthew Passion.
>
> The many chorales were beautifully done. Their texture was transparent, the voice parts all could be heard, the singers obviously meant the solemn words they sang--and the nuances of interpretation, retards, dynamic shadings, and so on sounded spontaneous and unfired.

For one who dedicates her life and talent to the perfection of musical excellence, recognition will eventually come, and Margaret Hillis was not to be denied. In the mid-fifties, Fritz Reiner, the conductor of the Chicago Symphony Orchestra, wanted to import her American Concert Choir from New York for a performance of the Verdi Requiem with the Chicago Symphony Orchestra. Although the American Concert Choir had been performing for three years with the Chicago Symphony, Miss Hillis refused because she believed a sixty-voice choir would not be sufficient. The cost of importing 120 New York singers was prohibitive, so Hillis suggested that Chicago recruit its own chorus. Reiner questioned, "Marr-ga-ret, ver do ve get the singers?" This was no problem since Margaret was prepared and anxious to develop a new group. She commuted weekly for five years from New York to Chicago. What she produced through her organization, talent, and genius is unbelievable. She held auditions, and then met the newly-formed chorus every Monday evening at Orchestra Hall. The chorus membership included church choir directors as well as singers, teachers, lawyers, music professors, secretaries, clerks, housewives, and on and on. She built from scratch, although there were a few outstanding musicians. The first two performances were Bruno Walter's Mozart Requiem and Reiner's Verdi Requiem.

Dr. Hillis re-auditions choristers yearly. As the caliber of the chorus has improved, the caliber of prospective members' proficiency also has improved. Members must be excellent sight-readers, have vocal training, vibrato control, and above all, a feel for voice color. At the present time, there are over one hundred professional choristers who are paid for both rehearsal and concerts. In addition, over one hundred amateurs do the same work free. It costs in excess of $700 per hour to rehearse this choral group, and every minute is used to advantage. Director Hillis is well organized and is always prepared to develop every possible musical nuance to perfection.

Her credo is simple and sound: "Whatever their religion elsewhere, when in rehearsal, members must be Presbyterians and have a strong sense of predestination. Singing must be absolutely clear. There's no place to hide; the chorus must think ahead to the goal note of the phrase in order to pull the whole phrase together."

Except for her own subscription concerts, Hillis rehearses the chorus for other conductors of the Chicago Symphony. It is a difficult responsibility to anticipate another conductor's interpretation, personal taste and expectation. Dr. Hillis is a "gem" on the podium. She prepares the singers to anticipate the conductor's style and smallest wish. When Hillis prepares the chorus for guest conductors, Sir George Solti (the permenent conductor of the Chicago Symphony Orchestra) trusts her implicitly. She uses a general approach that is concerned with diction, rhythmic and harmonic language, correct accents, tone color, dynamics, and all other effects necessary to produce vocal perfection. She has developed the ability of her choristers to think in terms of "mental imagery." Before a tone is uttered, each performer has a mental conception of what the results will be.

Her rehearsals are demanding and include preparing the physical body in terms of muscles and vocalization. No athletic team would compete without properly warming up, nor should any vocal group sing without the same consideration. Proper vocal preparation before rehearsing is of utmost importance. There are sectional rehearsals, full chorus rehearsals, and orchestra-chorus rehearsals which are held during performance week, after the singers have spent countless hours of their own time on the analysis of the music to be performed.

The key words to describe Margaret Hillis are "organized" and "patient." She is always courteous to her performers, and they in turn have developed a dedicated discipline to meet the arduous demands of a talented conductor. At the conclusion of every rehearsal and performance, the choristers are emotionally and physically exhausted, but they have deep pride in their association with Miss Hillis and the Chicago Symphony. The Chicago Symphony Chorus is the finest of its kind in the world.

The success of Chicago's Chorus is a reality because of the success of Margaret Hillis. She has all the musical skills and the gifts to communicate this knowledge in producing a tuned instrument. There is no competitor in the American conducting profession who can equal her skills. Sherrill Milnes, king of Italian baritones in opera, has spoken of Hillis with awe "as a great musician who taught me the deeper truths of music making and an incomparable education in symphonic literature." Robert Page, director of choruses for the Cleveland Orchestra describes his experience as a chorister and student of Miss Hillis: "Miss Hillis was the first conducting musician to drive home to me the point of the sanctity of the music notation and the resultant excitement and pleasure of having sounds and syllables accurately synchronized."

In January 1978 Bach's Mass in B Minor was programmed in observance of the Chicago Symphony Orchestra's Chorus twentieth anniversary. It was rededicated to the memory of Mayor Richard J. Daley, who had been a strong and loyal supporter of both the orchestra and the chorus. He had mediated the difficult and lengthy labor contracts for the musicians in the early 1960's. He also was instrumental in raising funds for tours and shared the cultural advancement of the group as an International Ambassador of good will in their European tours.

Margaret Hillis was also touched by the performance. She could recall struggling for six years to develop the chorus while many season ticket holders were turning in their tickets when they found the chorus was to perform. Twenty years later, no one could have predicted the chorus's longevity and success.

Thomas Willis, music critic for the Chicago Tribune, wrote the following review on January 6, 1978*:

> At first a commuter from the East, she has become a busy and irreplaceable local force, conducting Civic Orchestra concerts, extending herself into suburban complex as music director of the Elgin Symphony Orchestra and directing choral organization at Northwestern University where she is in her last year.
>
> Fritz Reiner summoned her to organize a permanent group worthy of regular performances with the Symphony, and she fashioned a flexible combination of professionals and devoted amateurs.

*Reprinted, courtesy of the Chicago Tribune.

> Today, it is not just the only chorus in the United States sponsored by a major symphony orchestra, it is acknowledged as the finest performing group of its kind.
>
> Its mastery of languages satisfies the most finicky foreign-born conductors. Its intonation, top to bottom, is nearly perfect. A disciplined precision and musical intelligence informs any work in its repertory. If it has any flaw, it is the very homogeneity which makes it so valuable. Passion is sometimes best expressed with timbral variety.

Miss Hillis' conducting experience has not been limited to vocal directing although that portion of her professional life has been most extensive. She conducted the community-based Kenosha Symphony in Wisconsin from 1961-1968. She is presently music director and conductor of the Elgin Symphony Orchestra in Illinois, a position she has held since 1971. Miss Hillis says, "This is a very fine semi-professional orchestra, and we do between five and eight concerts per season and repeat some performances in other areas." Frequently in the past twenty years, stepping in on very short notice for ailing scheduled conductors, she has conducted the Chicago Symphony Orchestra.

Based on her fine reputation, she has received many invitations to guest conduct, and she has proven her capabilities and talents on the podiums of the Cleveland Orchestra, Minnesota Orchestra, Akron Orchestra, National Symphony Orchestra, Milwaukee Symphony Orchestra, and many others.

There are no permanent women conductors of major symphony orchestras in the United States today, and this reflects societal issues and concerns. However, women are receiving guest conductor invitations, and they can thank musical pioneers like Hillis, Queler and Brico for paving the road.

What are the possibilities of women conducting orchestras today? "There is still pressure on young women to be better than their male colleagues, and I think that is healthy. They must be well-schooled and well-disciplined." Would Margaret Hillis accept a permanent position with a symphony orchestra? "Well, I find myself in a very peculiar position--I love the Chicago Symphony Chorus--somehow it is my mission in life, and when I realized I could not make a career as an orchestral conductor in the 1950's, I was determined that I would develop choruses that would be equal to the greatest orchestras. If a strong-enough offer was forthcoming from a large orchestra, I feel I would accept the opportunity."

In 1977 when Sir George Solti, Music Director and Conductor of the Chicago Symphony Orchestra, suffered a fall and was unable to conduct, the much-respected Margaret Hillis replaced the famous conductor on a few hours' notice in the long-awaited New York performance of Mahler's Symphony No. 8, the "Symphony of a Thousand." Karen Monson, critic for the (New York) Daily News, wrote the following in the Wednesday, November 2, 1977, edition:

SWEET "BRAVA!" FOR AN OLD PRO*

> Applause is not new to the Chicago Symphony's Margaret Hillis. But her Carnegie Hall triumph as a sub for George Solti has vaulted her to a special place in the musical world.
>
> The lady is a pro.
>
> "Well, if you have to do it, you do it," said Margaret Hillis on the morning after her triumphant, but unexpected return to Carnegie Hall.
>
> She took the podium in front of the Eastern musical elite, and turned to the Chicago Symphony Orchestra and Chorus, the Glen Ellyn Children's Chorus, eight star soloists, and the psychologically and technically complex score.
>
> Eighty minutes later, she finished to the cries of Brava!

Donal Henahan reviewed the concert for the New York Times on November 1, 1977:

WOMAN STEPS IN FOR SOLTI,
WINS CARNEGIE HALL OVATION**

> What an improbable scenario. Even a militant feminist editor might reject it as just too much. One of the world's most lionized conductors, sched-

*Reprinted with permission from Field Enterprises, Inc.

**© 1977 by The New York Times Company. Reprinted by permission.

uled to lead one of the great orchestras in a Carnegie Hall performance of Mahler's most complex and philosophically ambitious symphony, injures an arm and is forced to withdraw at the last moment. His place is taken by his woman assistant, and she conducts a triumphant performance that wins her a standing ovation.

Improbable or not, it happened last night at Carnegie Hall. George Solti, who fell in Chicago on Friday and suffered a sprained wrist and strained back, neck and shoulder muscles, turned over his Chicago Symphony Orchestra and the awesome Mahler Eighth Symphony to Margaret Hillis, the orchestra's choral director. Miss Hillis, who happens to be as famous in her own field as Mr. Solti is in his, built her performance carefully, but she built it well. What her Mahler Eighth sometimes lacked in Soltian fire and tension, it made up for in poise, clarity and ethereal detail.

If all the foregoing does not yet strike you as the fevered dream of a novelist, consider in addition that this is a symphony that closes with a Mystical Choir singing the final, famous words of Goethe's Faust: "Das Ewig-Weibliche zieht uns hinan"--"The Eternal Feminine leads us on." Or, as the Peggie Cochrane translation had it more prosaically in the program: "The ever-womany draws us heavenward."

Miss Hillis, it must be admitted, could hardly have chosen a more likely work for showing what she could do. The Mahler is one hour and 20 minutes, give or take a couple of minutes, of almost solid choral and vocal-ensemble music. Long before she was called by the late Fritz Reiner to Chicago to organize the orchestra's chorus, she had made her reputation with the Robert Shaw Chorale, the American Opera Society and other groups. She has often conducted the Chicago Symphony in the choral-orchestral repertory. So, finding herself faced with more than 400 singers and instrumentalists on this occasion was not a daunting experience: She had, after all, trained and rehearsed the two mixed adult choruses and the children's choir for this very production of the Mahler Eighth.

Of course, Miss Hillis had under her baton a battalion any Mahler conductor could yearn for: the magnificent Chicago orchestra, her own exceptionally

> polished and responsive Chicago Symphony Chorus and the Glen Ellyn Children's Chorus, which used girls as well as the boys that Mahler's score specifies.
>
> Wisely opting at first for certainty and control, which lent rather metronomic feeling to much of Part I, Miss Hillis gradually loosened up, and by the last ecstatic pages she had her forces working for her and Mahler with a burning enthusiasm that radiated a fine glow over the Faustian finale.
>
> The job of announcing to the audience that Mr. Solti would not conduct the Mahler fell to Carnegie Hall's panjandrum, Julius Bloom. He explained that the conductor (whose fan club in New York is famously vociferous and partisan) had suffered an accident and would need "at least another day's respite before returning to the podium." Groans could reasonably have been expected, if not actual boos; instead, Miss Hillis's name was greeted with nothing but friendly cheers. It seemed to this listener to be New York's musical audience at its most civilized. Happily, Miss Hillis's performance proved worthy of the occasion. She did not attempt to imitate Mr. Solti's tempestuous Mahler, but her professionalism was evident in the fact that her Eighth Symphony ran within a minute or two of the one recorded by the orchestra and its regular conductor in Vienna a few years ago.

Dr. Hillis is a perfectionist and a humanist; she shares her talents with audiences as well as professional musicians. An example was the Christmas Do-It-Yourself Messiah she conducted in 1978 at Orchestra Hall in Chicago. This participatory performance delighted the audience even though many were unable to "keep up" with the professionals on stage. It was reflection of a lesson known and shared for thousands of years. "Music belongs to people and people belong to music."

Margaret Hillis received the coveted Grammy award for "The best choral performance of 1977" for the Verdi Requiem (Chicago Symphony Orchestra and Chicago Symphony Chorus, Solti conducting). In 1978 she received a second Grammy, this time for the Beethoven Missa Solemnis (Solti conducting).

Margaret Hillis had been a distinguished faculty

member at several colleges, including chairing the Choral Department at Northwestern University and presently acting as Visiting Professor at the University of Indiana. Professor Hillis taught conducting skills to hundreds of young students during her tenure. She has ignited a spark of talent in many aspiring young conductors. Whether they can attain success on the prestigious podiums will be known with the passing of time. The road will be easier because Hillis has proven that women have the ability, talent, and dedication to wield the baton.

She has been honored by three universities and colleges with honorary degrees. In 1967, Temple University, and in 1972, Indiana University, conferred Honorary Doctor of Music degrees, and in 1977, Saint Mary's College, Notre Dame, Indiana, awarded her an Honorary Doctor of Fine Arts degree. In addition to these honorary doctorate degrees and the prestigious Grammy awards, Hillis has received other honors--

1947 Sigma Alpha Iota Sword of Honor
1960 Sigma Alpha Iota Ring of Excellence
1964 Professional Pan Hellenic Association award for outstanding achievement in the field of music
1965 Woman of the Year in Music, awarded by Who's Who of American Women
1969 Alumni of the Year, Indiana University
1969 Steinway Award for outstanding contribution to the cultural life of Chicago
1972 Chicago YMCA Leader Luncheon I award, outstanding women in the field of the arts
1973 Friends of Literature award for notable contribution to the cultural heritage of Chicago
1974 Sigma Alpha Iota Foundation "Circle of 15" award
1978 Kappa Gamma Alumni Achievement Award
1978 Woman of the Year in New Music Category Classical Music, Ladies Home Journal

Perhaps the most important award of all is the respect and admiration shared by the thousands of young people who have been fortunate enough to work under the leadership of Margaret Hillis. To know her is to love her, stand in awe of her great ability, and expend 110 percent energy to meet the demands she expects of herself and her musicians. Maestra Hillis has a positive attitude, and she has turned disadvantage into a positive career. Would she pursue the same goals if she had her life to live over? "I guess if I had another chance, I'd take the same path, accept the same challenges and, hopefully, make a few less damn-fool mistakes."

Recordings
(with Hillis as Choral Director)

Verdi's Requiem Mass, RCA label, ART 2476. Grammy award winner.
Beethoven's Missa Solemnis, London label, 12111. Grammy award winner.

JEAN EICHELBERGER IVEY

Composer-Teacher of Composition

Dr. Jean Eichelberger Ivey is an extraordinarily gifted musician who has composed for virtually every medium, and many of her compositions have literary themes. Her early career was established by her exceptional ability in the field of electronic music that placed her solidly among advanced American composers. Though occupied by electronics and the infinite possibilities of sound combinations that are exploding in the world of music, Ivey has prodigiously shared her talents with teachers and students. She knew by instinct everything to avoid and believed that composing was her destiny. Dr. Ivey explains,

> Writing for the voice has always been particularly dear to me, as is the setting of texts and the use of literary themes in general. Composing for particular performers, too, and writing in an idiomatic way for each performing medium, be it voice, instrument, or electronic tape, is a challenge I strongly respond to. In fact, the synthesis of many elements, many diverse influences, in a unified, coherent, and expressive whole, strikes me as the prevailing historical task of composers now at the end of this innovative century. I aim at combining tonal and atonal elements, and I consider all the musical resources of the past and the present as being at the composer's disposal, but always in the service of the effective communication of humanistic ideas and intuitive emotion.

Ivey's many compositions reflect her philosophy, and she has contributed her talent to the exciting twentieth-century repertoire. Her compositions are unique, well-balanced and properly porportioned, testifying to a remarkable creative talent. Her ability to explore is the result of visionary thinking which has resulted in her distinctive contribution to music.

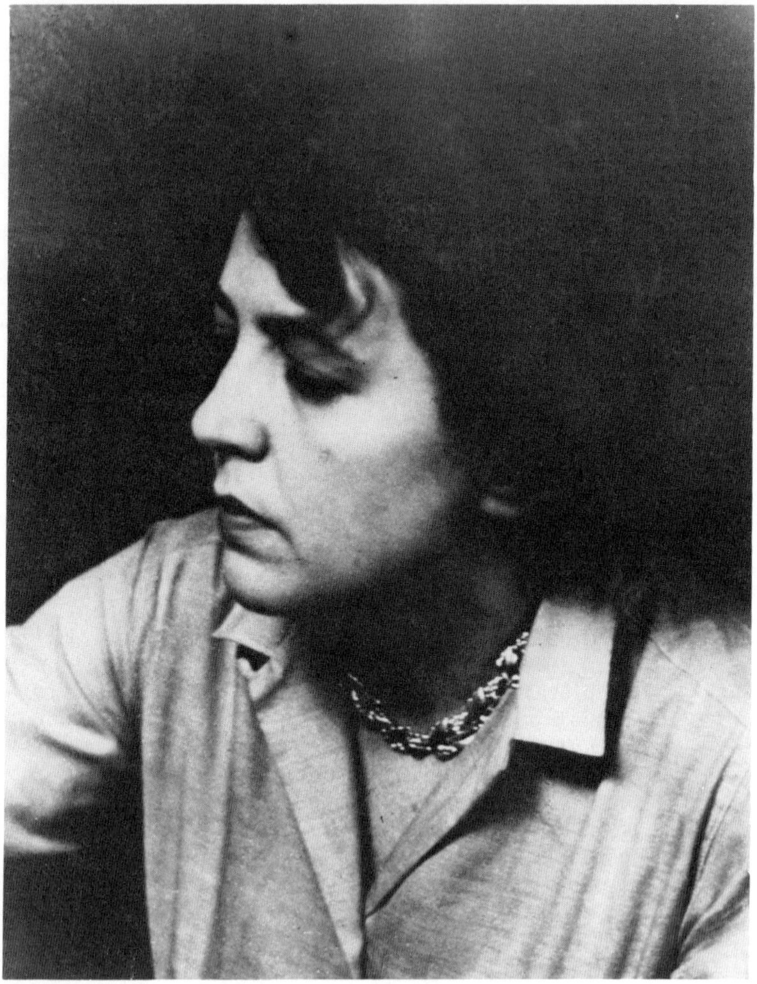

JEAN EICHELBERGER IVEY
(Photo by Wayne D. Sourbeer)

She was born in Washington, D. C., in 1923, the daughter of Elizabeth Pfeffer and Joseph S. Eichelberger. Her father was then editor of an anti-feminist newspaper. The paper folded, and the family was hard-hit in the depression of the 1930's. She was able to attend college only by winning, in a competitive examination, a full-tuition scholarship to Trinity College. Ivey earned her Bachelor of Arts degree magna cum laude in 1944.

Already teaching, and a church organist since the age of twelve, she went to Peabody Conservatory for her first Master's degree in piano, completing her studies in 1946. Jean Eichelberger Ivey completed a second Master's degree in composition during the summers at the Eastman School of Music. Wayne Barlow was her principal composition teacher, although she also studied with Herbert Elwell, Bernard Rogers, Kent Kennan, and Nicholas Nabokov. Her piano teachers included Pasquale Tallarico, Glenn Dillard Gunn, Katherine Bacon, and, briefly, Claudio Arrau. At the University of Toronto, where she studied electronic music with Myron Schaeffer and Hugh LeCaine, the Doctor of Music degree in composition was conferred in 1972.

Early in her career, she was engaged as teacher of piano, organ, and theory at several American colleges (Peabody Conservatory in Baltimore, Trinity College and Catholic University in Washington, and College Misericordia in Wilkes-Barre, Pennsylvania). During this time she gave piano recitals in numerous colleges and academies, and at the National Gallery of Art and the Phillips Gallery in Washington.

Paul Hume, writing for The Washington Post in June 1956, praised the young Jean Eichelberger (Ivey)*:

EICHELBERGER RECITAL DISTINGUISHED

> Jean Eichelberger returned to the National Gallery last night to play a recital distinguished in its high level of pianistic art.
>
> Starting on a wholly classical plateau, the musical artist included highly poetic readings of the F Minor Variations of Haydn, and the E Major Sonata, Opus 109 of Beethoven. The poetry was appropriate to each work, since they represent their composers in veins of unusually relaxed introspection.

*Reprinted by permission of the publisher.

> To the spacious measures of the Beethoven, Miss Eichelberger brought a clarity notable because it was achieved without any loss of singing line, and because the wonderful second movement of the sonata never lessened in its essential forward motion in order to remain clear. It is also always of note when a pianist can keep things distinguishable in the tricky acoustics of the Gallery.
>
> After the intermission, Miss Eichelberger displayed her solid talents as a composer in a classical Prelude and Passacaglia. Well conceived, the music builds with a steady and knowing hand, lacking the desire for innovation, but fully alert to the resonant potentialities of her instrument, and filled with touches of fresh figuration and harmony.
>
> Ravel's Oiseaux Tristes and Vallee des Cloches are among his most elusive works for piano, or, for that matter, from his entire repertoire. They require a maximum of variety in touch, and a command of the pedal as well as a constant attention to the rhythmic basis on which they are erected. To these, and to the more celebrated Toccata, Miss Eichelberger brought her keenly musical perceptions in playing that was highly rewarding.
>
> Wayne Barlow's Sonata is a solid piece of music in the manner of a conservative man knowing in his treatment of the piano. It made the American contribution to the evening's concert a worthy companion to the substantial works that surrounded it.

In 1957 she toured Mexico under the auspices of the Binational Center of the American Embassy. Her recitals included her own Prelude and Passacaglia, and works by American and Mexican composers. Later she recorded some of these works at the request of the Pan-American Union for use on their short-wave broadcasts to Latin America. In the same year, she was chosen, together with Carol Hoppe, young American mezzo-soprano, to make a joint concert tour of the United States under the sponsorship of the National Catholic Music Educators Association.

She undertook her first European tour in 1958, appearing in Germany and Austria in programs which included her own piano sonata. Wherever she performed, reviewers extolled her accomplishments both as a performer and composer. Her piano compositions Theme and Variations, contemporary in harmonic idiom and form, and Sonata, a sharply delineated and classically developed work, were acclaimed. She was praised as an outstanding interpreter of classical as well as modern works, demonstrated mastery in her technique and as a musician of great capacities.

During the years that followed, Ivey taught at several other American colleges while composition increasingly absorbed her interest. She has composed for orchestra, chamber ensembles, vocal and instrumental solos, chorus, electronic music, and music for live performer plus tape. Dr. Jean Eichelberger Ivey's music has been performed by the Eastman-Rochester Orchestra, the Houston Symphony in a Rockefeller Symposium, the League of Composers International Society for Contemporary Music in New York, the American Society of University Composers in national conferences and radio programs, the Bicentennial Parade of American Music at the Kennedy Center in Washington, and many others.

In 1968 she was the only woman composer represented at the Eastman-Rochester American Music Festival; Ode for Orchestra was premiered at this program. After considerable experience in composition for live performers, she turned to tape composition. Beginning the same year, she enjoyed excellent success with her electronic work Continuous Form, which has had thousands of performances in credited station breaks on Channel 13 in New York City and the leading educational television station, WGBH Channel 2, in Boston. This composition is in an endless cartridge from which sections were chosen at random for breaks and at the beginning of each day's opening. The tape is randomly combined with films by Wayne Sourbeer; no two station breaks can be alike.

In 1969 Ivey returned to the Peabody Conservatory faculty, this time as a major teacher of composition. She is also founder-director of the Peabody Electronic Music Studio.

The new and different has always gained acceptance through the efforts of the pioneer grass roots approach. Ivey established what is believed to be the first electronic music workshop for in-service public school teachers. The workshop was first held in the summer of 1967 at Peabody Conservatory, Baltimore, Maryland, and continued yearly for ten years. A complete review can be found in the Music Educators Journal, November 1968, written by Ivey. The following material highlights the workshop presentation in six brief steps*:

1) Electronic music was defined as music created in the laboratory using electronic sound generators and techniques made possible by magnetic tape recording.

2) The composer in the electronic music studio records his raw material and manipulates it. He selects and forms the results into an effective sequence that he records on his final tape.

3) Much practical information about tape recording was presented and attention was given to factors in the choice of tape recorder, a survey of kinds of tape, splicers, amplifiers, mixers, and filters. Also included was a review of basic acoustics.

4) Basic orientation in the concepts, sounds, and terminology of electronic music were presented.

5) The heart of the workshop was practical tape work. This and other experiments were both a challenge tc the imagination and a source of many insights into the nature of sound itself.

6) A workshop can only introduce a complex subject, but it gives enough basic practical information to make school music teachers feel able to go further on their own.

Electronic music can gain acceptance only if help and understanding are offered to fledgling music teachers, and Ivey provided just such an opportunity, through her workshops, lectures and articles. She was a contributor to Elliott Schwartz's book, Electronic Music: A Listener's Guide and the following is an excerpt (pages 230-232) from that writing**:

---

*Copyright ©1968 by Music Educators National Conference. Reprinted with permission.
**From Electronic Music: A Listener's Guide, rev. ed., by Elliott Schwartz. Copyright ©1973, 1975 by Praeger Publishers, Inc. Reprinted by permission of Holt, Rinehart, and Winston.

After considerable experience in composing for live performers and in tape composition, and with every intention of continuing both, I find myself at present most interested in works which combine the two. My first finished works of this kind, Terminus for mezzo-soprano and tape, and 3 Songs of Night for soprano, five instruments, and tape, were premiered at Peabody in the spring of 1971, and a recording of them is now in preparation. (The soore and tape of Terminus are available from Carl Fischer, Inc., publishers.) For some years I have entertained the notion of a series of pieces for various solo performers plus tape, partly because so many performers ask for such additions to their repertoire; and I have also done some work on a large monodrama for voice, orchestra and tape.

In some ways, writing for live performers plus tape seems to me the most difficult of all types of composition. It combines all the problems of composing for live performers and the problems of pure tape composition, with some special problems caused by their interaction. The challenge of coping with all these problems simultaneously may be one of its principal attractions for the composer.

A pure tape composition is like a painting--one puts it together alone in the studio, drawing on all one's resources of equipment, imagination, and taste. Unlike traditional composition, where the composer hears his work only in his mind until, often much later, performers bring it to life, the tape studio offers ready access to sound. The composer can test out his ideas on the spot, rearrange, manipulate, and structure, under the constant stimulus of hearing each successive step. Like the painter, he beholds his work taking shape before him. His finished tape, like the painting, needs no interpreting performer but embodies its creator's ideas alone. The composer's control over the final results, as well as his responsibility for them, are at a maximum.

Composing for live performers, on the other hand, involves a kind of forecasting of probable reactions. It requires an intimate knowledge of how voices and instruments behave, how performers react to each other, to notation, and to the whole performing situation including the audience. Whether the composer intends aleatory results or great precision, some unpredictability is inevitable; each performance differs, grossly or subtly, from every other; each performance differs, grossly or subtly, from every other. The appeal of this quality of change in live performance has, I think, been overrated. We do not expect of a painting, a literary work, or a film that it change each time we experience it.

If such a work draws us back to it again and again, it is because it offers such complexity, subtlety, and multiplicity of interpretations that it seems impossible ever to experience it completely. The same can certainly be true of a tape piece. Nevertheless, the possibility of the unpredictable is one of the special features which live performers provide.

A more serious lack felt by many in tape music is the lack of visual interest. One thing we have learned from tape concerts is the importance of visual aspects in concerts as a whole. Seeing the conductor raise his baton, watching the performers make their characteristic gestures, even the rearrangement of the stage between pieces, all contribute an interest of which we were scarcely aware until it was no longer there. It is quite a different experience to sit in a concert hall where nothing happens visually, where without warning sounds suddenly emerge from loudspeakers. A visual focus for attention can of course be supplied in many ways--by lighting or darkness, by the use of film, pantomime, or kinetic art objects. But the visual experience of watching a live performer is perhaps more directly appealing, more natural and unforced, and more integrated with the unfolding musical situation, than any other.

Linked with the unpredictable and the visual, as well as with less easily defined components, there are complex human interactions between audience and player to which both respond. The hearer delights in a virtuosity which he could never imitate but with which he imaginatively identifies. The player feels himself inspired, perhaps, to outdo himself, to bring off effects he would never think of in rehearsal.

The combination of live performers with tape

> seems to offer all the wealth of both worlds, plus a dimension which neither can reach alone.

Two of Ivey's purely electronic pieces have been recorded: Pinball, a piece of musique concrète (originally composed as a film score) is a study of sounds taken from a pinball machine including the clicks, rattles, and bells (it appears on the Folkways record FMS 3/3436); and Cortege-for-Charles Kent, a commemorative electronic score for a past Director of the Peabody Institute (recorded on Folkways record FTS 3/3439). Peter Davis wrote for the New York Times on March 16, 1970*:

> ELECTRONIC MUSIC AVOIDS THE UNUSUAL
>
> The International Society for Contemporary Music devoted its Carnegie Recital Hall program last night to what might be termed classical electronic music. There were no rock groups, dancers, projections, or other mixed-media effects to disturb the listener. Pure electronically manipulated sound was the order of the evening.
>
> Two pieces were given premieres, Jean Eichelberger Ivey's Cortege and Barry Vercoe's Synthesis No. 2.
>
> Cortege is a lament, economically but effectively constructed from gentle wailing figures and deep, booming cannonlike reports.

Ivey said, "My favorite medium is voice. It was mainly a historical accident that my electronic music tended to be featured in the late sixties and early seventies in connection with the Peabody studio. I prefer not to be too identified with electronic music." A glance at the list of recordings and compositions at the end of the chapter will readily support her statement. Outstanding composers all have an unlimited source of creativity and they express themselves throughout their lifetime via a variety of possibilities. Otherwise, there would only be a masquerade of uninspired, technical compositions.

Four of Dr. Ivey's works had premieres in 1973;

they were Tribute: Martin Luther King, for baritone and orchestra, commissioned by Margaret Laver and performed by the Peabody Conservatory Orchestra, Leo Mueller, conductor with Earl Grandison, soloist; Hera, Hung from the Sky, for mezzo-soprano, winds, percussion, piano and tape commissioned by the University of North Dakota's Collegium Musicum; Skaniadaryo, for piano and tape, the first piece commissioned by the New York State chapter of the Music Teachers National Association in a national commissioning program performed by Barbara English Maris; and Aldebaran, for viola and tape premiered in New York by Jacob Glick.

A perceptive listener will immediately be attracted to composer Ivey's pieces that combine tape and live performers. Hera, Hung from the Sky is scored for mezzo-soprano, seven wind instruments, percussion, piano and electronic tape. She used as the heroine for the piece the goddess Hera, punished for daring to rebel against her husband's authority. The composition was inspired by the poem "Hera, Hung from the Sky," published in 1961 in Carolyn Kizer's collection, The Ungrateful Garden. Kizer writes of life's tensions, especially those that reflect female conditions. She captures an artistic remedy for womanly woes and expresses these feelings in her poetry.

Gregory Levin reviewed Ivey's Hera, Hung from the Sky in an article in The Music Quarterly (vol. LX, no. 4), in 1974, p. 628*:

> Hera, Hung from the Sky is a sensitive handling of a difficult poem, with a generally syllabic setting of the text word painting, judicious use of musical underscoring, and textual and melodic repetition. It allows the text to be always understood and illuminates its abrupt contrasts in mood. Long, sustained harmonic plateaus give a spacious and relaxed quality to the music which counterpoints with the manic-depressive hysteria of the text. Ms. Ivey attains variety and breadth in her musical phrasing by varying the length of instrumental and electronic interludes which interrupt the text. By maintaining a subtle and constant dissymmetry between the lengths of sections with voice and sections

*Reprinted by permission of the publisher.

> without voice, she builds a gentle but insistent musical momentum.

Discrimination in higher education has been recognized and discussed for a number of years. Dr. Jean Eichelberger Ivey strongly believes that women composers are discriminated against in that area also. She says,

> One of the principal forms of sustained remunerative employment available to serious American composers is to be found in colleges and universities. How many women are listed as members of the composition faculty, or composers-in-residence? Very, very few. If a woman whose specialty is composition is hired at all, it is likely to be in some other capacity--as teacher of freshman theory or class piano. Another area that seriously limits women is the anti-nepotism policy. What is more natural than that college teachers should occasionally marry other college teachers? (This composer was formerly married to a college teacher.) But when it happens, the woman's job becomes infinitely precarious. Many, perhaps most, universities definitely prohibit the hiring of faculty couples. Others evoke vague unwritten policies that either reject altogether the "faculty wife" or limit her to some such category as part-time instructor, one year appointee, or the like.

One would readily agree that such outrageous happenings did occur and still occur. The Federal Affirmative Action, Executive Order 11375, as amended, was passed to prevent this type of discrimination. There has been some progress, though slow and small, but it is a step in the right direction. Colleges in violation of these regulations stand to lose all Federal monies. All college positions must be advertised as Equal Employment Opportunity/Affirmative Action Employers.

Jean Eichelberger Ivey and her contemporaries have all been products of discrimination in one or more of the following areas: Foundation grants, promotion to higher academic ranks, performance opportunities, publication of music and commercial recordings. One cannot condone discrimination, and every effort must be expended to quickly eliminate the inequalities. The field of music, particularly conducting and composing, is one of the last male bastions. When men and women are equally free, then will the world produce the ultimate medium in an all-encompassing musical art. Ivey tried in vain to receive a large commission so she could devote an extensive period of time to composing. Even when she had the assurance of the Baltimore Symphony for a performance of her composition, as well as supporting letters from the conductor, the soloist and others, she was turned down.

Yet, she did complete her composition Testament of Eve, indicating what history has proven: true artistic ability can never be stifled. Ivey explains, "I wrote the text about 1965, but I hesitated to embark on a work of such dimensions with no performance in view. When in 1974 Sergiu Commissiona promised a performance by the Baltimore Symphony, I set to work in earnest. By that time the mezzo-soprano Elaine Bonazzi had already recorded two of my pieces, and I greatly admired her work. So I tailored Testament of Eve to her special vocal characteristics and dramatic temperament." She writes in the program notes for the world premiere,

> The story of Eve and the Tree of Knowledge has always fascinated me. For at least a dozen years I have thought of composing a musical work on this subject. To "know good and evil," to leave the comforts of Paradise in order "to be as Gods"--how inexhaustibly rich in symbolism! One could see in this the evolution of the human species itself, with its unique concepts of conscience and rational choice; or that perennial human tendency to aspire, which has brought us out of the cave, and makes each generation seek to outdo the last, and which now, on the dark side, threatens us with unprecedented problems; or the personal evolution of each one of us from protected infant to responsible adult.
>
> To me as a woman, it is of special interest that in this myth, a woman makes the choice. She chooses knowledge and growth, as opposed to remaining a pampered pet forever in the Garden of Eden. And Eve, whose name traditionally means "Mother of all the living," makes this choice not for herself alone but for Adam and her children and all the human race to come. She is very like Prometheus; and yet while Prometheus is usually seen as heroic, Eve in a patriarchal culture was often dismissed as silly, sensual, bad.

> Lucifer, the "bearer of light," I have also reinterpreted. He appears here as a disembodied voice on tape, rising out of turbulent winds, an invisible spirit who ultimately is a part of Eve herself--her own dawning self-awareness and urge to grow and change.

The Testament of Eve offers the startling opportunity to rethink the myth of the Garden of Eden in terms of a woman's view. This new text made many traditionalists feel somewhat uneasy, but it is extremely thought-provoking and presents the female and her capacity for intellectual pursuit. The music reflects the genius of Ivey's ability to write for orchestral instruments, voice and tape.

The world premiere was performed by the Baltimore Symphony with Elaine Bonazzi, mezzo, and Leon Fleisher, conductor. It was reviewed by Elliott W. Galkin for High Fidelity/Musical America in August 1976*:

> Jean Eichelberger Ivey's Testament of Eve, the third work commissioned† for performance by the Baltimore Symphony this season, was heard in its premiere presentation on April 21 at the Lyric Theater under the direction of Leon Fleisher. It is a fascinating composition in terms of effect and amalgamation of traditional and innovative materials. Some twenty minutes in duration and scored for mezzo-soprano, tape, and large orchestra (with a colorful array of about two dozen percussion instruments), it tells the story of Eve's rejection of pleasure in preference to the Spartan quest for knowledge.
>
> The score is conceived in terms of a debate between Lucifer--the tape--and Eve, as personified by the voice. The dialogue is vivid, accompanied by picturesque electronic colors, mystical aleatory moments, and impressive climaxes utilizing a complex chromatic language which contains elements reminiscent of Mahler and Messiaen.
>
> The vocal assignment contains challenges of pitch, timbre, and meter of the most sophisticated sort, and as negotiated by Elaine Bonazzi--like Miss Ivey, a member of the faculty of the Peabody

---

*

> Conservatory--was a tour de force. She treated its intricate melodic angularities and ornate melismatic passages with elan and fervency. Fleisher conducted the work with obvious stylistic empathy, and the orchestra provided a partnership of refined resonances.
>
> †[The critic is mistaken about this work's being commissioned. It is not. I wrote the magazine on this point, and I think my letter was published in November '76 (Ivey).]

Ivey's Prospero, scena for bass voice, with horn, percussion (one) and four-channel tape, was composed for a concert at the Eastman School of Music on April 4, 1978, honoring Wayne Barlow (Ivey's principal composition teacher) on his retirement as Director of the Eastman Electronic Music Studio and Professor of Composition. The piece is dedicated to Barlow and contains in the tape section a quotation from his Sonata for Piano, as performed by Ivey.

According to the composer's program notes, "It takes its text from the last act of Shakespeare's last play, The Tempest. Prospero, having raised a tempest by his magical powers and gained his ends thereby, abjures the art of magic and bids farewell to his attendant spirits. Many critics have seen in this, Shakespeare's own farewell to the stage."

On January 25, 1979, Prospero was performed at Carnegie Recital Hall, League of Composers-International Society for Contemporary Music Concerts. Peter G. Davis reviewed the concerts for the New York Times on February 24, 1979*:

> By their very nature, concerts of contemporary music tend to be chancy affairs, containing as much, if not more, dross than quality. The last two programs presented by the League of Composers-International Society for Contemporary Music in Carnegie Recital Hall had their fair share of marginalia, but several works did stand out as being a bit special and well worth any open-minded listener's attention.

> In the League-ISCM concert of last January 25, the standout was Jean Eichelberger Ivey's Prospero, a setting of the Act V speech from Shakespeare's The Tempest, in which Prospero abjures the art of magic. Miss Ivey's choice of bass-baritone (Robert Kneefe), horn (Melissa Coren), percussion (Daniel Druckman), and tape gives a deliberately austere, rugged and unsentimental quality to her musical interpretation of this powerful speech. It was all not only appropriate, but added a distinctly original musical dimension to the words, and one with considerable expressive impact.

Ivey has received numerous grants including an annual ASCAP since 1972; several Meet the Composer awards; Martha Baird Rockefeller Fund; Composers' Assistance Program of the American Music Center; National Endowment for the Arts; recipient, Peabody Conservatory Distinguished Alumni Award, and her name was placed by Peabody Conservatory in Outstanding Educators of America. She has also been the subject of many articles, radio interviews, and a half-hour television documentary filmed by WRC-TV (NBC) in Washington, D. C., for their series A Woman Is, which has been shown throughout the country.

Her commissions include the following:

By Margaret Lauer, of New Orleans, a 30-minute work for baritone and orchestra in three movements, Tribute: Martin Luther King. Premiere by Peabody Conservatory Orchestra, with Earl Grandison, baritone, and Leo Mueller, conductor, 1973.

By the Collegium Musicum of the University of North Dakota, Hera, Hung from the Sky for mezzo, winds, percussion, piano, and tape. Text by Carolyn Kizer. Premiere 1973. Recorded by Elaine Bonazzi and the Notes from Underground Ensemble conducted by Andrew Thomas on CRI label, 1974.

By the New York State Music Teachers Association (their first commission) in conjunction with the Music Teachers National Association, an artist-level work for piano and tape entitled Skaniadaryo. Premiered at state convention, Buffalo, by Barbara English Maris, pianist, 1973.

By the Composers Forum of Albany, New York, to

compose a piece for Jacob Glick, viola, and Vivian Fine, piano, entitled Music for Viola and Piano. Premiere 1974.

By Sigma Alpha Iota (in conjunction with serving as Composer-Judge for the triennium ending 1978), Solstice for soprano, flute/piccolo, percussion, and piano. Text by composer. Premiere at National convention, Dallas, Texas, 1978.

By the National Endowment for the Arts, 1978. Work for orchestra and four-channel tape, SCA-Change (in preparation).

"The Composer as Teacher," an article written by Dr. Jean Eichelberger Ivey and published in the Peabody Conservatory Alumni Bulletin (fall-winter, 1974, Volume XIV, Number I), gives insight into Ivey's teaching. Too lengthy to reprint in its entirety, the highlights are presented below*:

> Composition cannot really be taught--but it can be learned. Out of this unique experience, each composer learns to steer his own course. What a teacher can hope to provide is a favorable environment for learning.
>
> Teaching composition, then, can have little in common with teaching a course that has a well-defined curriculum. It is more like setting out as guide on a journey of exploration, with a route never traveled before and the destination unknown. But this same sense of open-ended adventure is one of the fascinations of the creative life itself. So much is given by unconscious and intuitive elements, that a composer, poet, or painter finds his own development scarcely more predictable than another's. And so a composer may find in the teaching of other, less experienced composers, a gratification not far removed from that of his own journey of the soul.
>
> Another pitfall for the composer as teacher is the danger of imposing his own personal style on his pupils instead of helping them find their own.
>
> If a composer is not to teach his own style, what does he teach? It seems to me he functions

*Reprinted by permission of the publisher.

> something like a physician, who does not dream of treating all his patients alike, but from a breadth of knowledge diagnoses each, and prescribes what that patient seems to need. Some students, particularly in the earlier stages, are stimulated by more or less definite assignments. Others need to be given their head, with only a perceptive suggestion here and there. Nearly all need to extend their acquaintance with the music of their contemporaries, and one tries to recommend scores appropriate to each student's interests, experience, and project under way. Then there are specific facts and skills to teach as needed. A student's string quartet, for example, may involve reviewing string ranges and techniques (which he also encounters in orchestration class) as well as citing examples by Bartók or Carter, or Beethoven.
>
> In all, I look for signs of the student's special bent. By noticing, pointing out, and discussing the student's individual traits as they begin to emerge in his music, and perhaps by comparing them to similar things in the music of others, one helps the student become aware of his own tendencies and better enables him to develop them coherently and forcefully. He gradually acquires the conviction to say: This is what I think, this is what I like, this is what I am trying to do in my music. The composer who turns out works indistinguishable from those of a flock of other composers is the one we can do without. We value the one who has something personal and individual to say.

Ivey's well-defined article should serve as a model for schools of music. It is imperative that aspiring composers be provided the opportunity to develop their own creative abilities in a manner that reflects personal input. Composition deals with the intangible.

People lived in caves, today in solar homes. Composers must make choices and decisions if their music is going to reflect their creative potential. How boring music would be if it all sounded the same.

Dr. Jean Eichelberger Ivey, composer and teacher of composition, is held in esteem for daring experimentation, for the merging of diverse trends, for expressing a new vitality in fresh and exciting tonal combinations and a powerful personal imprint. Her position in twentieth-century music is prestigious.

Recordings

Pinball, Folkways record, Electronic Music, FMS 3/3436.

Pinball, excerpt, Columbia Special Products educational record, P 11597.

Music by Jean Eichelberger Ivey, for voices, instruments and tape, Folkways record FTS 33439. Terminus (mezzo and tape), Aldebaran (viola and tape), 3 Songs of Night (soprano, 5 instruments, and tape), Cortege--for Charles Kent (purely electronic).

Hera, Hung from the Sky, mezzo, seven winds, three percussion, piano and tape, Composers Recordings, Inc. CRI-SD 325.

Prospero Scana for bass voice, horn, percussion, and tape. Grenadilla records. In preparation.

Compositions

Ivey has composed numerous pieces, unpublished and published by several companies. Her principal publisher is Carl Fischer. The Fischer publications are listed below. (Including works placed in rental catalog of Carl Fischer, Inc.)

1954 Passacaglia for Chamber Orchestra
1963 Sonatina for Unaccompanied Clarinet
1967 Ode for Orchestra
1969 Tribute: Martin Luther King, baritone and orchestra
1970 Terminus, mezzo and tape
1971 Three Songs of Night, for soprano, five instruments and tape
1972 Forms in Motion, a symphony
1973 Hera, Hung from the Sky, mezzo, seven winds, three percussion, piano, tape
1973 Aldebaran, viola and tape
1973 Skaniadaryo, piano and tape
1974 Music for Viola and Piano
1976 Testament of Eve, mezzo, orchestra and tape
1977 Solstice, soprano, flute/piccolo, one percussion and piano
1978 Prospero, bass voice, horn, one percussion and tape.

BETSY JOLAS

Composer

Betsy Jolas is one of the leading creators of music in France. The American Academy/National Institute honored Jolas in 1973, along with three American composers, including Barbara Kolb, in recognition of their contributions in the field of composition.

Jolas was born in 1926 in Paris of intellectual American parents. Her mother, Marie Jolas, was a fine musician who studied singing in Berlin and Paris, where she became one of the devotees of James Joyce. She and her husband, Eugene Jolas, shared the same Paris literary preoccupations. They founded Transition, the famous avant-garde Left Bank international literary review.

The home environment, cultural opportunities, subtle Parisian cultivation, were to directly influence her life. As a young girl, she and her sister Tina had the opportunity to converse with the famous James Joyce, a childhood family figure. She saw portions of the score to Ionisation by Edgard Varèse about the time it was written (1934), and was often in the company of the literary giants of that era.

She studied piano and at an early age enjoyed sight-reading most anything at hand. Jolas often accompanied her mother at the piano for family and school recitals. This experience enriched her musical life as well as providing an opportunity to keep company with culturally aware people. She grew up feeling at ease and compatible with the field of the related arts.

Betsy Jolas says, "I knew I'd be a dancer, a painter, a musician--that I would have a career in the arts. But I never dreamed I'd be a composer. A composer was a genius like Beethoven."

BETSY JOLAS
(Photo by Alex Brown)

Jolas is a well-balanced feminist. She always had confidence in her ability to relate within the societal structure and from a young age found acceptance based on talent, not gender. That she had the advantages of being part of a cultivated and monied family could easily have influenced her outlook. She did feel some distrust when she first began to compose, but as her qualifications improved, she found her contemporaries became more relaxed and warm to her, and interested in her work.

It still took almost ten years for her to be recognized as a composer in France. For a period of time, she refused to have her compositions played on all-women programs. She wanted to be known as a composer, not a woman composer, but for hundreds of years only compositions written by men were regularly programmed.

The Jolases returned to the United States in 1939 when World War II broke out in Europe. She attended the Lycée Français in New York and the Dalcroze School of Music. Paul Boepple, who at that time directed the famous Dessoff choir, was to be an influence on the direction of her musical education. Miss Jolas credits her experience at the age of fifteen as a chorister, piano and organ accompanist with the Dessoff choir as an important influence in developing her career. She not only sang works most people did not know, but she became familiar with the musical scores as she accompanied the choir. Jolas was a devotee and admirer of such notable greats as Heinrich Schutz, Orlando Lassus, Josquin, and Perotin. Later in her career she would reflect some of their qualities in her compositions.

During her undergraduate years at Bennington College in Vermont, Jolas studied harmony with Boepple, organ with Karl Weinrich and piano with Hélène Schnabel. Bennington College has long been a haven for creative artists to teach and develop undergraduate students interested in the various fields of the arts. The college had for many years the dubious distinction of being the most expensive and most liberal women's college in the United States, though it is now a co-ed institution. In the early 1970's it was the first college in the United States to have a husband and wife team hold the two highest administrative positions: Gail Thane Parker was president, and her husband was Vice President.

During the time Jolas attended Bennington College, she composed her first important piece of music, a full-fledged Mass. This was performed by the student music groups with the help of local talent. It was during this period that she entertained serious thoughts of becoming a composer. Her composition MOTET I, To Everything There Is a Season, scored for seven voices, was performed during graduation exercises and then at Carnegie Hall.

It was many years later that Betsy Jolas discovered Virginia Woolf's book A Room of One's Own, an essay on female literary creativity. To quote from this book, "A woman must have money and a room of her own--with a door that locks--if she is to write fiction." The book develops the theory that literary success has been achieved by women not in the old forms hardened and set by men, but in the novel--a form that is still new and pliable, and a media that women can influence. The same is true in musical composition. Women will not contribute in the Bach to Beethoven period, but in the new forms and expression. Jolas says, "Now since I can write music better than I can cook, I decided to be a composer."

Following her graduation from Bennington College in 1946, she returned to France on her twentieth birthday. Shortly after her arrival she realized her training and background had not been extensive enough to compose on the level of proficiency she deemed necessary. However, Plupart du temps, her composition written in 1949, received honors from the National Society and was aired over French radio.

In Paris she studied analysis and aesthetics with Olivier Messiaen at the Paris Conservatoire. Jolas found Messiaen to be an astonishing and revealing teacher. Messiaen has been a musical giant in the field of contemporary music since 1944. She also studied composition with Darius Milhaud and counterpoint with Simone Plé Caussade. She continued to study with these master teachers for several years and credits Messiaen for his insistence that she listen with a new ear. There is no doubt that he helped her grow, and he molded her ability to hear exciting new tonal combinations. Still, Jolas was unable and unwilling to share in the experimental serialism being employed by Gilbert Amy, Stockhausen, Berio, and Nono. "I couldn't go through that purgatory--I couldn't do what they set out to do--create a musical language from scratch."

She entered a competition at the close of the school year in writing a fugue. The students were allowed eighteen hours to complete their work, during which time they were locked in a room with no piano, but allowed coffee and sandwiches. Jolas won second prize for her composition.

Miss Jolas married a French physician in 1949 and is the mother of three children. Although at times her family commitment slowed down her creative endeavors, she has always been able to continue her studies and her composing. This was possible because she is a member of an affluent as well as cultured family. Jolas admits that her career as a composer started slowly, not only because of her family responsibilities, but because of her own uncertainty as to just what musical medium could best express her feelings.

Her style evolved from changing compositional expressions. No creative person continually expressed herself via the same medium, and Jolas was influenced by both the French Renaissance composers, Debussyan music and choral compositions that were part of her culture, and to some small degree avant-garde serialism. She began to develop a contrapuntal style, with little thought of harmony, but with concern for rhythmic touches and unequal tempos.

In 1953 Jolas entered a conducting competition at Besançon, much as a joke. She was the only woman conductor and was chosen as a finalist, and eventually received honorable mention. As a result of this experience, she did not feel psychologically equipped to conduct all-male musicians because her training had not been extensive in the skills needed in this leadership position. Over the years she has conducted her own compositions and has been well received on the sacrosanct podium.

From 1955 to 1965 Jolas was editor of Ecouter Aujourd'hui, a periodical of the French Radio-Television Network. It was quite by chance that she was offered the position, but the results were most rewarding since this job projected the young Jolas into the mainstream of Parisian serious music. She met the important musicians in France at the time since all of them were contributing anonymously to this broadcast.

In addition to becoming acquainted with all the new musical compositions Jolas says of those years, "I got to meet absolutely everybody who was important in music. That is how I met Pierre Boulez. I would call or write to him in connection with my radio periodical requesting a presentation on a specific composer that I knew he was familiar with. I had this wonderful correspondence with him especially since he was writing the text anonymously, and there was no constraint, he felt free to write what he wanted." Eventually, Betsy Jolas did a series of programs called Que Savons nous (What do we know about...). Some of the subjects discussed were polyphony, sonata, concerto, and accompaniment music. The programs were music and talking and were aired every morning and Jolas feels, "I learned a great deal preparing for and hosting these programs. I spent a great deal of time listening and studying."

During this time, Pierre Boulez was also devoting his efforts to the programming of the avant-garde compositions of Stockhausen, Berio, Pousseur, and many others. This was a difficult task because the listening audiences were not in tune with musical changes being investigated by these composers. These concerts were known as the Domaine Musical. Jolas gathered her courage and requested that the demanding Boulez look over and comment on her work. This was to be the turning point in Jolas' career. He offered good technical suggestions, and a year later Boulez premiered her composition Quatuor II at the Domaine Musical. The composition was recorded, and with it Jolas' career as a serious composer was launched. Quatuor II is scored for coloratura soprano and string trio. The voice part is performed without text. Miss Jolas says of the work, "I was amazed with the emotion that developed during the performance. I didn't think I had written it." The burden of responsibility belongs to the performer. The voice is the only carnal instrument, and when scored with strings the final medium is awesome and spectacular, and one must hear it fully to appreciate its beauty. Within ten years Jolas attained status as one of the finest contemporary composers in France.

Betsy Jolas has contributed in many areas outside the field of composing. In 1961 she received the French author and composer award, contributed to an extensive poll on serial music, has been active in a number of national and international debates and discussions, has judged several important competitions, and is a contributor to the journal previews. Articles about Betsy Jolas have appeared in Dictionary of Contemporary Music (E. P. Dutton), The New Grove Dictionary of Music and Musicians, and Dictionnaire de la Musique Contemporaine.

The Domaine Musical conducted by Gilbert Amy performed Jolas' J. D. E. in 1966. The composition is scored for fourteen instruments and is based on sequences with a time duration between each related series. The conductor signals the performers to enter, but since there is no perfected way to indicate duration between sequences, the performance depends on how the music is interpreted by the conductor. Most performances are similar, but not precisely the same.

Miss Jolas has been in the process of writing two to three major compositions for almost twenty years. They are lyrical, but also highly structured and complete. She is generally regarded as belonging to the post-Boulez serial school. Her music is atonal in some aspects and yet there evolves a lyrical quality that is especially sensitive. There are indications that at times she utilizes a total chromatic spectrum that affords a new spirit of sound.

The Domaine Musical conductor Gilbert Amy, performed D'un Opéra de Voyage written by Jolas in 1967. Michel Gielen conducted the same Domaine Musical ensemble in the first performance at the Royan Festival of 1967. The piece was quite a success and had to be repeated. The concert held on April 30, 1968, was reviewed by Robert Siohan for Le Monde*:

> D'un Opéra de Voyage is the Mallarmean title chosen by Betsy Jolas to make clear a sort of instrumental transmutation of the substance and spirit of vocal cords. The word "opera" finds its justification in the fact that the various instrumental voices sing, laugh, talk, murmur, and declaim.... No doubt is possible as to this score; its success is total and a witness to an authentic power of communication.

Beginning in 1971 Betsy Jolas often substituted for Olivier Messiaen and taught his composition classes when he was on tour. She was appointed professor of Advanced Musical Analysis at the Conservatoire National Supérieur de Musique in 1975. This famous and academically demanding music college has no equal in all of France. The students are admitted only by audition by jury and must be talented as well as motivated to complete the rigorous requirements of an ambitious curriculum.

---

*Reprinted by permission of the publisher.

In 1978 Professor Jolas was appointed Professor of Composition replacing the world renowned Olivier Messiaen who had retired. That she is talented, has fine credentials, and is a creative genius with an international reputation was the sole basis for this prestigious appointment. She shares the responsibility of teaching composition with others and feels it is of great importance that young composition majors be offered the opportunity to study with more than one professor --this is most important in developing young talented minds.

Philippe Torrens wrote an article for the French Musical Courrier in 1973 on the eight star composers of contemporary music in France. Selection was based on the activity of each avant-garde individual as a composer, and the importance of the number of works achieved. Betsy Jolas received recognition for eight of her compositions between 1963 and 1970. This included Mots written for five voices and eight instruments for which Jolas composed the music and the text. The style is contrapuntal with certain word emphasis which in effect produces an overall super text. She has composed extensive compositions for voices and is an authority on contemporary vocal notation and the difficulties of the actual scoring of vocal parts.

Ten Concerts of Contemporary Music were presented by the Composers Theater at Washington Square Church in New York City in the spring of 1974. The Concord Quartet performed Quatuor III (nine etudes), a new work by Betsy Jolas. The composition dealt in contrasts and sounded richly coloristic and given the noted acoustics of the church, they were not as lyrical as many of her other works. She shared the program with all male composers.

In 1974 Betsy Jolas received the coveted Grand Prix National de la Musique Award. She shared the spotlight with the late Alexander Calder, Abel Gance and Jean-Louis Barrault. "I felt like a baby among giants," said Jolas. That she was recognized for her talent at a young age documents her status as one of the leading creators of France.

In 1976 and 1977 Betsy Jolas was composer in residence at Tanglewood, the summer home of the Boston Symphony Orchestra and the Berkshire Music Festival in Lenox, Massachusetts. During that summer, four of her compositions were heard: D'un Opéra de Voyage (1967) for chamber orchestra; Quatuor II (1964) written for coloratura soprano, violin, viola, and cello; Episode I (1964); and Fusain (1971).

The Jolas Quatuor II remains a hauntingly beautiful piece of music some twelve years after its premiere in France. The tone color using soprano voice with strings was strangely effluent and superbly performed by soprano Elizabeth Parcells and a string trio made up of BMCO students. It stretched the imagination of the listening audience and was acclaimed one of the finest pieces on the entire program.

Betsy Jolas' composition Quatuor III (nine etudes), a quartet for strings, has been recorded with the Composers Recording, Inc. (number 332) by The Concord String Quartet supervised by the composer. The recording was made possible by a grant to Jolas from the American Academy/National Institute of Arts and Letters Award in 1973. Jolas offers the following comments:

> I have attempted in this work to present a contemporary view of some characteristic elements of string technique in the form of nine etudes, each of which, following Debussy's example, deals with one particular aspect of this technique: pizzicato, harmonics, aleatory (No. 7 is in memory of Purcell's Fancy on one note), vibrato, etc. Several of the movements are played without pause.
>
> Commissioned by the Kindler Foundation, Quatuor III was completed in September 1973. The first performance was given at the Textile Museum in Washington, January 7, 1974 by the Concord Quartet, to whom the work is dedicated.

Jolas' compositions have been performed in the United States for many years, but during 1976 her music was extensively played and reviewed: she is climbing that same ladder of success in the United States that she had long ago attained in France.

In 1974 pianist Marie-Francoise Bucquet premiered Jolas' B for Sonata, which she had commissioned, for her four programs of twentieth-century music played in Alice Tully Hall. Also in 1974, the Serge Koussevitzky Music Foundation and the Library of Congress commissioned five composers to write works for the Chamber Music Society of Lincoln Center during the 1975-76 season. Betsy Jolas was one of the five composers honored. Her composition O'Wall for wind quintet was premiered in New York and performed the following summer at Tanglewood.

On August 17, 1977, the following review by Donal Henahan on O'Wall for wind quintet appeared in the New York Times*:

> O'Wall, a woodwind quintet by Betsy Jolas. Miss Jolas, who conducted, based this score on a scene from the last act of "A Midsummer Night's Dream" in which Thisbe apostrophizes the wall separating her from her lover. The Shakespearean fantasy, with its noctural creatures and its fanciful confusion among animal, human and spirit worlds, made an aptly rustic accompaniment to the rural drama played out in the audience.
>
> Miss Jolas calls her piece, which was given its premiere last season by the Chamber Music Society of Lincoln Center, a "puppet opera" in which each instrument portrays a separate though unrevealed role. This kind of dramatic expression, being strictly instrumental, lends itself to confusions and misunderstandings perhaps, but the Jolas piece is so fascinating as abstract listening that confusions turn out to be either unimportant or delightful. This listener, for instance, somehow heard the doleful braying of Bottom in the horn part throughout the piece, although that deluded ass actually sleeps through the scene.
>
> Miss Jolas' Quintet, like some works by Elliott Carter, gives a distinct character to each instrumental part and lets expression flow naturally from this role-playing rather than working from the more constricting formal patterns favored by many of her contemporaries. Not surprisingly, one heard suggestions of Messiaen, her teacher, although there was a gentle humor to much of O'Wall that is not to be found in the older composer's work.

Betsy Jolas received a Fromm Music Foundation Commission, and her composition Tales of a Summer Sea was premiered at the Berkshire Music Festival in August 1977. Her tone poem piece could easily depict the sea, the waves, the squalls, and the storms. This prolific piece of music will continue to be performed and has a tremendous audience appeal. Jolas was also in residence as a guest teacher at the festival.

Richard Dyer of the Boston Globe wrote the following comments published on August 18, 1977*:

> And Betsy Jolas' Tales of a Summer Sea, written on a Fromm Foundation commission especially for this festival, is some kind of masterpiece. The basic texture and volume and tessitura of the music remains constant throughout--the unplumbed, salt, estranging sea. But this is the constancy of incessant change ... surprising musical events, the sea-spray's thousand diamonds, solid yet barely perceptible. It is astonishing that a composer of this importance was almost unknown in this country until a year ago.

The Brooklyn Philharmonic Orchestra under the leadership of the eminent Lukas Foss presented a concert called Meet the Moderns in late January 1978 at the Brooklyn Academy of Music. Works by George Crumb, Barbara Kolb, Betsy Jolas, Olivier Messiaen, and Krzysztof Penderecki were performed. Lukas Foss has a strong commitment to presenting both old and new music, but through experience has learned that new music must be presented not only with pride, but also in a place on the program where it can be related to other compositions. Lukas Foss is also a composer which enables him to relate to his colleagues. He made the following comment, "They're looking toward me as one of the comparatively few people who know what it's all about. I'm not going to let them down. And besides, a conductor should be a little bit of an educator. I enjoy it."

Lukas conducted the New York premiere of Lassus Ricercare by Betsy Jolas. This composition used fragments of Orlando Lassus, the great Renaissance master, and one of Betsy Jolas' early idols, scored through contemporary techniques.

Peter G. Davis of the New York Times wrote on January 30, 1978**:

> In the Jolas composition a brass quintet provides the tonal anchor while two pianos, harp, and a

---

*Reprinted courtesy of The Boston Globe.
**©1978 by The New York Times Company. Reprinted by permission.

> variety of percussion instruments add a lacy overlay of ornamental filigree--a most attractive and ingeniously contrived web of sound.

In the late 1960's, Betsy Jolas, in an interview in Paris, France, readily agreed with many contemporary composers that the system of notation that had so long and faithfully served the needs of composers does not contain the necessary symbols to reflect the musical thoughts of modernistic compositions: vocal lines, new and varied uses of instruments, new time durations, and interpretation. However, Betsy Jolas says, "No composer today can picture a universal system of notation that would suit him as well. Most of them agree that the present system is proving inadequate, but since we are experiencing constant esthetic changing, no one system can be imposed at this time except by natural selection."

Ms. Jolas has been among the best known and most appreciated composers in France for a number of years. Her status in the United States gained momentum beginning in 1973 as recipient of the prestigious American Academy of Arts and Letters Award and her talents are in demand in this country. Betsy Jolas' music is performed with increasing frequency as a result of her residencies as visiting composer at the State University of New York in Buffalo in 1975, at Yale University in 1979, and the (almost unheard of) two summers as composer-in-residence at the Festival of Contemporary Music at Tanglewood. Her chamber opera, The Riverside Pavilion, toured not only England, Belgium, and France, but was heard in the United States in 1975 in Washington, D. C., Chicago, and Philadelphia. Since Jolas was in this country she appeared at each of the performances.

Betsy Jolas is a remarkable and articulate young women who has contributed an important repertoire to twentieth-century music. Her compositions are capable of moving audiences and are challenging to the musicians who perform them.

Recordings

Quatuor II, Mady Mesplé et le trio à cordes francais, VSM CVB 2190, aux USA Angel S-366-55 Prix de l'Academie Charles Cros.

D'un Opéra de Voyage, Orchestre du Domaine Musical, dir: Gilbert Amy, ADES I 200I Prix de l'Académie du Disque.

Iphigénie, Musique d'accompagnement.

Sonate à 12, Les solistes des choeurs de l'ORIF, dir: Marcel Couraud, Inedits ORIF 995-031 Barclay Prix de l'Académie du Disque.
Tranche pour harpe, Marcelle Decray, CORONET 850 C 2508.
Quatuor III, Concord Quartet, CRI 332.
Mon ami, Michèle Boegner, ADES 2001.
Autour, clavecin Elisabeth Chojnacka ERATO STU 710 10.
Points d'aube, Serge Collot: Alto. Ensemble Ars Nova, dir: Marius Constant.
J. D. E., Ensemble Ars Nova, dir: Marius Constant.
Stances, Claude Helffer: piano. Nouvel Orchestra Philharmonique ADES 14013 Prix de la ville de Paris.

Betsy Jolas has composed an extensive list of musical works (almost a hundred in number). Most of the compositions beginning in 1963 have been published by Heugel Company of France, and Theodore Presser Company is sole distributor of her music in the United States and Canada.

1949 Plupart du temps, mezzo soprano and piano
1956 Figures for 9 instruments
1959 Five poems of Jacques Dupin, soprano, piano/orchestra
1961 L'Oeil égaré, text by Victor Hugo, radio cantata
1963 Dans la Chaleur vacante, soloists and orchestra, radio cantata
1963 Mots, voices and instruments
1964 Quatuor II, coloratura soprano and string trio
1964 Episode, flute
1965 Motet II, 12 part chorus and small orchestra
1966 J. D. E., 14 instruments
1966 4 Plages, for string orchestra
1967 D'un Opéra de Voyage, twenty-two instruments
1967 Tranche, for harp
1968 Points d'aube, viola and thirteen wind instruments
1968 Diurnes, for chorus of 12-72 voices
1969 Etats, violin and six percussion
1970 Sonate à douze, twelve solo voices
1970 Lassus Ricercare, instrumental ensemble, brass, piano, harp and percussion
1971 Fusain, bass flute and piccolo (one flutist)
1973 B for Sonata, piano
1975 Le Pavillon au bord de la Riviere, chamber opera
1976 O'Wall, woodwind quintet
1974 Quatuor III, nine etudes
1977 Tales of a Summer Sea, symphonic orchestra
1977 Eleven lieder, for trumpet and small orchestra
1978 Stances, for piano and orchestra

BARBARA ANNE KOLB

Composer

In 1969 Barbara Kolb became the first American woman to receive the Prix de Rome, in composition. She opened the door for the equality of women in the creative world. Kolb is one of America's outstanding young composers whose music embraces a new expressiveness.

She was born in Hartford, Connecticut in 1939, the only child of Helen Lily Kolb and Harold Judson Kolb. Her father was a self-taught musician, director of music for a local radio station, and conductor of many semi-professional big bands of his time.

Kolb majored in clarinet at the Julius Hartt School of Music at the University of Hartford and earned a Bachelor of Music degree, cum laude, in performance, in 1961. She was a student of composer-conductor Lukas Foss and Gunther Schuller at Tanglewood in 1964. She received her Master's degree in composition, in 1965 from the same university, where she studied with Arnold Franchetti. She then went to New York City.

Barbara Kolb was the first woman to be recognized by the Fromm Foundation and was commissioned in 1970 to compose music to be performed during the Fromm Festival Concerts at Tanglewood, in Lenox, Massachusetts. She received the commission along with three other women because of excellence and not as a token gesture toward women. The concerts of contemporary music sponsored by the Fromm Foundation at Tanglewood are an important part of the Berkshire Festival. This portion of the festival concentrates for several days on contemporary music. Other women commissioned were Shulamit Ran, Joyce Meekel and Betsy Jolas (from France). The commission included a $400 cash award, a performance at Tanglewood, and publication of the composition.

She wrote Trobar Clus, scored for strings, brass, flute, harpsichord, guitar, marimba, vibraphone and chimes.

Grants, awards, commissions, and fellowships have long been a source of monies for creative people. They are a necessity, but the uncertainty of continual sponsorhip is questionable, and many awards are prestigious but offer only a small financial commitment.

Barbara Kolb played E♭ clarinet in the Hartford Summer Band and the Hartford Symphony Orchestra for six years. One cannot create without the necessities of life (food, lodging and sleep), hence, Kolb had to play in these groups to earn a livelihood. She comments, "Orchestra work did not provide for individual creativity, due to the fact that playing continually in an orchestra provides no stimulation and is basically a boring mini-intellectual experience, allowing no room for growth." She moved to New York City and supplemented her income for several years by working at the monotonous task of music copyist.

In the 1970's, as her music became more prominent, her compositions were programmed throughout the United States and Japan, awards became more frequent and of more financial value so she was able to devote most of her efforts to creating. All of the following awards are important and some are developed more extensively later in the chapter. She was recipient of commissions from the Fromm Foundation, Koussevitzky Foundation, the University of Wisconsin in Milwaukee, MacDowell Colony (background music for a documentary film), the New York State Council for the Arts, Washington Performing Arts Society, Music Teachers National Association, Portland Symphony Orchestra (Maine), and the University of Wisconsin (Fall River). This represents an impressive list of commissions received by an impressive composer.

In addition to the above she received three Tanglewood Fellowships, four MacDowell Colony Fellowships, the prestigious Prix de Rome, Fulbright Scholarship, two Guggenheim Fellowships, resident composer of the American Academy of Rome, resident composer of the Marlboro Music Festival, Ford Foundation Grant (to study electronic music at Mills College in California), two Creative Artists Public Service Awards, and the National Endowment for the Arts Award.

The technique of composing cannot be taught since the

BARBARA KOLB
(Photo by Jean-Luce Huré)

teacher only makes suggestions. It can be learned through the study of analysis of existing work, but the choice of material depends entirely on the composer's style, inventiveness and natural ability. All creative products are the result of a burning desire and obsession of the individual to bring to fruition her own personal taste. No artistic commitment requires costly academic degrees, although pressures from universities and other institutions of higher education more often than not do require earned degrees to attain professional status.

In 1973 Miss Kolb was summer composer-in-residence at Marlboro College in Vermont. She received her first full-time college appointment in the same year at Brooklyn College in New York, as professor of composition and analysis.

In 1975 there were less than one hundred women professors teaching composition full-time in prestigious colleges in America.

Ms. Kolb offered several comments on contemporary music and they are worth repeating: "It is really a sad state of affairs when you think of the few orchestras that exist and the limited number of conductors who would even think about programming a contemporary piece. Conductors of orchestras cannot take a chance on the unknown quality for they must please the audience as well as the board of trustees who give them their jobs. So, to program a contemporary piece is a thorn in everyone's side--you must educate your audience slowly with contemporary music because they are so filled with the classics. Part of the problem is the conductors who are not good enough, those who have not studied contemporary techniques and have had little, if any, experience with contemporary music. They have to spend too much time learning complicated scores and usually they don't want to be bothered. New music needs good conductors."

Barbara Kolb has an exclusive contract with Boosey and Hawkes Music Publisher. This company took an interest some years ago in such prominent twentieth-century composers as Igor Stravinsky, Béla Bartók, Aaron Copland, and Benjamin Britten. Ms. Kolb says, "A tremendous revelation occurs when you realize that a company of the stature of Boosey and Hawkes is truly interested in you and will publish everything you write. Suddenly you begin to think--I'm not just a crazy composer who sits alone writing music that nobody will ever hear or cares about. There is a whole new attitude that develops when you discover that people actually like your music. Writing music is a very painful process and it is very solitary. With the recognition from Boosey and Hawkes there is a feeling of responsibility to them, and not just to myself, which is a tremendous incentive to continue."

Barbara Kolb is a young woman who has not yet reached her fortieth birthday but has attained international acclaim for her compositions. The combination of youth, extensive training and international recognition places the talented Kolb in the position of being one of America's foremost composers. Millions of men have composed for hundreds of years, but only a tiny percentage have received international status. She is a model role for women and men in undergraduate studies who aspire to a career in composing. Only a talented few will attain her level of creativity, but the fact remains that it can be accomplished.

All awards are important, but when she received the Prix de Rome award in 1969-71, Kolb joined an impressive group of contemporaries, including Lukas Foss, Randall Thompson, Samuel Barber and Howard Hanson. That she was the first woman ever to receive this award in composition denoted recognition of her significant talent as one of the outstanding young composers of the century. Rome Prize Fellowships are awarded to individuals on evidence of ability and achievement in several fields including musical composition. The award provides for a period of economic leisure in Rome, Italy.

At the age of thirty-six, Barbara Kolb was composer-in-residence at the American Academy in Rome. She spent the academic year composing Spring River Flowers Moon Night for ensemble and the revision of Soundings (two versions are available, one for ensemble and the other for orchestra).

The second Festival of Contemporary Music at the Berkshire Music Center on August 19, 1970, was conducted by Gunther Schuller. He chose to conduct two world premieres: Mario Davidovsky's Synchronisms No. 6 and Barbara Kolb's Trobar Clus. Kolb used a poetic form taken from the troubadours in the 11th and 12th centuries. The composition was orchestrated for thirteen instrumentalists divided into four mini-orchestras. The reviews were excellent indicating that the first woman to receive a Fromm Foundation commission had been a well-qualified recipient.

Mr. Daniel Webster, writing for the Philadelphia Inquirer on Wednesday November 22, 1978, describes Trobar Clus thusly*:

THREE SOLUTIONS TO SONORITY
IN ENSEMBLES

> The mark--and the necessity--of contemporary composers is their ability to reinvent the orchestra. In the search for new sounds and combinations and

*Reprinted by permission of the author.

> the need for economy, composers have devised small combinations capable of great variety and novelty.
>
> Three composers whose work was presented yesterday by the Contemporary Players at Temple University showed their solutions to the problem of sonority. The interest centered on Barbara Kolb, a much-honored composer who is spending the semester as a visiting professor.
>
> She conducted the ensemble in her own Trobar Clus, a concise work for 13 instruments that explore contrasts between plucked instruments and fundamentally sustaining ones. Her ensemble included harpsichord, guitar and percussionists playing marimba and vibraphone and chimes. Three brasses and a flute were the sustaining elements while a string quintet moved between the two camps.
>
> Her exploration was built of intimate combinations of sounds and led to an ecstatic moment that used all the instruments. Along the way was a downgrade glide in the trombones and the other instruments capable of sliding, which was a striking moment in a piece that had strong sense of structure and progress.

Trobar Clus has been recorded by The Contemporary Chamber Players of the University of Chicago, Ralph Shapey, music director and Barbara Kolb, conductor (Turnabout Label, Vox Productions number TV-S 34487). Solitaire is also recorded on the same record. Ms. Kolb provided notes to accompany the recording:

> Trobar Clus, to Lukas, was commissioned by the Berkshire Music Center and the Fromm Foundation. It is a Provençal poetic form which was developed by the Troubadors (Trobar meaning Troubador in Provençal) during the 11th and 12th centuries. Essentially, it is an uncrystallized Rondeau form, as Trobar Clus was the predecessor to the rondeau, and by its formative nature it allows one to be flexible within the boundaries of an extremely free, yet (paradoxically) strict pattern.
>
> The disposition of instruments relates to the variations of the internal form. Repetition functions more through the rotary recurrences of various groups of instruments than through a literal repetition of thematic material. However, each group

> retains its own personality and proceeds in a continuous state of evolution just as one does in life.
>
> One should feel a rather positive staticism. In other words, the work should convey various statements which are complete in themselves, yet imply continuation ... perhaps, there is no ending.

The School of Fine Arts of the University of Wisconsin-Milwaukee commissioned Barbara Kolb in 1973 to compose music to commemorate the tenth anniversary of its founding. The composition Frailties, orchestrated for the Symphony Orchestra, was premiered on May 9, 1973, at the University's Fine Arts Festival. Mark Starr conducted.

Kolb received a Koussevitsky Music Foundation Award and her composition Soundings was programmed on October 27, 1972, conducted by Gunther Schuller. The world premiere was performed by the Chamber Music Society of the Lincoln Center in New York at Alice Tully Hall. This was the thirtieth anniversary of the Koussevitsky Music Foundation which commissioned six new works to be performed by the society. Soundings utilized a prerecorded tape as the twelfth participant in the double sextet, including a string quartet, woodwinds, harp and chimes. This composition was eventually rescored by Kolb when she realized the potential of the materials for full orchestra. Two major symphony orchestras have played the composition.

On December 12, 1975, Barbara Kolb's evocative composition Soundings was performed under the baton of Pierre Boulez and the New York Philharmonic Orchestra. Ms. Kolb based her composition on the extrasensory marine-sounding technique, where the water depth is determined by measuring the echo time of signals bounced off the bottom of the sea. The composition has a mysterious effect on the listening audience as it develops strong tone color clusters and combinations of instrumental sounds that "lifts" the ears to new levels of appreciation. The very same evening the piece was performed in Rome by the Rome Radio Orchestra. Kolb was a trustee of the American Academy of Rome from 1972-75, and was a resident composer.

The same exciting orchestral composition was performed by the Boston Symphony Orchestra in 1978 during the regular concert season. Conductor Seiji Ozawa chose Soundings to represent music of the United States on the orchestra's Japanese tour during that season.

Richard Dyer, writing for the Boston Globe on February 18, 1978, said:

BSO STRIKES GOLD WITH SOUNDINGS*

> The BSO hasn't had particularly good luck with its new pieces this year.
>
> But, in Barbara Kolb's Soundings the orchestra has found itself a piece of real music as well as a new work. Kolb uses the technique that everyone has at hand nowadays--multiple orchestras, fragmented and insistently repeated melodies, criss-crossing and overlapping rhythmical patterns. But she has used procedures to make a piece that has a beginning, a middle and an end, something that to atmosphere, texture and color adds destination. The music makes sense and leaves mysteries, which is what art is supposed to do, it leaves you with an insistent urge to hear it again, which fortunately I shall, since Seiji Ozawa has chosen it for frequent performance on the forthcoming Japanese tour.

Ms. Kolb wrote the following notes as they appeared on the Boston Symphony Orchestra's Program**:

> Soundings is scored for three orchestras, two of them replacing channels of electronic music on tape in the original chamber version; it requires two conductors. Each of the three orchestras includes flute, oboe, clarinet, bassoon, horn, three violins, three violas, three cellos and two basses. Orchestras I and II each have a harp and orchestras II and III include chimes.
>
> This composition is in three sections. The first begins with a linear ostinato in the strings, from which further patterns evolve in successive layers. The texture becomes increasingly rich through extended chromaticism, although the original patterns retain their character as they emerge and disappear from the sound matrix. The whole descends to a climax where the patterns dissolve in the texture.
>
> In the second, or soloistic, section the original patterns are isolated and treated individually as

---

*Reprinted courtesy of The Boston Globe.

> though seen through a microscope. Here linear movement is replaced by spurts of motivic ideas which could not actually be heard within the texture of the previous section, but which are now clarified and developed by the solo instruments. The motivic ideas become increasingly chromatic and the section culminates in a passage for two violins which resolves into a brief transition in the strings of orchestra II and III where all movement is entirely suspended.
>
> The final section is characterized by an ascending linear movement which contrasts with the first section. Here the roles of the strings and winds are reversed with the winds ascending in chordal clusters and the strings carrying the melodic ideas. The upward movement toward the surface becomes faster and faster through a rhythmic acceleration until the climax is reached. The signal has not returned to its starting point, and it is not clear what has been measured. Suggestions of motivic ideas from the first section quietly appear and disintegrate.
>
> The performances were dedicated by Kolb to the fond memory of a loyal friend of generous artistic sensibility, Olga Koussevitsky.

The Monday evening concerts in Los Angeles are best known for presenting musical esoterica. On December 10, 1974, Barbara Kolb's West Coast premiere of Solitaire, written in 1971, was performed at the County Art Museum Bing Theater. Composed for piano and accompanying electronic sound it provided the audience with an evening of coloristic contrasts.

The Gregg Smith Singers performed Kolb's Looking for Claudio in July 1975 at St. Stephen's Church on West 69th Street, New York City. It was the most widely acclaimed composition during the three-day festival, a twentieth-century legacy. The beautiful tonal combinations easily soothed the listeners into a world of dreams of long lost beloved ones.

Music critic Donal Henahan of the New York Times wrote on July 31, 1975*:

> The prize offering turned out to be the United States premiere of Barbara Kolb's Looking for Claudio (1975), a haunting piece for guitar and tape. There were distant bells, soft humming, and near the end a section in which the guitar and tape join in a disquieting insistent duet--all adding up to a mood of loss and restrained sadness. A lovely spellbinding piece.

Kolb's Appello had its world premiere on October 10, 1976, at the John F. Kennedy Center for the Performing Arts in Washington, D.C. As with her previous compositions, this too was widely accepted and acclaimed. The freshness and vitality of this work is inspiring.

The year 1978 was an exciting one for Barbara Kolb. She received two commissions: one from a Chicago FM radio station to write a series of songs (Songs Before an Adieu for flute, guitar and soprano) and the second from the University of Wisconsin at Fall River to compose Chromatic Fantasy for narrator and chamber ensemble (based on the poetry of Howard Stern).

The most important and prestigious prize of this period was the Honored Alumna of the Year Award conferred by the University of Hartford, Hartt College of Music. Too often our institutions of higher learning wait until it is too late to recognize living alumni or more often they tend to recognize elderly graduates. The University of Hartford produced a fine example for aspiring undergraduates by honoring the young, exciting, talented and intellectually stimulating Barbara Kolb. Composer Kolb conducted at the Kolb Festival of Music, presented as part of the award ceremony. The program included her compositions Homage to Gary Burton and Keith Jarrett, Looking for Claudio, Songs Before an Adieu, and the world famous Trobar Clus.

Under the terms of the Willamain McPhee Thaxter Memorial Composition Fund, the Portland (Maine) Symphony Orchestra, conducted by Bruce Hangen, performed the world premiere of Barbara Kolb's Grisaille, on February 13, 1979. Kolb was the first composer ever honored under this fund, which was established in honor of Willi Thaxter. She had been a major factor in the decision to have a full-time resident conductor, an originator of the Youth Concerts and an enthusiastic believer in the role of the arts in the quality of the urban environment. She was also President of the Board of Trustees in the early 1960's.

Barbara Kolb comments, "Grisaille is my first orchestra piece, and it was a tremendous learning experience--it was the first time I ever thought of the orchestra conceptually as a whole. My composition Soundings, performed by both the New York Philharmonic and the Boston Symphony Orchestra, was originally written for chamber ensemble and tape and then rescored. I had an incredible amount of fear of writing for the full orchestra because I didn't think I could do it, but I am pleased with the results."

Many of the great master composers shared this same fear expressed by Kolb. For example, when Brahms composed his now famous D minor Concerto, he promptly experienced a setback, a hostile to indifferent reaction. He described it as a brilliant and decided failure. But history has proven otherwise. Kolb explains further,

> I was determined to write an orchestral composition that was not like the usual--and this is not like the usual--you don't have clearly delineated parts where there are isolated sounds and soloistic instruments. The basic idea has to do with layers of sound juxtaposed, emerging and dissolving continually, over a harmonic-matrix which changes slowly. There are lots of rapidly moving notes in clusters throughout the entire orchestra to be played simultaneously and in time. As the piece is based on one chord, which changes in disposition and transposition, the idea is one which is monochromatic, yet, should be subtle in color.

Kolb wrote the following program notes for Grisaille:

> "The intensity of expression should vary in degrees. At times it is necessary to paint in monochrome and limit one's self to gray tones ..." Debussy.
>
> A music devoid of melody, harmony, rhythm and meter in the traditional sense, yet incorporating a sense of structure through a variety of colors which continually repeat themselves kaleidoscopically is my intent in Grisaille.
>
> Grisaille (a technique depicting monochromatic, decorative painting), was inspired by a painting in graphite by Hans Schiebold. The arbitrary, yet controlled development of various lines and textures set in a quasi-relief background made me think that

> controlled pitches expressed rhapsodically without concern for rhythm or meter, would be the comparable statement in music--texture which creates a statement--a blending of ideas incorporating color.
>
> In effect, lines emerge and disappear from the sound matrix, according to an underlying logic which generates the structure. The effect evoked should be like looking through a dense, tropical foliage rising in different arcs towards the sky.

The Portland Symphony Orchestra in Maine is one of the finest of its kind in the world. The caliber of performance is amazing. The credit for this must be shared by Bruce Hangen, conductor, Russell I. Burleigh, manager and the performers. Membership of the orchestra is comprised of residents of Portland and the immediate areas and musicians who commute from Boston, Massachusetts. Principal performers are often members of the Boston Pops or Boston Symphony Orchestra--local musicians realize the importance of importing some instrumentalists and have a deep pride in the organization. Even more important is the friendliness expressed by the musicians that is interwoven throughout the entire organization.

Says Barbara Kolb, "My experience with the Portland Symphony Orchestra was very positive--they work hard and they are delightful to work with, nobody suffers from delusions of grandeur. Mr. Bruce Hangen is a lovely person and a terrific conductor. He understands contemporary music, is interested in it, has experience and conducts very well."

Conductor Hangen had done his homework well, he interpreted the score of Grisaille to the tiniest detail and he accepted the responsibility for helping the audience to prepare themselves for this contemporary premiere. Conductors must assume a leadership role if America is to promote new musical experiences.

Mr. Hangen's Notes from the Podium,* printed in the Portland Symphony Orchestra's program, are well worth repeating for listeners and could serve as an excellent model for other conductors:

---

*Reprinted by permission of the author.

Tonight's concert marks the first occasion in more than a year that an entirely new composition has been presented by the PSO, so I would like to offer a few comments and/or tips on just how one should be listening to Barbara Kolb's GRISAILLE, or to any other brand new composition.

Probably the most important suggestion I can offer is that you not listen in any different a way than you would to anything else. No matter in what specific musical language a certain composition may be written, it is nevertheless music. And all music is based on the same principles of tension and release; of activity and repose; of sonic colorings and their myriad shadings; of the horizontal and melodic principles of sound progressing in time, as opposed to, or in conjunction with the vertical or harmonic aspects of any one particular moment. These same principles of composition can be applied to practically every style of music known to the western world the last five centuries--Palestrina, Bach, Haydn, Beethoven, Brahms, Strauss, Stravinsky, Boulez, Kolb--in that all should be listened to in the same way.

But, alas, they are not, and it's our fault. All too often we, especially the "first time" listeners, come with the incorrect expectation that we should be listening to yet another statement of something we already know. In other words, Beethoven's music wasn't so popular in his own lifetime because his audiences were expecting to hear more Haydn; in turn, Brahms' audiences wanted Beethoven and I wouldn't be surprised if many of Kolb's audience tonight are displeased if her music doesn't sound more like Stravinsky's.

Consequently, you should approach Ms. Kolb's composition on the assumption that, yes, indeed it will be entirely new; and that it should be listened to and appreciated for what it is, rather than what you think music is supposed to sound like. Only then will it become a lively, challenging and positive experience. But do remember that above all, it's unfair to all concerned to expect something new to not sound new at all.

Next, please be forewarned that I have little sympathy for those who may come complaining about "all that dissonance." After all, you will have to agree that the terms consonants and dis-

> sonants are entirely relative and subjective in their application. Maybe as an experiment we should enter City Hall tonight on the premise that Ms. Kolb's musical language is in fact just as consonant with itself and its environment as was Schumann and his FOURTH SYMPHONY in their own time. And as a still greater experiment, may I suggest that we consider ourselves to be a totally enlightened community for at least the next couple of hours. Now, having absolutely no preconceived notions about music, about so-called proper ways to form melodies, harmonies, phrases or balances, let's sit back and allow each composer's creation to play upon our natural instincts. Let's let ourselves be carried by the thoughts, ideas, the play-of-sound that each composer is trying to express. Open up! Be receptive! "Careful! No preconceived notions!" If you can do that, there will be some hope.

The concert was an evening to remember, sub-zero temperature, howling winds and still a full house of adventurous music lovers--who extolled with thunderous applause the gifted young Barbara Kolb and Grisaille.

Headlines in the Portland Press Herald on February 14, 1979, read: "Kolb's Composition: Eerie Yet Eary." The review was written by Clark T. Irwin Jr. and the following are excerpts*:

> Grisaille proved eminently listenable, interesting and not at all alarming. The audience, apparently feeling very receptive, applauded the piece warmly and greeted Ms. Kolb cordially as she received a congratulatory Hangen Hug.
>
> Grisaille is an experience difficult to convey in words. The name is taken from a painting technique which uses shades of a single color to convey textures and structure.
>
> In the musical analogue of the painterly technique, orchestration seeks out block effects and eschews abrupt transitions of tone or tempo.

*Reprinted by permission of the author.

> There is a pervasive, subtle humming quality to the work. Tones advance, then recede, scales ascend, then descend, leaving a tingling aura behind them.
>
> Although Ms. Kolb disavows straightforward rhythms, Grisaille undergoes almost organic progressions of sonic growth and decay, tension and relaxation.
>
> At length, the brasses break through the shimmering mist of strings with pulsing chords that drive the piece to a crescendo complete with the thunderous rattling of snare drums. Then silence.
>
> It works and will certainly repay hearing or rehearing when WCBB (Channel 10) broadcasts the taped performance.

Barbara Kolb has never actively participated in the women's movement. She has contributed to the cause, however, because she is talented and determined to pursue a career in composing. Kolb explains, "Music is a matter of art not gender. If anything, composing a piece of music is very feminine. It is sensitive, emotional and contemplative. By comparison, doing housework is positively masculine." She has succeeded in earning international praise, invading what was once a man's world.

Professor Kolb is one of America's youngest and most successful composers. She has climbed the ladder of recognition, but not without pitfalls. Her Fulbright Scholarship to Vienna in 1966 was a disaster. She found herself living in a cellar apartment with spiders as uninvited company, permitted one bath per week, and the cultural conditions were almost decadent. She returned the Fulbright. She has lived for years in a walk-up brownstone two-room apartment, on a small amount of money to provide for her personal needs. This is less than ideal living conditions, but creative ability can never be stifled even when personal and physical conditions are difficult. In all probability such existence added fuel to Kolb's determination to compose.

She has been the synthesist for over twenty-five years of experimental composers. The avant-garde compositional ideas of serialism, tone clusters, and other modern idioms are fused and blended by the insight and keen ear of Kolb into compositions of expressivity, sensitive elegance and lyrical beauty. She could become the most prolific composer of the twentieth century.

Says Kolb, "Someday I would like to write background music for film because I like film people for one thing and I like theater for another and I like drama in general. It also pays money and I enjoy money as much as I enjoy the others."

Composer Kolb has the uncanny ability of writing beautiful lyrical music that is light, sensitive and emotionally descriptive. It has a direct audience appeal which has provided for repeated performances. The height of creative achievement is to share a given talent with others, and she has reached that peak and still continues to express her musical genius. The conceptual orientation of the twentieth century deals with multiple components, including rhythmic motives, multiple sonorities, and multiple orchestras and conductors. The composer must forge all of these parts into a whole with feeling and unobstructed freedom. Barbara Kolb has the talent and artistic unity to lead the field of young American composers.

Since July 1976 she has had an exclusive publication contract with Boosey and Hawkes. Her earlier works are available through Carl Fischer and C. F. Peters.

Recordings

Figments-for-Flute and Piano, Three Place Settings, Chansons Bas, on Desto Label number 143.
Looking for Claudio, Spring River Flowers Moon Night, on Composers Recording Industry number S361.
Rebuttal, Opus number I.
Trobar Clus, Solitaire, on Vox (Turnabout number TV-S 34487).

Compositions (partial list)

1964	Rebuttal, for two clarinets
1966	Chansons Bas, for soprano and chamber group
1967-69	Figments, for flute and piano
1968	Three Place Settings, for narrator and chamber orchestra
1968-69	Crosswinds
1970	Trobar Clus, instrumental ensemble

1971 Solitaire, for piano and tape
1971 Toccata, harpsichord and tape
1972 Soundings, two versions, ensemble or orchestra
1973 Frailties, orchestra
1974 Spring River Flowers Moon Night, ensemble
1975 Looking for Claudio, guitar and tape
1976 Appello
1977 Homage to Keith Jarrett and Gary Burton, duet flute and vibraphone
1977 Vernissage, for flute, violin, guitar and soprano
1978 Songs Before an Adieu, flute, guitar and soprano
1979 Chromatic Fantasy, for narrator and chamber on the poetry of Howard Stern
1979 Grisaille, for orchestra

WANDA LANDOWSKA

Concert Artist, Master Teacher, Writer

Wanda Landowska was born in Warsaw, Poland, on July 5, 1879 and died on August 16, 1959, in Lakeville, Connecticut. Landowska--the woman, the artist, the genius--is held in awe for her great contributions to music. It appears to be humanly impossible for one person to attain and share the great wealth of knowledge and expertise that Landowska has given the world.

She was the daughter of Marian Landowska, a lawyer and a musical amateur. Her mother, Ewa, was a linguist. Landowska studied piano at the age of four with Jan Kleczyski. She attended the Warsaw Conservatory and studied piano with A. Michalowski. In 1896 she went to Berlin and studied composition under J. Urban.

Landowska eloped in 1900 with Henry Lew, a writer and an expert on Hebrew folklore. They lived in Paris, which at that time was an exciting center for the arts. This love and sustained support from Henry Lew lasted 19 years until his death in an automobile accident.

In 1925 she settled at Saint-Leu-la-Foret near Paris, where she founded her own Ecole de Musique Ancienne, intended primarily for experienced musicians desiring to improve their knowledge of the styles and to learn the technique of the old instruments. There were both private and public courses, the latter taking place during the summer months only and specializing in the aesthetics of interpretation of the 17th and 18th centuries. The students, both singers and instrumentalists, took part in the performance of the works concerned as well as in discussions, analysis, and criticism. Wanda Landowska built a large concert studio in her garden where the public lectures were held. She conducted one concert a week for twelve weeks followed by twelve weeks of Master Classes.

WANDA LANDOWSKA
(Photo by Otto Hess)

In the 1940's when the Nazis were approaching Paris, Wanda Landowska had to abandon her school, her library of more than 10,000 volumes, and her collection of old instruments. In 1941, after a short sojourn in the Pyrenees and later in Switzerland, she found herself in the United States. Her first recital, after an absence of fourteen years, took place in the Town Hall, New York.

MUSIC BY VIRGIL THOMSON*

New York Herald Tribune
Thursday, October 22, 1942

Wanda Landowska, harpsichordist in recital last night at Town Hall, playing the following program:

Prelude and Fugue in E flat minor from "The Well-Tempered Clavier." Book I.....Bach
Suite in E minor ....Rameau
Lament composed in London to dispel melancholy to be played slowly with discretion ..J. J. Froberger
Chromatic Fantasy and Fugue......Bach

A Shower of Gold

Wanda Landowska's harpsichord recital of last evening at the Town Hall was as stimulating as a needle shower. Indeed, the sound of that princely instrument, when it is played with art and fury, makes one think of golden rain and of how Danaë's flesh must have tingled when she found herself caught in just such a downpour.

Madame Landowska's program was all Bach and Rameau, with the exception of one short piece by Froberger. She played everything better than anybody else ever does. One might almost say, were not such a comparison foolish, that she plays the harpsichord better than anybody else ever plays anything. That is to say that the way she makes music is so deeply satisfactory that one has the feeling of a fruition, of a completeness at once intellectual and sensuously auditory beyond which it is difficult to imagine anything further.

On examination this amplitude reveals itself as

the product of a highly perfected digital technique operating under the direction of a mind which not only knows music in detail and in historical perspective, but has an unusual thoroughness about all its operations. There are also present a great gift of theatrical simplicity (she makes all her points clearly and broadly) and a fiery Slavic temperament. The latter is both concealed and revealed by a unique rhythmic virtuosity that is at the same time characteristic of our century and convincingly authentic when applied to the execution of another century's music.

It is when this rhythm is most relentless that I find Madame Landowska's work most absorbing, free recitativo, and the affetuoso style she does with taste, and she spaces her fugal entries cleanly. But music becomes as grand and as impersonal as an element when she gets into a sustained rhythmic pattern. It makes no difference then whether the music is dainty, as in the Rameau suite, or dancey and vigorously expository, as in both the Rameau suite and the Bach Partita. It is full of a divine fury and irresistibly insistent.

There is no need of my reviewing the works played, which are all great music, save perhaps to pay tribute to Rameau, who got so much of the sweetness of France, as well as its grace and its grandeur, into his E minor Suite. And to mention the romantic and rhapsodical beauty of the Froberger Lament. There is even less occasion to point out stylistic misconceptions and interpretative errors on the executant's part, because there weren't any. At least, it seemed to this listener that every work was fully possessed by her. If the audience was as fully possessed by these superbly convincing renditions of some of the grandest music in the world as this auditor was (and certainly it appeared to be), there really isn't much that any of us can do about it further, except to make sure of not missing this great artist's next performance. Last night's was as complete as that.

It is important that a person of her ability be recognized; however, the amount of space allocated to her is in no way sufficient to present all of her work. Readers should pursue this musical giant by reading some of the other books published by and about her and by visiting Lakeville, Connecticut, home of the Wanda Landowska Center.

Wanda Landowska is a legend in the history of music. She was known as the high priestess of the harpsichord, an interpreter of many composers (especially Bach), a lecturer at learned gatherings of the musicological congress, a critic, and author of several books of music. Most of them are available now in Landowska on Music (published by Stein and Day of New York, collected, edited, and translated by Denise Restout, assisted by Robert Hawkins).

Her ability to communicate and her compassion for human beings are extensive. She possessed a sincere love of people. It was important for her to share with the world her vast and varied understanding of music. She will always be known as a musical genius because a great volume of recordings of her artistry will be forever known and respected. One may not always believe the written word, but what ears hear is truth, and the recordings of Wanda Landowska will always assure mankind of the quality of her ability. One of her greatest achievements is the recordings she made from 1949 to 1954 of the whole of Bach's Well-Tempered Clavier on the harpsichord.

The first modern works composed for the harpsichord were written especially for Wanda Landowska by Manuel de Falla and were composed and dedicated to her, including his Concerto for harpsichord, flute, oboe, clarinet, violin and cello. Francis Poulenc also composed and dedicated to her his Concert Champetre for harpsichord and full orchestra. Madame Landowska's recording produced by the International Piano Archives IPA 106/7 includes this Poulenc work.

She is credited with the revival of the harpsichord at the beginning of this century. This has to be considered important, since without her great efforts, the listening public would have never shared the beauty of the many programs she performed on this instrument. It is equally important that she has been a recognized authority on the keyboard music of the 17th and 18th centuries. Virtuoso and musicologist, she interpreted music with words as well as sounds. She believed that music belonged to all people and words helped her share this feeling. They likewise helped the audience understand more fully the true meaning of the music which was forgotten when she entered the musical scene. There are only a few listeners who do not need this type of understanding.

On January 14, 1950, Wanda Landowska performed a benefit concert in honor of Dr. Albert Schweitzer's seventy-fifth birthday. She wrote the following notes for two of the works performed*:

Bourrée d'Auvergne............. Wanda Landowska

Many years ago, the Auvergne colony of Paris asked me to take part in a regional festival of music and dances of Auvergne. Marius Versepuy (scholar who devoted himself to the folk-music of Auvergne) who knew my fondness for folk-music, sent me a collection of authentic bourrées, and I began to read them. The motives of the bourrée fascinated me, and I was struck by their resemblance to certain Polish dances. I composed a chain of bourrées and transcribed them for the harpsichord. But this resemblance to the Polish Oberek continued to obsess me, and I asked myself, anxiously, if, in playing the bourrée, I was accenting it in the true Auvergne spirit. At this time, I lived in an 18th century house, in the Latin Quarter, where there was a large fireplace in my music room. Every week a coal man from the bistro across the street brought me a sack of coal. In Paris, many bistros sell drinks in the front and coal in the rear, and these are almost all owned by Auvergnats.

I shall put to the test my way of playing the bourrée, I said to myself as I sat at my harpsichord, awaiting the arrival of the coal man. A knock at the door and there he was with his sack of coal on his back. I broke into the bourrée. The man stood still, looked around to see where this music which he knew so well was coming from. He put down his sack and began to dance. Happy, I gave a sigh of relief.

Italian Concerto........................ J. S. Bach

Bach travelled very little in his lifetime, never even once leaving the confines of his native country. At most he would, upon occasion, quit his home and his work to hear a Reinken or a Marchant improvise. Yet, though withdrawn from the world, he kept in complete touch with musical movements in foreign countries. He knew thoroughly the French Masters

*Reprinted by permission of The Landowska Center, Lakeview, Connecticut.

> and delighted in reworking the compositions of the Italians. Bach was fascinated particularly by the concerto grosso, a form which was created about the year 1700 by Albinoni and Torelli and established definitely by Vivaldi. The essential feature of this form was the opposition between the tutti and the soli. Bach, who had transcribed for solo harpsichord Vivaldi's orchestral concerti grossi, accomplished an extraordinary tour de force: he composed his Concerto in Gusto Italiano the complex work which contains within itself all the elements of a concerto grosso. With royal authority, he attacked and settled the question of tutti and soli, and in bestowing upon a single instrument the execution of this opposition, he elucidated in a decisive fashion, the structure of all 18th century concerti grossi and the manner in which they were performed in that epoch; thus the Italian Concerto is, in fact, a concerto grosso for solo harpsichord. It is the most living of documents, the most eloquent of all explanations. On the harpsichord which--with its double keyboards and its varied registers--unfolds and multiplies en orchestre or is transformed into a solo, according to the fluctuations of the work, the Italian Concerto achieves full reality. The contrasts between the tutti and the solo, the dialogue passed from group to group, the juxtaposition of shade and light, all this mosaic of richly varied tones, finds new life on the instrument for which the music was originally created.
>
> Wanda Landowska
> Lakeville, Conn.

Only a handful of her contempories were in favor of her pursuing the harpsichord, probably because the instrument was not only forgotten after a whole century of romantic music written for the piano, but because attempts at reviving the harpsichord around 1900 were so badly done that they gave a poor idea of what the harpsichord really is. It took several years to complete the harpsichord that Landowska had commissioned the piano firm of Pleyel to build. Imagine the amount of knowledge and research she had to undertake to even begin this project. Denise Restout, Director of the Landowska Center, recalls,

> Madame Landowska visited most of the museums

in Europe to study the harpsichords that had been in use. She then met with the chief engineer from Pleyel and studied the plans of all the instruments she had seen. In agreement with the engineer they devised this instrument which is based on a typical harpsichord of the time of Bach, two keyboards, the two usual 8-foot registers, plus a 4-foot register, and the most important addition was a 16-foot register.

In 1912 the new instrument was completed and Landowska's dream, to build an instrument that would produce as closely as possible those used in the middle of the 18th century when they had reached the height of their glory for richness of the high registers and the beauty of sonority, became reality.

She authored many prolific articles, but in 1909 her book Musique Ancienne was published and created a sensation in the world of music. The material was basically an overall defense of the music of the past. True genius that she was, the book remains an excellent source of information. It can be found today in a new version of English translation in Landowska on Music (Stein and Day).

All artists pass through various stages of interest and creative powers--the extent of such undertakings are subjected to a variety of external and internal forces. The history of music is a history of change developed by countless musicians living and creating through cycles of growth and discovery. Wanda Landowska's ability to interpret music was of the highest caliber. As a prolific writer, she competently presents scholarly opinions and interpretations on teaching, working, fingering, phrasing registration, ornaments, rubato, allargando, criticism, and dozens of other areas.

The chronological writings and concerns that evolved throughout Landowska's lifetime can be perceived as issues that forever kept her mind active and pulsating with the challenges to meet the needs of a perceptive listening audience. The following is a partial list of her essays:

"Pourquoi la musique moderne n'est-elle pas mélodique?" S. I. M., 15 Mar. 1913.

"Comment faut-it interpréter les Inventions de J. S. Bach?" Monde Musical, July 1921.

"Le Concerto en mi bemol majeur de Mozart," Tribune de Genève, 7-8 Jan. 1923.

"Les Musiques d'aujourd'hui," Revue Contemporaine, 1 Oct. 1923.
"A propos du 25e anniversaire de la Societe Bach," Guide Musical, 1930.
"Les Suites de clavecin de Handel," Radio Magazine, 3-10 Jan. 1937.
"A Note on Bach," New York Times, 15 Feb. 1942.
"Tribute to Rameau," New York Times, 15 Feb. 1942.
"Strings Plucked and Struck," New York Herald Tribune, 28 Feb. 1943.
"Note on a Great Neapolitan," New York Times, 24 Oct. 1943.

The multiplicity of her contributions were obviously enhanced by extensive touring and travel. There is no finer teacher than travel and conversation to activate the probing mind to exquisite and meaningful experiences. Wanda Landowska toured throughout the United States and Europe including France, Germany, Spain, and Russia. Her performances as a harpsichord virtuoso are unparalleled. She spent years studying and interpreting the great masters, especially the polyphonic music of Johann Sebastian Bach. A professed lover of the music of Bach, Landowska was a firm believer that the expert performer must also know and understand the music and the intimate surroundings of the composers, musicians, and friends who lived and worked within a given time. To her it was impossible to be a perfectionist if one isolated a particular composer and became a specialist. She was an astute learner who devoted her life to intellectual pursuit of the many aspects of music and performance.

Her knowledge and ability to relate to audiences afforded her many opportunities to lecture before her contemporaries. She was held in esteem by the great European minds and more often than not spoke to packed audiences. Not only musicians but also writers attended her master classes, because they were fascinated by the richness, precision, and poetic beauty of her speech whether in French, Polish, or German. Her ability as a musicologist permitted her to speak fluently not only on interpretation and keyboard music, but on random composers such as Tchaikovsky, Couperin, Dvořák, Stravinsky, Gershwin and Poulenc. Wanda Landowska was an absolutely amazing person. There are many gifted people in the world, but only a few ever attain the pinnacle of success and dedication that was epitomized by her life.

One knows of Wanda Landowska as a superb performer,

both on the piano and harpsichord, perhaps as an interpreter and maybe as a musicologist, but her contributions as a composer are less well known. Her compositions could not be considered extensive in comparison to the classical giants such as Bach or Beethoven, but nevertheless she did compose and create in a style that again indicates genius status.

Her compositions vary from a folk approach found in Polish Folksongs a cappella (composed for the Orfeo Catala of Barcelona), Polish Folksongs for Solo Voice with Choir and Orchestra, Polish Folksongs for Harpsichord and Small Ensemble, and The Hop (Polish folksong for harpsichord solo) to a sophisticated and contemporary Liberation Fanfare for band. Her composition Bourrée d'Auvergne is recorded by her on Veritas VM 104 sponsored by the International Piano Archives. Her Liberation Fanfare was chosen for performance by the Goldman Band of New York on July 16, 1943*:

> Wanda Landowska, the world's greatest harpsichordist, wrote the Liberation Fanfare while in the South of France, during the Summer of 1940. This composition opens in a minor key and, in a heroic mood, voices grief, despair and revolt. Yet, faith in liberation persists. The minor key yields to a major one, for an inextinguishable hope sustains the countless martyrs. Gradually, joy overwhelms and illumines all: the Liberation Fanfare closes with a song of jubilation.

In July of 1978, I had the privilege of visiting the Landowska Center in Lakeville, Connecticut, and spent priceless time with Denise Restout, its director. Miss Restout's contributions are by far above what we as Americans consider director's responsibilities.

Denise Restout is a charming, intelligent and warm individual. She is also an outstanding musician in her own right. In 1933 she was recipient of a scholarship for Miss Landowska's Master Class in Paris, France. That scholarship was to span twenty-six years until Landowska's death in Lakeville in 1959. Miss Restout did not remain her student in the "pure sense" of the word, but became her assistant in

---

*Reprinted by permission of The Landowska Center, Lakeview, Connecticut.

1935. As I visited the Center, I had a feeling that Wanda Landowska never really died. She lives through her writings and teachings. Many of Wanda Landowska's contributions to the world of music will be preserved as a result of the tireless efforts of Denise Restout and her foresight in taking a stack of notes written by Landowska when they escaped the Nazi invasion in May 1940. Left behind and mostly all destroyed were Landowska's priceless music treasures from her music school. Included were her instruments, her library, and priceless correspondence. One valuable harpsichord from that music school that the Nazis destroyed in northern France in 1940 did eventually find its way to America. Miss Restout recalls it in this manner: "The instrument, Landowska's favorite, was found by a friend, Doda Conrad, who had served in the American Army and had been sent to Munich to look for works of art confiscated by the Gestapo." That very instrument was in the room when I visited the Landowska Center.

Landowska was a linguist, but Restout, when she came to America with her beloved teacher, neither spoke nor understood English. She asked Landowska how to learn and the response was, "answer the phone, read the paper and go to the grocery store." This she did and today she is in complete command of the language.

I can best capture the devotion of Denise Restout to Wanda Landowska if I relate her escape after returning to northern France where she discovered the horrors of the Nazis' destruction of the Landowska School. Receiving a message from Landowska, who was a refugee in Nice, that she had decided to leave for America and wanted her to go also, Denise Restout had to undertake a risky journey through the demarcation line between occupied and so-called "free zone" in France. She accomplished this by riding a big truck hidden under a heavy canvas with cows loaded into the back of the truck. They passed the German guards and were left in a section of land between the two zones. Then she ran about a mile through a plowed field to the French side and freedom, to accompany Landowska to America. Landowska and Restout arrived in America on Pearl Harbor Day, December 7, 1941, with little else but one harpsichord purchased by a former student who sold her life insurance to buy the instrument.

Recordings

In addition to the list of Wanda Landowska's recordings

published in Landowska on Music (collected, edited, and translated by Denise Restout; assisted by Robert Hawkins (paperback); published by Stein and Day) are the following:

Veritas VM 104 (1967) sponsored by International Piano Archives, excerpts from live performances at the Frick Collection and from the Wisdom Series film (NBC 1953)
- Praetorius: Volte du Roy
- Martin Peerson: The Fall of the Leafe
- Telemann: Bourée
- D'Anglebert: Gavottes
- Couperin: Les Ondes, La Pantomime
- Landowska: Bourrée d'Auvergne
- Bach: Third Movement of the D major Concerto for Harpsichord
- Vivaldi--Bach: Second Movement of the D major Concerto
- Bach: First Movement of the Italian Concerto
- Francisque: Bransle de Montiranda

International Piano Archives IPA 106/7
- Mozart, Concerto No. 13 in C major K. 415 (Rodzinski, conductor)
- Mozart, Concerto 22 in E♭ major K. 482
- Mozart, Sonata No. 12 in F major K. 332 (piano solo)
- Poulenc: Concert Champetre, harpsichord and orchestra (Stokowski, conductor)

Bruno Walter Society No. 720 (excerpts from Radio Broadcasts)
- K. P. E. Bach: Concerto in D major (Koldofsky, conductor)
- Handel: Concerto in B♭ major (Stokowski, conductor)

Bruno Walter Society: IGI-273 also excerpts from the Frick Collection Concerts
- Bach: English Suite in A minor (1947)
- Handel: Suite in G minor (1949)
- Handel: Suite in E major (1943)
- Rameau: Suite in E minor (1949)

EMI of Japan has reissued HMV DB5007/8 (Bach) and DB-4941-6 (Couperin)

THEA MUSGRAVE

Composer, Conductor

Dr. Thea Musgrave, composer and conductor, was born in 1928 in Edinburgh, Scotland. She was from a cultured family, the only child of Joan and James Musgrave. There was a time when she was attracted to the medical field because she had a deep feeling of responsibility to humanity. Following the completion of her public school education, she entered Edinburgh University as a pre-med student. That she changed her educational directions and studied music would, within a period of time, project her as the most prodigious and best known serious women composer of the twentieth century. Her ability to compose for opera, ballet, orchestra, chamber ensembles, vocal and choral pieces is recognized in twenty-four countries. She is a composer of international fame and recognition and as a conductor has received respect on the prestigious podiums in both opera and orchestral performances.

She received her Bachelor of Music Degree from Edinburgh University. Her undergraduate education was a traditional musical approach under the teachings of Mary Grierson in harmony and analysis, and counterpoint and history of music with the Viennese composer Hans Gâl. Traditional as her background may have been, it provided her with a solid understanding of the art of music and a base to build her individuality as a composer. As an undergraduate she received the coveted Tovey Prize in honor of Donald Francis Tovey, celebrated Scottish musicologist. That she was to change directions from medicine to music as an undergraduate student was to benefit mankind.

On a postgraduate scholarship she studied in France for four years, two years at the Paris Conservatoire and from 1950 to 1954 with Nadia Boulanger both at the conservatoire and as a private weekly pupil. The talented musicians,

THEA MUSGRAVE
(Photo by Martha Swope)

composers, and conductors of our century have had the opportunity to study under the world-renowned Boulanger, considered to be the finest teacher in the world of music and a musical goddess of the twentieth century. Musgrave says of the class Nadia Boulanger taught at the conservatoire, "It wasn't the piano accompaniment class, we never did any accompanying on the piano, but it was so much more. We did score reading, figured bass, transposition and of course Stravinsky; it was a wonderful general music education." This was a solid, stimulating background for the talented Musgrave, who also became familiar with the work of Bartók, Dallapiccola and eventually Pierre Boulez and Karl Heinz Stockhausen.

Thea Musgrave's next comment is shocking: "The distinguished Nadia Boulanger was not allowed to teach composition at the Paris Conservatoire because they (the conservatoire) had a rule that only composers could teach composition. So one of the greatest teachers of the century could not teach at the conservatory, except for piano accompaniment." Yet, this amazing teacher influenced almost all of America's leading twentieth-century composers, as well as many leading European composers.

The talented Thea Musgrave has been inundated with commissions from both European and American foundations since she completed her studies in France over twenty-five years ago. She must turn down commissions each year since it is humanly impossible to accept all of them. "Quality is the most important factor in my music," Musgrave feels.

Musgrave has always spent the major part of her time composing although she was on occasion an extramural lecturer at London University from 1958 to 1965; was visiting professor of composition at the University of California in Santa Barbara in 1970; and subsequently is a guest professor (when time from composing permits) for the College of Creative Studies at the University of California in Santa Barbara.

One of the earliest professional performances of Musgrave's music was heard at the Edinburgh Festival in 1955. Her composition Cantata for a Summer's Day, sung by the Saltire Singers, was a large diatonic and tonal piece, superbly performed and well received by the music critics and audience.

The British Broadcasting Company was also responsible

for projecting the talented Musgrave into the mainstream of serious twentieth-century music. She comments,

> The BBC is a fabulous organization. London's famous Third Program broadcast classical music all day. But it is different from America because most of the music is live. The BBC in Scotland, Wales, Ireland and regions in England all have their own orchestras. The unions allow only a certain amount of needle time [recordings]. I was very fortunate, coming from Scotland, many of my earlier works were performed by the BBC in Scotland, conducted by Colin Davis. Then, when I moved to London my music was performed by BBC in London. To be able to start a career under these conditions is absolutely fabulous.

In 1973 she did a series of eight broadcasts for British Radio III concerning the possibilities of electronic music for a wider audience. The programs not only provided excellent material for the listening audience but afforded Musgrave many opportunities to explore and research material that would be of value in her composing career. She had used prerecorded tape for several years previous to these programs with exciting success.

Thea Musgrave thus had achieved prominence as a composer in Europe before coming to America. She considers composing to be a unisexed profession and never encountered any particular problems as a women in the field of professional composing or conducting. Musgrave is recognized for her talent, the only basis upon which any artist should be judged. She has the uncanny ability to compose with a variety of beautifully balanced timbres that have a far reaching effect on the listener. One remembers the music and the virtuosity of Musgrave. There are only a few prominent composers in the world today and she would certainly be at the top of the list.

To describe and categorize Musgrave's compositions is utterly impossible. Her works cover a variety of musical possibilities each written with total commitment to the final product. There were periods of serial technique, free chromaticism, abstract instrumental forms, prerecorded electronic tapes, tonal division and a combination, delectation, or expansion of many musical idioms. Thea Musgrave's music can never be neatly pigeonholed. That is exactly what makes her music unique. Musgrave explains,

> Nobody influenced me to compose, I always liked music and it grows from that. You don't become a composer for practical reasons you do it because that is what you have to do. My style develops and I do different things at different periods of my life. For example, my Clarinet Concerto is based on "dramatic personage," the clarinet player walks throughout the orchestra and takes on a certain dramatic attitude. The soloist must have a special pizzazz. It's a combination of instrumental ability and personality.

Thea Musgrave has been attracted throughout her career to opera and ballet as a means of transcribing dramatic ideas through music, and large dramatic forms have influenced her other compositions. A special article in Opera News on February 14, 1976, on "Prominent Women," quotes her in the following manner*:

> In my instrumental music, I have gradually evolved a style where at times certain instruments take on the character of a dramatic personage, and my concern is then directed toward the working out of a dramatic confrontation.
>
> I have also been interested in the use of electronic tape; new sounds, echo effects, etc. become easily possible and can in a simple and evocative way show another level of experience which can then be integrated into the score. This concept was the starting point for my Voice of Ariadne.

There are certainly fresh, exciting, and vibrant compositions being written under Musgrave's philosophy. Her music roams freely, and she composes a new kind of musical art, exciting to perform and exciting to hear. Her esoteric settings are far different than those credited to the old master composers. Society is continually in a state of change, and our arts reflect similar changes. The world of electronics has opened an exciting new era for music. The tyranny of the bar-lines, meter signatures, major-minor tonality and other musical aspects have been changed or completely dissolved to permit a new dimension of sounds. No longer can one's ears take a nap--the hearing process is challenged.

Thanks to composers like Musgrave, the world of

---

*Reprinted by permission of the publisher.

musical composition has grown, expanded, and exploded to meet society's expectations. The artistic concepts, the musical techniques, the capacity for innovation attained by Musgrave have programmed her compositions in prestigious concert halls throughout the world. Her music has been performed and broadcast in the United Kingdom, France, Germany, Switzerland, Scandinavia, Australia, the United States, Canada, and Russia. Musgrave's compositions have been included in Edinburgh, Cheltenham, Aldeburgh, Zagreb, Venice, and Warsaw music festivals.

While teaching composition, at the University of California at Santa Barbara, in 1970, to replace a colleague on sabbatical leave, Thea Musgrave met Peter Mark. He subsequently became general-director and conductor of the Virginia Opera Association in Norfolk, Virginia. Thea Musgrave and Peter Mark were married in London in 1971. That artists have for centuries extolled in uniting their creative abilities is known throughout history, and Musgrave and Mark exemplify this union. She commuted from London to Santa Barbara for a period of time, but the difficulties of distance proved exhausting and expensive so she gave up her home in England.

In 1970 Musgrave's From One to Another was premiered at the Monday Evening Concerts in Los Angeles, California. Scored for viola and tape and written for her husband Peter Mark it has been performed both in America and abroad by him. Musgrave comments, "The viola part is accompanied by a pre-recorded tape composed of altered viola sounds. The music is similar to a concerto with stress on rhapsodic phrases and rich textures." When this composition was performed at the Ojai Music Festival failure of the electronic equipment resulted in the rescheduling of the piece for the next day.

One of the most exciting musical performances takes place when the composer conducts her own composition. In 1969, because of a problem, it was suggested that she conduct her composition Beauty and the Beast. She thought the idea a bit crazy since she had only six hours of formal instruction in conducting with Jacques-Louis Monod and a little experience conducting symphonic and chamber music. However, since that time she regularly conducts her own music.

The premiere of new works often requires a tremendous amount of rehearsal time and energy from both the musicians and the conductor. Most often the composer is in attendance during rehearsals so the conductor can confer with the writer for suggestions and changes. It is not unusual for a conductor to spend several months studying a new score and many conductors are hesitant to present new compositions because their busy schedule does not permit enough time for necessary preparation. According to Musgrave,

> A composer has a keen perception of the music she has written and it makes sense for her to conduct, especially a new work. As I compose I try to be very practical and not to make unreasonable demands on time that is very expensive in terms of orchestral rehearsals. However, I never compromise with the artistic importance. The rehearsals are tremendous learning experiences for both the musician and the composer-conductor. The musicians can offer advice on the technical aspect of their particular instrument and immediate changes can be made. The musicians are best qualified to determine certain aspects. I have trained as a musician, I know the score since I wrote it, and I respect and understand the performers, therefore conducting is not difficult.

The combination of composer-conductor is certainly not a new idea. It was successfully employed for centuries by the old masters, who not only composed and conducted their compositions but at times performed with the ensemble, too. Thea Musgrave has attained prominence on the podiums of the Scottish Opera Company, the Los Angeles Chamber Orchestra, the New York City Opera, the San Francisco Opera Company, Scottish Opera, the Scottish Ballet, the Philadelphia Orchestra and others. She was the first woman to conduct her own composition with the Philadelphia Orchestra in 1976. Her Concerto for Orchestra, written in 1967 and premiered in London, England, was performed. She says, "I rehearsed the orchestra for two hours and their caliber of musicianship was such that it could be accomplished. I would not be able to do that with an orchestra of less standards. This was a fabulous experience, the Philadelphia Orchestra is everything people say it is, really marvelous."

Musgrave has been commissioned several times by the British Broadcasting Company and one of the works written (in 1969) was Night Music, for chamber orchestra. The world premiere was performed by the BBC Welsh Orchestra and reviewed by Stanley Sadie of the London Times, 1969*:

> The work is some 17 minutes long, a continuous movement for chamber orchestra with specially prominent parts for two horns--a continuation, Miss Musgrave says, of her series of works using and extending the traditional concerto principle. It is a strong shapely piece. (It) avowedly has no programme, but her vivid graphic writing invites description in emotive adjectives. Music, in fact, underlaid by a strong feeling, and also lucidly laid out: not a big work, but another notable token of her originality and distinction of thought.

Professor Andrew Frank, of the University of California at Davis, wrote the following article published in Notes (Ann Arbor) on Musgrave's Night Music**:

> Night Music by Thea Musgrave is a beautifully constructed, masterfully composed work for chamber orchestra. The one-movement, multi section piece features the two horns players who are asked to assume various stage positions in the course of the work. The various positions correspond to the different types of musical gesture: when two players are seated adjacently, the music is flowing and lyrical; the music becomes more agitated and dramatic when they change position and move to the opposite sides of the conductor. The changing stage positions are put to excellent use at the coda as the first horn, offstage and fading into "niente," is contrasted to the second horn still on stage.
>
> There are moments in Night Music when the players are playing independently of the conductor and two different types of notation are presented on the page. Conventional notation is juxtaposed against a free, "senza misura" notation which allows the players considerable freedom. There is a system of cues which help the players keep the parts moderately synchronous.
>
> The one-movement work begins "Andante Notturnale" and progresses through several more sections: "Svegliato," which supplies the first real

*Reprinted by permission of the publisher.
**Reprinted by permission of the author.

contrasting music in the piece (violins with sfz attacks on a pitch, E, which gradually expands to a cluster); "Andante Amoroso," an extremely lyrical, free-flowing section; "Calmo," a short section in which the two horn players stand and go to their new stage positions on opposite sides of the conductor; "Tempo Libero: Minaccevole," in which the first horn plays relatively free material over the second horn's fast march and the violins' and violas' "Adagio" in 3/4 time. The two remaining sections are "Tempestuoso," and "Tempo di Andante Amoroso," which functions as a coda. In the last section the first horn moves offstage and gradually disappears altogether while the second horn remains on stage. Set against this is the orchestral tutti which plays wisps and snatches of the previously heard music.

Night Music is busy music, and while the individual parts are not rhythmically complicated, the players are generally kept quite active. Of course, the two solo horn parts would require professional players of the highest caliber. There is no doubt that Musgrave possesses the technique of a master as this work so ably demonstrates. As for the actual gestural content of the music, it would not be hyperbolic to say this music is hauntingly beautiful, elusive, nocturnal, and deserves to be in the front ranks of the contemporary chamber orchestral literature.

In 1970 the British Broadcasting Company commissioned Musgrave to write a composition for the celebration of the Beethoven Bicentennial. The Piece was titled Memento Vitae: a concerto in homage to Beethoven. According to the composer, "the work is an exposition of the struggle between the old and the new. Using references and quotations from Beethoven's era as the old, and extended segments of exciting orchestral improvisation as the new, the conflict of themes swirls and ultimately ends with the timpani blasting the last sound." The Memento Vitae is classifiable as a one-movement piece of program music. The United States premiere was performed by the Milwaukee Symphony Orchestra in September of 1975, conducted by Sarah Caldwell.

Music Viva of Boston, Massachusetts, is noted for its performance of twentieth-century music. On April 17, 1973, at Harvard's Busch-Reisinger Museum, Thea Musgrave's composition CHAMBER CONCERTO NO. 2 was performed and there was tremendous enthusiasm from the audience. Written in homage to Charles Ives, one can readily trace the style and tonal effect with Ives' compositions Fourth of July and Three Places in New England. The conflict, rhythm, and tonal expression of the bass clarinet, piano, viola, flute, the eventual sounds of churchy pianissimo, and the addition of practical American folk tunes readily identify this composition with Charles Ives.

The Royal Opera House commissioned her to compose an opera for the English Opera Group that resulted in her third opera The Voice of Ariadne based on Henry James' book The Last of the Valerii. The plot develops around two cultures, an Italian Count, his American wife, and their love relationship. A statue depicts the person who is not there and was a perfect instrument for Musgrave's ability to compose for tape. She comments, "I taped the voice so the words could be clearly heard and added electronic sounds that depicted the sea and distance." (The use of tape had been most successful in her previous ballet, Beauty and the Beast.) The libretto was the work of Amalia Elguera who, in Musgrave's opinion, "writes beautiful poetry." When the opera was premiered in 1974 at the Aldeburgh Festival, it had a woman composer, conductor and librettist, yet none of the sixteen newspapers that covered the opening mentioned the roles of the women. Only the performance was of importance.

Thea Musgrave made her New York conducting debut on September 30, 1977, at the New York City Opera with The Voice of Ariadne. The performance was reviewed by Mr. Harold C. Schonberg for the New York Times, on October 1, 1977*:

> Thea Musgrave is a British composer, now resident in the country, whose operas are beginning to attract a great deal of attention. Last night the New York City Opera introduced Miss Musgrave's The Voice of Ariadne to this city. She herself conducted the performance.
>
> The Voice of Ariadne brings to the fore once again an old problem involving contemporary opera. Which is more important: words or music? Theo-

retically opera is a fusion of many elements, of which the word--the libretto--is but one. But as things have worked out so often in the last half century, many contemporary operas have foundered on the dominance of the word, with the music taking a subsidiary role.

Composers protest that they are indeed writing melody; they say they have included set pieces and all the traditional paraphernalia in their works. The public continues to say no. To most of the public, contemporary opera does not "sing"; there is no real melody, singers never are allowed to let themselves loose.

The chances are that The Voice of Ariadne will join the ranks of forgotten operas that do not "sing," and in some respects that will be a shame, for it has many things going for it, especially in this production. The key word here is intelligence. Everything is intelligent about The Voice of Ariadne.

Miss Musgrave knows how to set the English language infinitely better than most of her colleagues. Never is the natural accent of words wrenched askew; never is the natural flow interrupted. She also is enough of a traditionalist to work within established operatic conventions, and The Voice of Ariadne is built around solo, duet and other set pieces.

The libretto, too, is extremely intelligent. It has been adapted by Amalia Elguera from a Henry James story--The Last of the Valerii. Naturally, James being involved, there are all kinds of relationships. But basically the story tells about a Count infatuated with the Ariadne legend. He alone can hear her voice, and he falls in love. At the end his wife takes on Ariadne and conquers.

This is a bald synopsis of a very literate libretto, one that is capable of being interpreted on many levels. Nothing much really happens; there is no violent action or, indeed, much action of any kind. Yet the character development is so strong that the story holds the attention. And the entire production strives for a period quality that transcends the period. The sets and costumes by Carl Toms are naturalistic, handsome and rich-looking, and Colin Graham's direction points everything toward the denouement. For once, in Henry James, an American can meet the European aristocracy on even terms.

> Miss Musgrave's music uses a small orchestra, has taped sections--Ariadne is never seen, only her voice on tape is heard--has a good deal of aleatory and plenty of dissonance. Yet it is anything but avant-garde. Miss Musgrave constantly tries for melody.
>
> Whether she succeeds is another question. She still writes in a style that sounds very old-fashioned, with all those seconds and ninths. She favors a type of melodic declamation, and even the big numbers, where she wants to get a soaring line, manage to sound tight and constricted. Basically her resources are very limited. Textures sound monotonous after a while, and the musical materials are just not very interesting. What Miss Musgrave does, she does with integrity, but this is still another opera that does not "sing."
>
> The production was representative of the City Opera at its best: a handsome cast, musicianly, with more than enough voice to take care of the vocal problems, and completely creditable on stage. There were patches where diction went by the boards, but enough came through to keep the plot lines clear.
>
> Miss Musgrave, who has been the conductor of many of her operas, this one included, went about her business with confidence. When she came on stage at the end, there were cheers. The audience liked what it had heard. Thus this very likely is a minority report--on the music, at any rate.

Again in 1973 the BBC commissioned Musgrave to write for the Promenade Concerts (the famous summer series performed in London). Concerto for Viola was composed and had its United States premiere performance in 1975 by the Pasadena Symphony Orchestra. Peter Mark, Thea Musgrave's husband, played the demanding solo parts both in this country and abroad. The composition is humoresque and can best be appreciated in live performance. The assumption would be that Musgrave took into consideration her talented husband when composing the concerto. The instrumentation provides for varying tone colors within the orchestra. Of particular interest is the master class offered by the soloist to the viola section of the orchestra. In this work the viola players sit where the violins usually are placed. The work provides many interesting and varied tone colors.

Thea Musgrave was the recipient of a Koussevitsky Award in 1972 which resulted in the composition Space Play, and in 1974-75 she received a Guggenheim Fellowship and composed her miniature ballet Orfeo III and scored her Scottish Dance Suite for band.

The Lincoln Center Chamber Musical Society opened its 1975 season on October 17 with the United States premiere of Space Play. The concert was held in the Alice Tully Hall. The world premiere was given in London, England, and it was also programmed at the Monday Evening Concerts in Los Angeles. There were several reviews of the piece, the most interesting appeared in the November 3, 1975, issue of the New Yorker, written by Andrew Porter*:

> Thea Musgrave's Space Play--A Chamber Concerto
>
> It is a musical game for nine players. Flute, oboe, clarinet, and bassoon are stationed around the platform; violin, viola, cello, and double bass cluster at the center; just behind them, as a kind of referee and genial master of ceremonies, is the horn. The wind players have most of the fun. The oboe stands up to lead the first episode, andante espressivo, con molto rubato. Then the horn takes charge, rising inviting the others to emulate his cadenza like flourishes, and sets the new tempo for a piu-mosso section, in which the flute and bassoon play leading roles. The clarinet, silent on the sidelines during these exchanges, comes forward at the close of this, musing on a two-note figure, and proposes a calmo episode under his direction. This ends with some skyrockets from the instrument and leads to an altercation with the horn. The latter enlists the flute and the bassoon as his followers; at his summons, they imitate his call. He turns to the clarinet next: "as if about to lead him in," the clarinet is stubbornly silent, so the horn, "turns pointedly away ... and toward (the) oboe," who proves more bidable. The clarinet interrupts furioso, but the argument is won by

*From Music of Three Seasons, by Andrew Porter. Originally appeared in the New Yorker. Reprinted by permission of Farrar, Straus & Giroux.

the horn, who celebrates victory in a big declamando melody. There is an amicable coda, in which the violin is allowed a say of his own.

In a series of recent works--notably the Clarinet, Horn and Viola Concertos--Miss Musgrave has explored the play of music through space, and dramatic dialogue involving mimicry, parody, and what sounds like straight-forward conversation, or quarrel, between instruments. There is a moment in the Viola Concerto when the soloist seems to be giving a master class to the viola section of the orchestra. Space Play, which lasts about twenty minutes is slighter than those works--a happy diversion in which the composer holds an adroit balance between letting the players do what they like and making sure that they do so within bounds that define the piece she has devised. The rules for each stage of the game are cunningly framed. Many of the moves--though not always the speed or volume or pitch level at which they must be executed--are obligatory. The shape of a musical gesture, and often the precise note on which it begins or ends, may be indicated, while inflections are left to the individual's fancy. Only three measures are strictly metered; for the rest, the ensemble takes its cues from whoever happens to be the leader at the moment. There is a good deal of twiddle and twirl and flourish, but also--and this, perhaps is what gives the work its endearing character--a recurrent vein of lyricism, in the form of fully composed melodies. Space Play, commissioned by the Serge Koussevitzky Music Foundation in the Library of Congress, was first played by the virtuosi of the London Sinfonietta, a year ago. The virtuosi of the Chamber Music Society gave a musically deft performance, just a little inhibited on the "acting" side, which should reinforce the scenario of the score. The "independent musical personalities" that the composer had in mind did not emerge very strongly. Space Play is a game that could become popular with ensembles, and their audiences. The score is published by Novello.

Thea Musgrave's fourth opera, Mary, Queen of Scots, with the story line from Amalia Elguera's unfinished play, Moray, had its world premiere on September 6 and 8, 1977, at the Edinburgh Festival. She was not only the composer and the conductor, but also the librettist. It is her most successful opera and solidly places her as one of the leading composers for lyric theater today. The opera is most likely to remain in the repertoire because of its interest and musical inspiration and dramatic appeal. Musgrave and the opera had dozens of positive reviews all indicating the genius talent of her creative ability.

In the September 29, 1977, issue of Country Life, published in England, Stewart Deas reviewed the musical scene:

A Scots Queen at Edinburgh*

> It is not always the things that are trumpeted loudest at a festival that turn out to be the most exciting or rewarding. Undoubtedly the greatest fuss at this year's Edinburgh Festival, and the greatest amount of money, was lavished on its star-studded production of Carmen. But, after all, Carmen is one of the best-known and most often performed operas, and it seemed a little strange to require such an expensive production of it. As a result, the seats in the grand tier could cost up to £20. They were not nearly so expensive for the other operatic venture of the season, the staging of a brand new opera, Mary Queen of Scots, by the Scottish composer Thea Musgrave.
>
> In the event, it was really the new opera that stole the thunder. With the composer conducting and with a fine cast drawn from the Scottish Opera, there was a quality about it all that held the attention and carried the conviction. The action deals with the period between Mary's arrival in Scotland and her unwilling flight to England, and Musgrave has had to pack a great deal of action into quite a tight space. Indeed, although she herself has said that no opera could hope to include all the historical events of even this crucial part of Mary's life, it does seem at times that she has tried to embrace too much.
>
> It is an opera of violent contrast and swift changes. At one moment we may be listening to

*Reprinted by permission of the publisher.

> an enchanting chorus about Peace ("Peace in the city, On the moor, for the rich, for the poor"--the libretto is the composer's own), when Gordon (William McCue) rushes in shouting "Treason." At another time the gentle strains of a dance are broken into by violent quarrels. As yet another quiet lullaby, sung by Mary to her child is broken into (by Gordon again) urging the Queen to take refuge in Stirling from the armed forces of James Stuart (Jake Gardner) a character brought to somewhat unlikeable life in the Musgrave conception of him. There is much fighting and killing and stabbing in the opera, but they are nearly, though not quite balanced by beautiful moments of repose such as the exquisite scene of Mary's Supper Room with the four Mary's singing in a group round the ill-fated Riccio portrayed by Stafford Dean.
>
> At the head of a strong cast stands Catherine Wilson as the Queen, surely the embodiment of all the composer intended to convey through her in the opera. The even, pure soprano tone of her beautifully controlled voice is turned to wholly expressive ends, and her features match her every mood. This was a performance to watch and listen to in every detail.
>
> David Hillman was a most convincing Darnley, and Gregory Dempsey a sturdy tenor Bothwell, although, curiously enough, I should have expected Bothwell to be a bass. The director of the production, Colin Graham, has been particularly successful in the swift transition from scene to scene, and in seizing upon the restful moments to provide exceptionally beautiful stage pictures. The orchestra, itself full of the most fascinating detail, followed the composer's beat as if devoted to her to a man.

The United States premiere of Mary, Queen of Scots was performed by the Virginia Opera Association, general-director and conductor Peter Mark, in March 1978 in Norfolk, Virginia. Thor Eckert Jr. reviewed the production for The Christian Science Monitor on April 27, 1978:

> Magnificent new opera on
> Mary of Scotland
>
> It is rare to be able to acclaim the arrival of a major new opera in this day and age. But such is

Thea Musgrave's Mary, Queen of Scots--an imposing, magnificent work which proves that hope must never be abandoned.

But the good news is also that the Virginia Opera Association, which mounted the United States premiere, is an exceptional little company, thriving in Norfolk, Virginia. It is companies like these that are demonstrating opera's viability in other than the cultural meccas, and that newer and broader audiences than ever are hopping onto the opera bandwagon.

Miss Musgrave has been impressive in the past with such works as the Clarinet Concerto.

Her chamber opera, The Voice of Ariadne, was last seen at the New York City Opera. It is an uneven work that only hinted at the magnificent qualities to come in her full-fledged historical opera.

Miss Musgrave penned her own libretto--not always the best policies; but she has crafted a lucid, dramatic prose frame for her music. The words flow with poetic insight and dramatic credibility, as is not the case with some of her contemporaries, whose librettos are full of awkward clashing phrases and clumsy word-usages. The story tells of Mary from her arrival to claim the throne in Scotland through her forced departure for eventual imprisonment in England. There is much condensing of the action for dramatic purposes, but there is nothing that betrays history psychologically, nor that betrays the theatricality of the drama.

But the music is the thing, and in a superb orchestral fabric, Miss Musgrave weaves a spell of compelling power and magical impact.

There is a constant undercurrent of turmoil throughout the score; she is uncanny in her ability musically to depict clashes in style--Mary's French elegance vs. her rough-hewn Scottish courtiers, etc. And her use of melody is rare by any current standards.

There are several large monologues--the closest the work comes to having arias--that fit snugly into the continuous stream of musical and textual action. Each reveals a stunning facility to stop action and capture the subconscious feelings and undercurrents of both character and situation. Here is, clearly, the work not just of a master orchestrator, but a theatrical master as well. And whereas so many

> new lyric dramas are notable, just for their professional competence, Miss Musgrave's must be reckoned as one of the precious few new operas of imposing artistic merit. *

Thea Musgrave is without doubt a musical genius; she is not only talented, articulate, and intelligent, but has been honored by her country for her outstanding creative achievements. Prince Charles of England presented her with an honorary doctorate degree from the Council for National Academic Awards in 1976. She is a leader not only for her country, but for the exciting twentieth century of composers.

Dr. Thea Musgrave has participated and contributed her energy and talents to many organizations: the Executive Committee of the Composers Guild of Great Britain; the Awards Committee for the Commonwealth Fund of New York (the selection committee for the Harkness Fellowship); advisory panel for the British Broadcasting Company. She is also an honorary fellow of the New Hall, Cambridge, England.

Thea Musgrave has been acclaimed throughout the world by music critics, musicians, other composers and audiences. She ranks in the top percent of twentieth-century composers, both men and women. Only time will tell her final place on the roster of famous composers, but history will prove her a leader of her contemporaries.

Recordings

Triptych for Tenor and orchestra (HMV ALP2279/ASD2279), Scottish National Orchestra conducted by Alexander Gibson, tenor Duncan Robertson.

Night Music for chamber orchestra (Argo ZRG 702), London Sinfonietta conducted by Frederik Prausnitz, horns Barry Tuckwell & Anthony Chiddell.

Clarinet Concerto (Argo ZRG 726), London Symphony Orchestra conducted by Norman Del Mar, clarinet Gervase de Peyer.

Concerto for Orchestra (Decca Head 8), Scottish National Orchestra conducted by Alexander Gibson.

---

*Reprinted by permission from The Christian Science Monitor.

Horn Concerto (Decca Head 8), Scottish National Orchestra conducted by the composer, horn Barry Tuckwell.
Colloquy for violin and piano (Argo/ZRG 5328), Manoug Parikian and Lamar Crowson.
Trio for flute, oboe and piano (Delta SDEL 18005), Mabillon Trio.
Chamber Concerto No. 2 (Deloa DEL-25405), Boston Musica Viva.
Monologue for solo piano (Argo ZRG 704), The composer.
Excursions for piano 4-hands (Argo ZRG 704), The composer and Malcolm Williamson.
Primavera for soprano and flute (Caprice Riks LP 59), Dorothy Dorow and Ulf Bergstrom.
Soliloquy for guitar and tape (DGG 2530 079), Siegfried Behrend.

Partial List of Compositions

Her impressive list of compositions are published by J. & W. Chester, LTD Eagle Court, London, EC1M 5QD, England; with United States sales representative, Magnamusic-Baton, Inc. 10370 Page Industrial Boulevard, St. Louis, Mo. 63132. Also published by Novello & Company, 1-3 Upper James Street, London, WIR 4BP, England; United States representative, Novello Publications, Inc., 145 Palisade Street, Dobbs Ferry, New York, N.Y. 10522. Overseas agents are found in Argentina, Australia, Austria, Belgium, Brazil, Canada, Denmark, France, Germany, Holland, New Zealand, Czechoslovakia, Israel, Norway, South Africa, Spain, Sweden, and Switzerland.

1953	A Tale for Thieves, a ballad
1953	A Suite O'Bairnsangs, voice and piano
1954	Cantata for a Summer's Day, chorus and piano
1955	Five Love Songs, soprano and guitar
1955	The Abbot of Drimock, chamber opera
1958	Obliques, orchestra and string quartet
1958	A Song for Christmas, aria
1959	Colloquy for Violin and Piano
1959	Scottish Dance Suite, for orchestra
1960	The Phoenix and the Turtle, for chorus and orchestra
1961	Serenade, flute, clarinet, harp, viola, cello
1962	The Five Ages of Man, for chorus and orchestra
1962	Marko, The Miser, written for children to sing and play

1964	The Decision, opera
1964-65	Nocturnes and Arias, for orchestra
1966	Chamber Concerto No. 2, in homage to Charles Ives
1966	Concerto No. 3, octet - drama for instruments
1967	Concerto for Orchestra
1967	Music for Horn and Piano
1968	Clarinet Concerto
1968	Beauty and the Beast, ballet
1969	Night Music
1969	Soliloquy for Guitar and Tape
1970	Memento Vitae, a concerto in homage to Beethoven
1970	From One to Another, for viola and tape
1971	Horn Concerto, with orchestra
1972-73	The Voice of Ariadne, chamber opera
1973	Viola Concerto
1974	Space Play
1975	Orfeo II, opera
1975-77	Mary, Queen of Scots, opera
1978-79	A Christmas Carol, opera

PAULINE OLIVEROS

Composer, Professor of Music and Director of the Center for Musical Experiment

The inventive and gifted Pauline Oliveros is an internationally known musical genius. Long recognized for her contributions in the field of electronic music and mixed media, she has more recently established her credentials as a pioneer in the exploration of meditative states in relation to music, particularily in her ceremonial works. She explains, "Most of my work is rooted in improvisation and primary process imagery. As a beginning composer, I searched laboriously with the aid of the piano for the sounds I heard. This was a kind of a slowed down improvisation. As I found the pitches I wanted, my mind constantly formed images of the instrumental colors I wanted. From the beginning, sound quality has been a prime concern."

Pauline Oliveros was born in Houston, Texas in 1932. The strange joy of listening to noise permeating from her grandfather's crystal radio, telegraph keys and a wind-up Victrola during the late 1930's entertained the young Pauline. She was receptive to the acoustical phenomena of electrical systems and vocal sounds. Many young children develop a keen sense of hearing, but Oliveros developed a remarkable insight and devotion to sounds and their relationship within a total hearing pattern. Her talent was manifested and nurtured by sound effects employed by radio. Two of her favorite radio programs were "Fibber McGee and Molly" (the hall closet) and "Inner Sanctum" (the squeaking door). Her curiosity and imagination responded to exciting tonal combinations which made an indelible mark on childhood memories.

When asked who encouraged her to compose, Oliveros simply states, "Nobody." Her interest developed as the result of a high school English class that was devoted to creative projects. "I was reading Tennyson and decided to write

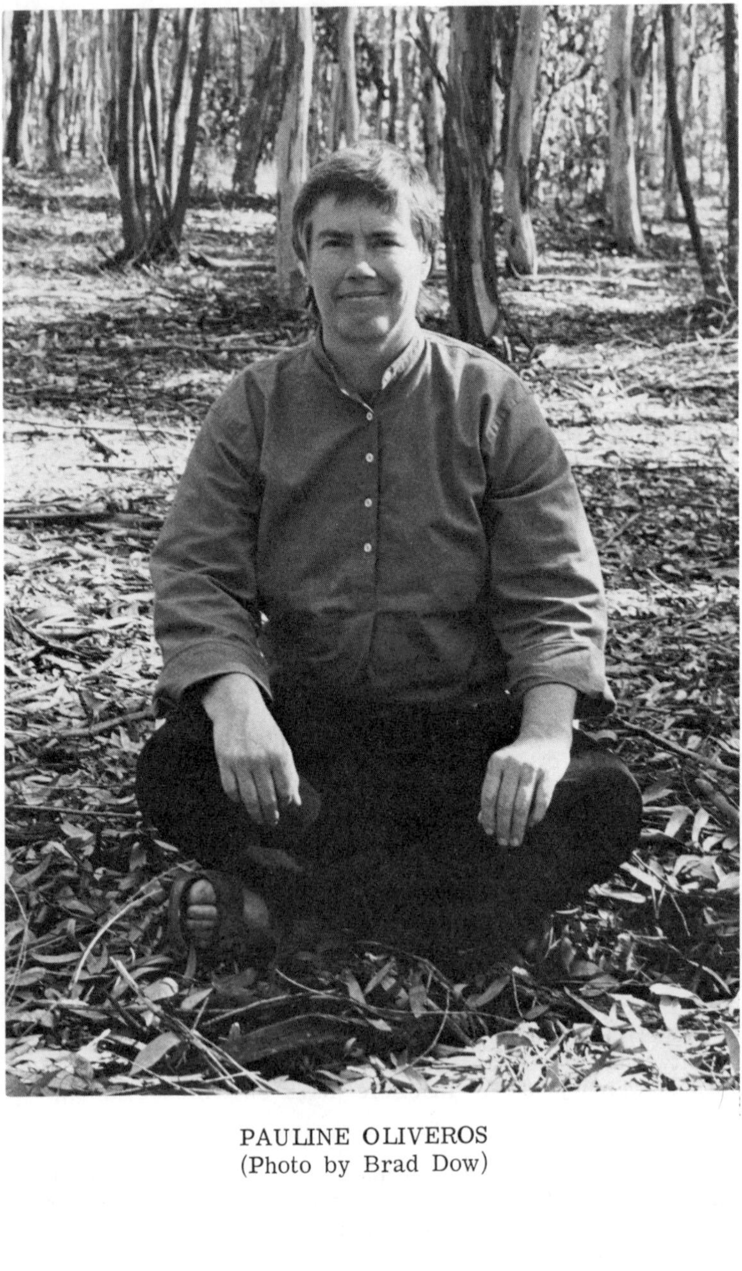

PAULINE OLIVEROS
(Photo by Brad Dow)

music set to poetry. Naturally I couldn't do this because I had been taught as a performer (accordian and French horn) and did not have the skills to notate what I was hearing because it was complicated and couldn't be notated within the traditional system. I was hearing sound qualities which only much later became accessible to me through electronic means. At this time I was out on a limb and I've since been there many times."

Pauline Oliveros was a child genius and a natural innovator who pursued her career with dedication and devotion to conquer the challenges of modern sound possibilities. She studied composition with Dr. Paul Koepke at the University of Houston in 1951. In 1952 she began six years of study with composer Robert Erickson in San Francisco. She credits Mr. Erickson with influencing her in three ways: 1) he reinforced her interest in sound quality, 2) he encouraged her to improvise her way through compositions rather than to rationalize, and 3) he introduced her to the concept of organic rhythm, which is rhythm that shifts, expands, contracts, and is not periodic in the metrical sense. There is a sense of simultaneous fast and slow tempos.

Oliveros received her Bachelor of Arts Degree in composing from San Francisco State College. Following graduation she was involved in group improvisation and her composing was an interesting and revolutionary process. Oliveros explains, "When I first began to compose I was interested in the way sounds could be mixed, and the resulting colors. I struggled to find the most interesting timbre patterns."

Pauline Oliveros' first public recognition as a composer came with the reading of her Variations for Sextet, for flute, clarinet, trumpet, horn, cello, and piano, conducted by Thomas Nee at the American Composers Workshop held in 1960 at the San Francisco Conservatory of Music. She received the Pacifica Foundation National Prize for this composition. Alfred Frankenstein reviewed this piece in the San Francisco Chronicle in 1960:

MODERN MUSIC FESTIVAL OPENS*

> The San Francisco Conservatory of Music started something new and important yesterday afternoon

*Reprinted by permission of the author.

> when it presented the first concert in a seven-program festival of modern music. Since it was the start of a locally unprecedented venture, several mistakes were made, but the committee in charge made no mistake at all when it selected Morton Subotnick's Serenade to open the program and Pauline Oliveros' Variations to conclude it.
>
> Both of these are ensemble pieces in the tradition of Anton Webern, a tradition which places heavy emphasis on sparks, spangles, flutters, and coruscations of sound, brings tone, color and nuance into the central place formerly occupied by harmony, and rarefies rhythm to the point at which it becomes something else for which, as yet, we have no term.
>
> Similar as these two pieces are in idiom, they are totally different in effect, and therein lay the value of playing them on the same program. The Subotnick is light, gracious, playful, lyrical--everything one thinks of in connection with the word "serenade." The Oliveros is intensely serious, forceful, vastly dramatic in its implication, and truly symphonic in its breadth of values. Like the music of Webern himself, it convinces you that the crack of doom rides on the 64th-note, and the softer that 64th-note, the more awe-inspiring in its delivery. Webernism is fashionable nowadays, but Subotnick and Miss Oliveros transcend that. Both pieces are quite good, but the one by Miss Oliveros is, I think, the most remarkable I have yet heard by any of the younger American composers.

Alexander Fried wrote the following for the San Francisco Examiner, in 1960 on the Modern Music Festival*:

> Pauline Oliveros' Variations for mixed instrumental sextet was by miles the most impressive work in a Pacifica Foundations Awards Concert of new American chamber music, Friday night at the San Francisco Museum of Art.
>
> This young San Franciscan is evidently a brilliantly talented composer, and a lot can be expected from her in years to come.
>
> Incidently, Miss Oliveros proved that any musical

*Reprinted by permission of the publisher.

> idiom at all in which a piece is written (be it ever so strange or experimental) can be acceptable, so long as the inner feeling that goes into it is sensitive and creative.
>
> Her Variations is a very avant-garde sort of "colortone" music. It doesn't aim to be melodious. Rather it presents its tone patterns in spurts, murmurs, splashes and meaningful pauses of abstract sound.
>
> In this manner, her piece was alive and fascinating every moment. It had emotional value and a continuing suspense and fulfillment.

A gift of a tape recorder from her mother, Edith Gutierrez, in the late 1950's was to profoundly affect the talented Oliveros.

> I recorded hundreds of sounds, changed the speeds and became fascinated with the number of transformations and began to lose interest in acoustic sounds. I went through a long period, until the end of the 1960's, of working with electronic media. From 1958 I spent a great deal of time consciously listening to the environment. I made a major commitment to my own form of meditation. It was to listen to everything all the time; a difficult and expansive task. At that time the rhythms of the urban and natural environment began to affect my work. It was possible to work with these ideas on tape but not necessarily with the musicians of that time.

Oliveros felt there was a problem of attitude on the part of musicians of the time, who either could not, or would not, explore the possibility of expanding their sound vocabulary. She soon turned toward electronic sounds and the world of tape music.

In 1962 Oliveros received the prize for the best foreign work from the Foundation Gaudeamus in Bilthoven, Holland, for her composition Sound Patterns, for mixed chorus. Oliveros describes the piece: "It was distinguished by its lack of text and overall electronic/orchestral sound of an abstract nature. (Some people think this work is electronic rather than vocal.) My central concerns for time structure and tone quality were the same, however. I abandoned precise control of pitch for the first time in order to gain the possibility of complex clusters of sound which would have been undoubtedly too difficult for the chorus to reproduce from the notation of exact pitch."

Sound Patterns was one of the first compositions to explore vocal sounds in this way by a twentieth-century composer. This was only the beginning of the explorations of the young musical genius whose inventiveness would continue to sprout through a variety of media that would be recognized by numerous awards and commissions. (Sound Patterns is available on recording by Odyssey number 32160156 and Ars Nova number AN1005.)

In 1961 Pauline Oliveros and composer Morton Subotnick and Ramon Sender founded the San Francisco Tape Music Center, the only accessible electronic music studio in the area. In 1966 this center, with support from the Rockefeller Foundation, became the tape center at Mills College and Oliveros was named director.

Pauline Oliveros adopted a practical and different habit early in her composing career to write and create music for specific instruments, situations, and musicians. That this may sound a bit revolutionary is simply mundane, one needs only to reflect the lives of the old masters who composed for a given performance with both instruments and performers predetermined, and many of these same composers either joined the group in concert or conducted the performance.

Oliveros carries her composing approach one step further than the old masters by fitting the work to the personality of the performer. This is an extremely complex and susceptible argumentative device that the talented and determined Oliveros has successfully employed for many years. She says,

> I always spent time with the persons I wrote for in order to learn their special gifts or idiosyncrasies. This suggested ways of approaching the piece--for instance, when I wrote Theater Piece for trombone player, commissioned by Stuart Dempster trombonist, he first recorded lots of his own instrumental sounds. Then the piece really evolved around those sounds. I've had requests from musicians over the years to use this particular piece but I would not grant permission because it was uniquely Dempster's piece.

Written earlier in Oliveros' career, Theater Piece was reviewed on March 27, 1968, for the New York Times by Theodore Strongin*:

> Last night was trick night in the Evenings for New Music series held at Carnegie Recital Hall.
> Some of the tricks were more musical than others, but all had elements of fun.
> Pauline Oliveros's Theater Piece made use of taped distorted trombone sounds, oddly pleasant, mournful ones. Meanwhile, a live trombonist lighted candles on the dark stage and caused what looked like garden sprayers set up vertically, to whirl around by blowing through plastic tubes that at the same time made trombone-like noises. The trombonist finally blew out all the candles, also through the plastic tubes.
> If this sounds ridiculous, it was not. Somehow Miss Oliveros mixed her media with imagination and humor creating an absorbing fey atmosphere.

Whether composing for conventional instruments or other media, Oliveros is a sensitive person concerned with the performers and the listeners. She writes and seeks answers to societal mores, by releasing tension through humor, often placing herself in unique and different situations to discover new creativeness within herself. She is quoted as saying, "I had some people come over, got them a little drunk, and they belched." She used one of the belches as sound material to be processed and transformed. She has also spent an entire night recording a noisy toilet in a hotel. One must be quick of wit and possess a bit of humor to follow the dictates of their creative talents! Oliveros knows no boundaries nor limits that would deter her quest for new sound dimensions.

Individuals have always been influenced by other people, and their infinite creative abilities, and Oliveros' association in 1963 with David Tudor, pianist, and Elizabeth Harris, dancer-choreographer, ignited still another spark in her talented quest for innovation. This friendship reinforced her interest in the manipulation of sounds, musical and non-musical, and in collaborative performance. This resulted in mixed media compositions of diverse sonoric and theatrical elements in a relaxing, inventive situation.

Oliveros continued to develop, expand, and elaborate and in the 1960's her interest had shifted to electronic and mixed media. One of the most representative works of this period was Pieces of Eight (dedicated to Long John Silver), a theater piece for wind octet, objects and tape which contained the seeds of many of her later theater pieces. She describes this piece, "It was the first theater piece I wrote without collaborating with someone else. It was my own fantasy at work, with dramatic and visual elements."

Arthur Bloomfield wrote the following review for the San Francisco Examiner in 1965*:

> The San Francisco Tape Music Center paid its respects to Beethoven last night. But not exactly in a manner that would have gladdened the heart of Josef Krips.
>
> A bust of Ludwig perched on the piano as Pauline Oliveros' Pieces of Eight unwound admidst a concatenation of alarm clocks, cuckoo clock, cash register and assorted glissandos, burps and bellows from an ensemble of eight performers who looked rather more plausible than they sounded.
>
> The bust has a wretched expression on its face, as if Ludwig has just heard one of his symphonies played upside down, backwards, or maybe at 62 rpm.
>
> And we doubt if he enjoyed being paraded up and down the aisles, eyes blinking red, while feverish "ushers" rattled collection bowls and organ music filled the hall.
>
> It's not that we don't get the jest, but Miss Oliveros didn't quite hit the jackpot of whimsy on this one.

Another representative piece of this period is I of IV, electronic music composed directly on electronic tape and recorded on Odyssey Label number 32160160. Pauline Oliveros describes I of IV as,

> a two-channel, purely electronic piece which is a solo studio improvisation in real time. In this

---

*Reprinted by permission of the author.

> work I proceeded to elaborate a strong mental sonic image. First, I connected a special configuration of electronic equipment which would produce my idea. There was a climax in this particular improvisation of a feeling which had long been developing in my work; that I was a medium or channel through which I observed the emerging improvisation. There is a careful continuation in this piece of the idea mentioned by Frankenstein in Stimulating Sounds Too New to Be Named: that is that "the past becomes the substance and subject for the improvisation," in this case through various tape delay techniques.

Stimulating Sounds Too New to Be Named was a review written by Alfred Frankenstein for the San Francisco Chronicle on March 26, 1962*:

> Tape recorder music was the latest thing until Saturday night, when it was capped by something newer still in a concert at the San Francisco Conservatory of Music.
>
> This thing that is newer still has no special name as yet. It was exemplified by an improvisation wherein two musicians, Pauline Oliveros and Morton Subotnick, worked with two others, Lynn Palmer and John Graham, who know how to act and speak and have a gift for saying things that are so outrageously inconsequential as to take on a strange kind of meaning.
>
> While the musicians were busy, mostly with percussive sounds, and the two others were acting and singing and whatnot, Ramon Sender was taping the goings-on, and the taped sound came back, often in greatly altered forms, on speakers located at various points in the hall. As a result, the past of this improvisation became part of its present, and this use of the past as both substance and subject for an improvisation in the present seems to me a most remarkable idea.
>
> Like all new ideas, it needs polishing, and its demonstration Saturday night was long over-due. But it is probably going to go somewhere. I found it, even in the overextended form of Saturday night's

*Reprinted by permission of the author.

> program, one of the most stimulating things that has happened in years.

In 1967 Oliveros received an appointment as faculty member at the University of California at San Diego. Her position was as lecturer on the composition faculty. (She is now a full professor.)

Oliveros ended her fifteen-year stay in San Francisco with a twelve hour "Tape-a-Thon," a program in which she presented most of her electronic music. This end of an era was meaningful to her. Oliveros notes, "My new position on the faculty at the University of California provided a financial security which I had never known before. My work took a turn. I became increasingly concerned with theatrical and visual materials as part of the music."

From Pieces of Eight came such works as Night Jar for viola d'amore player (Jacob Glick), Double Basses at Twenty Paces for two string bass players, referee/conductor and two seconds (Bertram Turetsky), The Wheel of Fortune for clarinet player (William O. Smith), Aeolian Partitions for flute, clarinet, violin, cello and piano (The Aeolian Players).

Oliveros explains, "It is common to all of these works that the musicians' actions as performers and the visual elements are as important as the sounds produced. My concern with stage behavior and its unusual nature tends to disorient audiences and is intended to bring about in varying degrees a new understanding of how to listen. It is also intended to disorient the performer and break stereotyped approaches to performance, at the same time there is a desire for the individual personality of the performer to come through and take a vital role in the music." Her approach to performers and performances is exemplified in the following description of a concert by her. The review appeared in the Seattle Times and was written by Arts and Entertainment Editor, Wayne Johnson in 1969*:

> OLIVEROS CONCERT IS FASCINATING FUN
>
> The Contemporary Group had fun last night, and it seemed apparent that the large audience in the Hub

*Reprinted by permission of the author.

auditorium (the biggest crowd I've ever seen at a Contemporary Group concert) had fun, too.

The evening was devoted to music-theater pieces by Pauline Oliveros, a witty, entertaining, highly imaginative woman who teaches at the University of California at San Diego and is firmly established as one of the leaders of the avant garde in this country.

The program had nothing to do with traditional music and the traditional concert-hall experience. Unlike most "serious" concerts which are firmly rooted in the past, last night's concert (which for all its fun-and-games was still essentially serious) lived actively and vitally in the present and spun off hints of the future.

The intent of the concert was not only to explore new sound combinations, new music, but also to suggest new ways of presenting musicians--not just as musical performers but as total performers in a total-theater situation. The execution was as fascinating as the intent.

The most interesting, most substantial portion of the program was the premiere performance of The Wheel of Fortune, which was commissioned and performed by William O. Smith, the director of the Contemporary Group and a clarinetist and composer of some renown.

The piece which is partly scripted and partly improvisatory, presents not only various aspects of Smith the Musician but also various facets of Smith the Man.

In the piece Smith comes on stage wearing a costume which integrates in a striking, amusing manner the traditional black concert performer and the motley of the fool. In a manner that is partly ritualistic and partly fun-and-games. Smith outlines a "magic circle" (which is defined by masking tape, a chalk mark and nine blinking yellow lights of the kind used on construction barricades).

Working within this circle, Smith explores and explains the various features of his personality and experience. He talks about himself (in French and Italian, as well as in English), does some simple (and funny) magic tricks, discusses his name (and all other kinds of "smiths," in a virtuoso verbal "aria"), reveals his fascination with procedures and complex operations, and ends the piece with about 10 minutes of improvising (great playing!) on the clarinet in a variety of styles which expresses his own musical history.

The piece is fun and funny, but it's more than an extended gag. It adds up to a fascinating, entertaining portrait of a man who expresses himself primarily through his clarinet but whose expression --and need for expression--are shaped by many non-musical influences.

Stuart Dempster, another U. W. faculty member associated with the Contemporary Group, had wild fun with Theater Piece for Trombone Player and Tape, which Miss Oliveros wrote for him in 1966. On a stage which is semi-darkened most of the time, Dempster crawls under and around (seemingly through) a piano, scrapes the piano's strings, yaps and barks like a dog, and plays two Rube Goldberg contraptions; one consists of three lengths of garden hose fitted on one end with trombone mouthpieces and on the other with reflecting bells in which candles are burning, the other has hose fitted to twirling lawn sprinklers which when Dempster makes them spin, spew out something that looks like smoke and smells like talcum powder.

All this is accompanied by a wide variety of trombone sounds on tape--sounds which Dempster pre-taped and which were then arranged (and sometimes distorted) by Miss Oliveros. The Dempster piece is great good fun, but it lacks the human depth and fascination of the piece Miss Oliveros created for Smith.

The program opened with a taped piece called Bye Bye Butterfly. The Butterfly of the title is Puccini's Cio-Cio-San, the sound of whose first aria gets surrounded--and ultimately swallowed up--by a variety of electronic sound squiggles.

The other piece on the concert was called Events, which consisted of the showing of a generally uninteresting film accompanied by an interesting sound environment created by live musicians on stage (Miss Oliveros playing the accordion and Lynn Lonidier, the filmmaker, playing the cello) and by members of the Contemporary Group moving throughout the audience playing various instruments.

The droning, enveloping sound was highly effective for seven or eight minutes--but the piece lasted twice that long.

Pauline Oliveros was commissioned by Bowdoin College of Brunswick, Maine, to compose a composition for the Aeolian Players, a group consisting of flute, clarinet, violin, cello and piano performers. Unable to personally meet the individuals in the group she worked by means of a photograph and used this as the medium to project the personalities of the performers. Oliveros says, "The piano player was changed after I had received the picture and the part I wrote did not fit the new person." This was corroborated by composer Elliott Schwartz who commented, "The new pianist's physical appearance and personality were totally unlike that of his predecessor; strangely enough, the lone flaw in the Bowdoin performance was that the piano part was entirely wrong for some reason I couldn't explain at the time. Now that I think of it, it would have been a beautiful vehicle for the man in the photograph."

During the 1960's Oliveros' reputation was solidly based on her contributions in electronic music, theatrical pieces and mixed media. She was a prodigious composer and received numerous commissions and grants.

It is of interest to note a few of the commissions received during this period, but perhaps more revealing are the titles and the parts scored as a result of these commissions:

In Memoriam Nikola Tesla, Cosmic Engineer, for several musicians with extensive electronic devices, commissioned by choreographer Merce Cunningham.

Music for Expo 70, for two cellos, accordian and three tapes. Tape version to be modified by the acoustics of the Pepsi Dome designed by Experiments in Art and Technology. Commissioned by EAT for the Pepsi Cola Company pavillion at Osaka, Japan.

Please Don't Shoot the Piano Player, He Is Doing the Best He Can, a theater piece for an ensemble of soloists. Commissioned by Daniel Lentz for the California Time Machine.

Valentine, a theater piece for four players with amplification. Commissioned by Gordon Mumma for the Sonic Arts Group.

The Bath, for soloist and four tape recorders. Commissioned by Ann Halprin for the Dancers Workshop.

The Chronicles of Hell, two-channel tape. Commissioned by R. G. Davis for the San Francisco Mime Troupe production of the play, The Chronicles of Hell, by Gelderohde.

Lulu, for prepared piano, flute and actors. Commissioned by Leonard Woolf for the San Francisco Poetry Festival.

Oliveros worked not only as a creator, a professor, and writer but was awarded two prestigious grants during this period to further develop the technical aspects of electronic sound possibilities: in 1968-70 she received two thousand dollars for design and development of a voltage controlled audio mixer for use in electronic music composition and performance; and in 1969-70 she received four thousand dollars for the development of an electronic environment, including design sound and light control devices, applicable to automatic or manual response to the presence of performers and/or visitors.

In 1970 Pauline Oliveros' interest in the total act and environment of performance caused her work to change considerably although the base remained the same. Oliveros conveys her philosophy,

> I began to get interested again in acoustic sounds and particularly natural sounds, non-technological in origin. Then I began to develop meditation techniques--I became interested in the way people were relating. What could you create [in the 1960's] where people could do things together, make music without being skilled musicians or could you mix the complete range from non-skilled to highly skilled? I shed all my skills and radically changed. I began to explore ritual and ceremony and to look for ways of composing for unspecialized performers. I was composing underground in a sense because when I started this work, the materials seemed so simple that I felt alienated from the musical community and its virtuosic concerns. I was most interested in the tuning of souls.

In 1970 Pauline Oliveros formed the ♀ Ensemble, a group of ten women, devoted to the explorations of meditative states of consciousness and their relationship to performance practice. This group met weekly for two years and she composed XII Sonic Meditations for them. According to Oliveros, "The instructions are intended to include altered states of consciousness and slow moving, richly textured sonic events. Anyone may participate with immediate results but these meditations are meant for repetition by a group over a long period of time. The programs consist of training in advance a portion of the potential audience in a workshop, then instructing, in writing, all persons in advance who come to the program in how to participate. No one is a spectator."

Out of this experience she developed, over a period of years, Sonic Meditations, which includes over thirty pieces that are simple and are transmitted through the oral tradition. Pauline Oliveros' quest for new musical experiences has always involved the unexpected, she built her reputation on unorthodox approaches. Her Sonic Meditations and other pieces that include the audiences, may well shock the establishment but one need only to recall that the sophistication of society produced passive listeners. A person's basic instinct to participate in the arts can be traced to participatory involvement in tribal ceremonies and other activities not influenced by Western civilization.

Oliveros' humanistic approach to the musical arts meets a basic need of the individual, to be part of and involved in events and happenings. As a final result the individual is in tune with the artistic commitment and not spoon-fed a performers' musical skills and emotions.

Oliveros received international acclaim in the 1970's for her explorations, awards, commissions, coverage by the Associated Press and a ten-day seminar on Sonic Meditations in Berlin, which culminated in a program performed at the Metamusik Festival at the National Galerie.

In 1973 she received a three-month tenure as a Faculty Fellow in the Project for Music Experiment (now the center for Music Experiment and Related Research), which was funded by the Rockefeller Foundation at the University of California at San Diego. This enabled her to devote full time to exploration of meditative techniques as applied to composing, performing and listening. "Simple instructions can result in something new. I worked with a group of people for nine weeks, two hours per day, five days per week researching the project at the University. First on relaxation techniques, then meditative techniques and finally my own sonic meditation. This is what has primarily occupied me for the past nine years."

In 1973-74 Oliveros received a Guggenheim Fellowship in composition, to continue her research begun during the meditation project. The fellowship resulted in the composition

Crow Two: A Ceremonial Opera. She explains, "It was a combination of meditations both new and old (from Sonic Meditations). I was now composing with my meditations. Combinations of meditations could vary from performance to performance depending on circumstances."

One of her first meditations was Teach Yourself to Fly, dedicated to Amelia Earhart. She comments, "The piece is based on breathing and observing one's breathing cycle by gradually allowing the vocal chords to vibrate in a way that is natural. There is no concern for placing the voice on any pitch, but gradually one does increase the intensity with a large group--it sounds like an airplane. There is no audience because everyone is included in the meditation. The object is to become more concerned with one's relationship to the environment and helping oneself to feel good." Tom Johnson reviewed Oliveros' work for the Village Voice on May 24, 1976*:

> One important genre of new music is consistently overlooked because it never takes place in widely advertised public events, but rather in workshops and relatively intimate gatherings, where everyone can feel free to take part. It involves meditation, and thus overlaps somewhat with the activity of meditation groups and sensory awareness groups, but it has been developed by composers and must be considered primarily a form of music.
>
> In a way this is a new form of religious music. Of course, it has nothing to do with organized religion, but it does owe much to Eastern religious teaching, such as one finds in Sufi Inayat Khan's "Music," and it is oriented toward spiritual values. It is not a popular activity, and never will be anymore than Zen meditation or philosophical debate ever will. Yet it is an important development--particularly since it has independently attracted two of the most stimulating musical minds I have ever come in contact with--Pauline Oliveros and Philip Corner.
>
> Oliveros is a California composer who has been working in this direction for some time. Several years ago I attended a session she led at the Cun-

*Reprinted by permission of The Village Voice. Copyright © The Village Voice, Inc., 1976.

ningham studio. Much of the evening was devoted to Teach Yourself to Fly, an absorbing situation in which one is asked to breathe normally, very very gradually allowing one's breath to become vocal sound. I gained some useful nonverbal insights that night, but one shouldn't expect much to happen without an appropriate atmosphere and an experienced leader. I don't think you can really "teach yourself," despite the title.

Recently I have been studying Oliveros' Sonic Meditations XII-XXV, published in the winter issue of the Painted Bride Quarterly. They are clearly expressive, and rich in implications. One meditation involves saying a single word very, very slowly, others involve group chanting, some deal with imaginary sounds or remembered sounds, and any one of them could probably keep serious meditators busy for several sessions. One can be quoted in toto, since it is defined so briefly. But don't confuse brevity with simplicity: "Re-Cognition--Listen to the sound until you no longer recognize it."

Other recent Oliveros works are intended for formal presentation to an audience, but these, too, sometimes involve elements of meditation. In a large theatrical work called Crow II, for example, part of the music is for four flute players, who are asked to determine which pitches to sustain by attempting to send and receive telepathic messages. The audience is also invited to try to tune in on any psychic messages and anticipate what pitch the flutists will play next. Regardless of whether any psychic communication actually takes place, the problem becomes an absorbing meditation, especially for the flute players, and brings an air of intense concentration into the performance situation.

Pauline Oliveros was awarded the prestigious Beethoven Prize in 1977 for her piece Bonn Feier. There are similarities between the old master and the adventurous young Oliveros, they both established new means of expression which stretch the ear and the imagination of the composer, performers and the listeners. Dedication and determination are part of both philosophies even though they lived and created two centuries apart.

She received the Beethoven Prize at Bonn, Germany, awarded by the City of Bonn during the International Society of Composers and Musicians world music days festival. Bonn Feier is a city music piece representing a portrayal of the citizens of Bonn and the everyday occurrences that happen in ordinary life. Joan La Barbara reviewed this composition for High Fidelity/Musical America in September 1977.*

> One was not sure at times whether the man standing on his head in the middle of a square, singing and clapping his feet together, was a part of the Oliveros city-piece or a part of the constant piece that is any city, complete with characters and oddities and wonderful occurrences. The man and woman giving mustaches to those women who would wear them on the spot (and selling them to those who had to take them home and think about it) created quite a stir with the elderly female population, who seemed to find it highly undignified to see women sprouting large black mustaches, and prompted amused and bemused glances and much shaking of heads from all ages.
>
> As I wandered through the streets and pedestrian malls one day in search of a post office, I passed a young street artist chalking a madonna on the sidewalk, quite detailed and lovely. Several yards on, I saw some other children painting manhole covers. I got a bit upset, worried that the police would come and drag them away (after all, chalk is one thing and paint quite another). I found out later that the manhole painters were part of Oliveros' piece and the chalk artist was a daily street artist whose work had been amplified by many other participants. There were princesses with fantastic headdresses, a Ghanian drummer, a sailor with his parrot on his shoulder asking all who would listen if they'd seen his anchor or his ship, old people and pensioners sitting in shop windows, making use of all the wonderful, soft furniture that is usually occupied only by dust and scattered rays of sunshine.
>
> Oliveros' music is of the people, for the people, and by the people, challenging them to reach into themselves to discover their own means of enhancing the ideas suggested and challenging the viewers

---

*Reprinted by permission of the publisher.

> to examine the particular societal mores and rules, perhaps to release some of the bonds and laugh at life. Enjoy each other, she seems to say, look at all the wonderful things around you. Don't just race past them on your usual path, at your usual pace. Slow down, take a look, think a little, and smile. I thought I saw a pleased glint in Beethoven's eye as he gazed down from his frozen position on the mild revolution taking place at his feet. Maybe it was reflected sunlight.

Oliveros was commissioned by Wesleyan College of Connecticut for the Wesleyan Singers, Neely Bruce, director in 1977. She wrote Rose Moon, a ritual choral work. She conducted the premiere performance as well as lecturing at the Connecticut campus. The Wesleyan Singers performed Rose Moon on a tour made possible by funding from the University, the University of Illinois, Oberlin College, Brown University and in part through a grant from Meet The Composer, a state-wide service program of the New York State Council on the Arts, with support from the National Endowment for the Arts, Helena Rubenstein Foundation, Martha Baird Rockefeller Fund for Music, and the Alice M. Ditson Fund. Since Rose Moon is in the oral tradition a true performance requires the presence of Oliveros the composer. The complete score for this composition is published by Smith Publications (2617 Gwynndale Avenue, Baltimore, Maryland 21207).

Other commissions received during this time include The Flaming Indian (dedicated to Joan of Arc), for voices, instruments and electronics, commissioned by Gerald Shapiro for the New Music Ensemble of Providence, R.I.; Link, an environmental theater piece for Palomar College, commissioned by Larry Livingston; and [untitled], a ceremonial meditation for large group, commissioned by the Experimental Intermedia Foundation, New York City (the title used for this work is a spiral-type drawing with many spokes from the hub).

An article printed in the Santa Fe Reporter on October 12, 1978, provides the reader with an excellent insight into the workshops presented by Oliveros:

> NOT WHAT WE THOUGHT MUSIC WAS
>
> Unless music involves people, it ceases to exist, much like the sound of the falling tree in the

uninhabited forest. With this idea of basic involvement, the College of Santa Fe's Music Division has arranged a weekend of workshops with avant-garde experimental composer Pauline Oliveros.

Ms. Oliveros is part of the very contemporary school that seems to be telling us that music is not what we have always thought music was, but something more. Right or wrong, they invite us to try it on and see for ourselves.

These two workshop sessions are promised to be very much of a participation affair, and everyone is invited to be part of them. To paraphrase an old joke, you don't have to be a musician to get a lot out of this experience--and you may, in fact, get more out of working with Oliveros if you are not a musician (in the traditional sense) than if you are.

Oliveros is a 46-year-old Texan now heading the Center for Music Experiment of the University of California at San Diego. She views music as an all-encompassing ritual and thus an important part of the life of every human being--not a formal situation.

This whole view seems optionally to include the technical side of music that has developed over several centuries. But it is rooted in the simple fact that for all its methods, music is basically an emotional medium. It is at this primitive level that Oliveros seeks to involve us all in her conception of music.

Beyond this, any description starts to border on the psychological. A brief review of the history of music, from ancient Greek ritual through American Indian religious dance and Afro-American jazz, shows that music has never been far from the most fundamental areas of human consciousness.

The clearer your understanding of the central core of music, the more (despite a classical or jazz or whatever background) you should be ready to explore new variations in the basic experience. With an open mind, you can learn almost infinitely. This Exploration in Music series offers a chance to do precisely that. You may or may not like the new territory you see, but you won't know until you visit. *

*Reprinted by permission from The Santa Fe Reporter, Sante Fe, New Mexico.

Articles by Pauline Oliveros have been numerous and frankly express her concerns as a member of society as well as her thoughts as a leading composer of twentieth-century new music. "And Don't Call Them Lady Composers" was an explosive article written in 1970 that rocked the establishment. Published in the September 13th issue of the New York Times, this article by Oliveros elucidated the subjugation of women composers, conductors, and instrumentalists as she had lived and experienced the happenings. Oliveros notes in the article*:

> Why have there been no great women composers? The question is often asked. The answer is no mystery. In the past, talent, education, ability, interest, motivation were irrelevant because being female was a unique qualification for domestic work and for continual obedience to and dependence upon men.

At the time this article was published there was a great need for society to evaluate such issues and Pauline Oliveros, never one to be shy, projected her voice loud and clear.

When an individual reaches out and presents new works it is often completed against trying obstacles. Fortunately, Oliveros is fiercely individualistic and has the courage to utilize and present that which is unusual. She occupies a unique position among American composers since she has the reputation of being the most radical one to attain genuine musicality.

How does one describe Pauline Oliveros? Perhaps she can best be understood in her book Pauline's Proverbs, compiled and edited by Rosita (Linda Montano) in 1976 (Printed Editions, distributed by Truck Distribution, 1645 Portland Avenue, St. Paul, Minnesota 55104). Pauline Oliveros has already carved a large spot in the twentieth-century avant-garde music based on her ingenuity in the field of electronic, theatrical and meditation music. It will take the many writers of the history of music to fully develop the spectrum of her genius capabilities as a composer and as an individual. The freshness, the vitality, and the incomparable quality of her music and new sound possibilities have no limit.

She is a young energetic person, still in her forties, and one cannot predict her future contributions to the arts, but she will certainly contribute and people will be listening.

Published Compositions

Rose Moon (1977), ceremonial for chorus and percussion. Smith Publications (1978).
Bonn Feier (1971). An environmental theater piece for specialized and unspecialized performers. Smith Publications, published date 1978.
The Yellow River Map (1977). A ceremonial meditation for a group of 50 or more people. New Wilderness Newsletter.
Crow Two (1975). A ceremonial opera included in *Desert Plants Conversations with 23 American Composers*, Walter Zimmermann Aesthetic Research Center, Canada, 1977.
Trio for Flute, Piano and Page Turner (1961), Smith Publications.
Willow Brook Generations and Reflections (1976), for winds, brass and vocalists, Smith Publications.
To Valerie Solanis and Marilyn Monroe in Recognition of Their Desperation (1970), for orchestra or chamber ensemble, by Smith Publications.
Sonic Meditations (1971-72), for voices and instruments and unspecialized performers. Smith Publications, 1974.
Meditations on the Points of the Compass (1970), for large chorus, 12 solo vocalists and percussion. Media Press.
Outline for Flute, Percussion and String Bass (1963), Media Press.
The C(s) for Once (1966), for flutes, trumpets, vocalists and tape delay system. BMI Canada Educational Journal Canavangard.
Aeolian Partitions (1968), a theater piece for flute, clarinet, violin, cello and piano. Bowdoin College Press.
$\int \Upsilon^* \Upsilon dT = 1$ (1969) for 4 cellos, 4 bassoons, 4 reader singers, amplified heartbeat and shakuhaci. Source Magazine #7.
George Washington Slept Here Too (1965), a theater piece for four players. Soundings I.
Why Don't You Write a Short Piece (1968), for solo performer or group. Soundings I.
Sound Patterns (1961), for mixed chorus. Joseph Boonin, Inc., Edition Tonos.

Recordings

New Sounds in Electronic Music (Odyssey 32 16 0160), including *I of IV* by Pauline Oliveros.

Electronic Essays (Marathon Music Incorporated MS2111 Canada), including Jar Piece by Pauline Oliveros.
New Music for Woodwinds (Advance Recordings FGR-9S), including Trio for Flute, Piano and Page Turner, by Pauline Oliveros.
Extended Voices: New Pieces for Chorus and for Voices Altered by Sound Synthesizers and Vocoder (Odyssey 32 16 0156), including Sound Patterns by Pauline Oliveros.
20th Century Choral Music (Ars Nova Antigua Recordings (AN-1005), including Sound Patterns by Pauline Oliveros.
The Contemporary Contrabass: New American Music by John Cage, Pauline Oliveros, Ben Johnston (Nonesuch H-71237), including Outline by Pauline Oliveros.
New Music for Electronic and Recorded Media (1750 ARCH S1765), including Bye Bye Butterfly by Pauline Oliveros.

Compositions

1957 Three Songs for Soprano and Piano
1960 Variations for Sextet, flute, clarinet, trumpet, horn, cello, and piano
1961 Sound Patterns, mixed chorus
1961 Trio for Flute, Piano and Page Turner
1961 Time Perspectives, four-channel tape, electro acoustic music
1963 Outline, flute, percussion and string bass
1963 Seven Passages, two-channel tape, mobile, dancer, and electro acoustic music
1964 Apple Box, two performers, amplified apple boxes, and small sound sources
1964 Apple Box Orchestra, ten performers, amplified apple boxes, and small sound sources
1964 Five, trumpet and dancer
1964 Duo for Accordion and Baudoner with Possible Mynah Bird
1965 Cat O Nine Tails, theater piece for mimes with two-channel tape
1965 Winter Light, two-channel tape, mobile and figure
1965 Mnemonics V, two-channel tape, electronic music
1965 Mnemonics III, two-channel tape, electronic music
1965 A Theater Piece, fifteen actors, film projections and tape
1965 Rock Symphony, two-channel tape
1965 Covenant, two-channel tape for film sound track
1965 George Washington Slept Here, amplified violin, film projections and tape
1965 The Chronicles of Hell, two-channel tape
1965 Pieces of Eight, theater piece for wind octet and tape.

1965 Before the Music Ends, two-channel tape and dancer
1965 Light Piece for David Tudor, four-channel tape, amplified piano, and prismatic lighting effects
1966 The Bath, soloist and four tape recorders
1966 Hallo, theater piece for Halloween, tape delay system, instruments, amplified piano, mimes and light projections
1966 I of IV, two-channel tape, electronic music
1966 II of IV, two-channel tape, electronic music
1966 The Day I Disconnected the Erase Head and Forgot to Reconnect It, two-channel tape, electronic music
1966 5000 Miles, two-channel tape, electronic tape
1966 Big Mother Is Watching You, two-channel tape, electronic music
1966 Participle Dangling in Honor of Gertrude Stein, two-channel tape, electro acoustic music, mobile and film
1966 The C(s) for Once, trumpets, flutes, voices, organ and tape delay system
1966 Theater Piece for Trombone Player, garden hose instruments, constructed by Elizabeth Harris and tape
1968 Engineers Delight for Piccolo and Seven Conductors (Not Electric), piccolo, seven conductors with light projections and tape
1968 Circuitry, five percussionists, voltage controlled light score and light events
1968 Music for Lysistrata, two-channel tape, electronic music
1968 Mills Bog, two-channel tape, electronic music
1968 Beautiful Soop, two-channel tape, electronic music
1968 Alien Bog, two-channel tape, electronic music
1968 Evidence for Competing Bimolecular and Termolecular Mechanisms in the Hydrochlorination of Cyclohexene, a modular theater piece for specialized and unspecialized performers, sonic and mixed media events with audience participation
1968 Valentine, a theater piece
1968 Night Jar, a theater piece for viola d'amore player
1968 Festival House, theater piece for orchestra, mimes, light, film and slides
1968 O HA AH, a theater piece for chorus, conductor and two percussionists
1968 Double Basses at Twenty Paces, a theater piece for two string bass players, conductor/referee, seconds, tape, and slide projection
1969 AOK, accordion, eight country fiddlers, chorus, conductors and tape delay system

1969 The Dying Alchemist Preview, narrator, violin, trumpet, piccolo, percussion and tape sequence by Lynn Lonidier

1969 ∫Y*YdT=1, four bassoons, four cellos, four sight readers, amplified prepared piano, heart beat and shakuhaci, lights and theatrical events

1969 In Memoriam Nikola Tesla, Cosmic Engineer, seven musicians with extensive electronic devices

1969 Aeolian Partitions, theater piece for flute, clarinet, violin, cello, and piano

1969 Events, a live sound track for the film by Londier for accordion, cello, voices and other instruments. The audience participates in the singing

1969 Please Don't Shoot the Piano Player, He Is Doing the Best He Can, a theater piece for an ensemble of soloists

1970 Music for Expo 70, accordion, two cellos, three voices

1970 Music for Tai Chi, improvisation instructions for accordion, strings, winds, percussion and voices

1970 To Valerie Solanis and Marilyn Monroe in Recognition of Their Desperation, chamber version for strings, flutes, pipe organ, electronic music system and lighting

1970 Arrangement, by Douglas Leedy with further arrangements by Oliveros and Roger Davis. A collaborative theater piece for organ, flute, conductor, string quartet and magician

1970 Bog Road with Bird Call Patch, tape and live electronic music system, four channels

1970 Why Don't You Write a Short Piece?, theater piece for one player

1970 Meditation on the Points of the Compass, chorus and percussion

1971 XII Sonic Meditations, for group work over a long period of time, performers may be unspecialized

1971 Link, an environmental theater piece

1972 Post Card Theater, for unspecialized performers, mixed media events involving post cards

1972 What to Do, for any number of performers. Performers may be unspecialized. Sonic and mixed media events

1972 Phantom Fathom, an evening ritual, mixed media events including meditations and an exotic potluck dinner

1972 1000 Acres, string quarter

1973 Sonic Meditations XII-XXV

1973 Phantom Fathom (II), from the theater of the Ancient Trumpeter: A ceremonial participation evening

1976 Willowbrook Generations and Reflections
1975 Crow Two: A Ceremonial Opera
1977 Theater of Substitutions: Blind/Dumb/Director
1977 Horse Sings from Cloud, song for voice and accordian
1977 King Kong Sing Along, chorus
1977 Rose Moon, a ceremony for chorus and percussion

EVE QUELER

Conductor

Eve Queler was the first woman to conduct at the Lincoln Center's Mostly Mozart Festival in 1971. She opened another room for aspiring women conductors, proving that the sex of the conductor is unimportant. What is significant is the ability of the person on the podium to raise the orchestra's performance to the height of professionalism. If one closes one's eyes, one cannot determine the sex of the conductor. Queler is a perfectionist with the baton, and her triumph on the podium is of particular value since success in this male bastion has been extremely limited.

Queler's inventiveness, patience and persistence has established her as one of America's prominent conductors. She shares the distinction of being part of "Music's Distinguished Triumvirate" with Sarah Caldwell and Antonia Brico. The powerful inequities inherent in professional conducting were overcome by Queler as a result of her determination, versatility, and sheer talent. There is a continuing need to improve conducting opportunities in the United States for women and Queler will share these opportunities.

The resourceful Queler founded the Opera Orchestra of New York in 1967 to give aspiring young singers the opportunity to experience operatic roles with orchestral accompaniment and to help instrumentalists learn operatic repertoire. The opera orchestra has grown from its fledgling, uncertain beginning to the auspicious and prestigious position it enjoys in 1978. The credit belongs to the adventurous and independent Queler.

The only sexists in the concert world are outside the membership of the orchestras. They can be found in the audience, on the Board of Directors, and among the critics and writers. Women have the same difficulties as men in

EVE QUELER

finding an experienced conductor to apprentice themselves to and in finding an orchestra upon which to practice. Women have proven they have the talent and stamina to be on the podium.

Eve Queler has an impressive list of "firsts" in her repertoire of personal accomplishments. These include Conductor of the Opera Orchestra of New York; Associate Conductor of the Fort Wayne Philharmonic, and the first woman appointed to a metropolitan orchestra in the United States; First American woman to conduct a major orchestra in Europe in over 35 years; First woman to conduct a concert at New York's Philharmonic Hall (Lincoln Center for the Performing Arts); Assistant to Julius Rudel at the New York City Opera; The first woman to conduct the Philadelphia Orchestra, Montreal Symphony, San Antonio Symphony, Hartford Symphony, the New Jersey Symphony and many others; She received an honorary Doctorate Degree from Russell Sage College in 1978; Musician of the Month in Musical America in May 1972.

The list will continue to grow since Queler's talent and energy are illimitable. At the age of forty-two she is youthful and society is slowly coming of age in realizing and recognizing talent. In our generation, men have landed on the moon and women on the podium. I wonder which person traveled the most turbulent road? Astronaut Neil A. Armstrong uttered the historic words, "It's one small step for man, one giant leap for mankind." I paraphrase that quote and suggest that Eve Queler's one small step to the podium was one giant leap for all women.

Eve Rabin Queler was born in 1936 in New York City, one of two daughters of Benjamin J. Rabin and Harriet Hirsch Rabin. She was reared in the confines of an orthodox Jewish home in the Bronx. Except for the area of music, Queler lived a typically sheltered life within her family, synagogue and music. At the age of three she showed signs of being a child prodigy and at five received her first scholarship to a Bronx music school to study piano.

The second scholarship was received at the age of twelve to study at the world renowned Curtis Institute of Music in Philadelphia with Isabelle Vengerova. The scholarship was turned down since it covered only tuition and her family's lack of funds made it impossible to meet living expenses. Perhaps, also, the Rabins were reluctant to permit her to live so far away from home.

Following graduation from a high school of music and art in Manhattan, Eve Rabin attended the City College of New York, the Mannes College of Music and the Hebrew Union School of Sacred Music. During her undergraduate years she met a young man named Stanley Queler, a law school candidate. Although she never planned to marry, love was the victor and she became Mrs. Stanley Queler on December 23, 1956. Eve Rabin Queler followed the accepted trend of the time and went to work to financially help her husband through law school. She accepted such mundane jobs as playing the organ in local bars, churches and temples, even when she was pregnant. Experience is a great teacher, and as boring as these jobs may have been, they were to have an effect on her direction and musical career. All of learning is a combination of both positive and negative. It is the melding of these two opposites that create the individual. These experiences were an important growth period for the famous Queler, if not by musical standards, then certainly in the area of confidence and the ability to relate to people.

The Quelers have produced a winning combination, somewhat unusual given the conditions of society at the present time. Attorney Queler has supported his wife's career, as business manager of the Opera Company of New York in its early years, financially when she worked as the associate conductor of the Fort Wayne Philharmonic, and as both a father and mother to their children when she traveled. Eve Queler eventually returned to graduate studies and developed a portfolio of excellent credentials. She is a fine sight reader which led to the position of studio accompanist for the distinguished baritone Martial Singher during her student days. The experience she garnered during this time expanded her musical talents and opened new horizons. With his help she learned the French language repertoire and developed an insight into vocal coaching. She went to Marlboro, Vermont, during the summer with Singher and then to Tanglewood in Lenox, Massachusetts, with a fellowship in the opera department.

She received a job coaching at the New York City Opera in 1958 which influenced the direction of her life, for it was during this time that she developed a burning desire to conduct. To accomplish this goal she returned to graduate school and studied conducting with Carl Bamberger and musical analysis with Paul Emerich. Thanks to a grant from the Martha Baird Rockefeller Fund, she was able to study for two years with Joseph Rosenstock of the Metropolitan Opera.

Under the tutelage of Maestro Rosenstock, Queler expanded and further developed her conducting talent. In 1970 she was a recipient of an award--the only woman of eight finalists--to study at the American Institute of Orchestral Conducting with Walter Susskind in St. Louis. Maestra Queler's musical training is similar to the training experienced by the great European conductors. She spent demanding and arduous years developing her conducting talent and her comprehension of the great operas at the New York City Opera and musical compositions, under the supervision and direction of world renowned conductors. Experience received under master conductors is incomparable and extremely difficult to attain.

Queler comments on reading scores:

> Well, I read scores quite easily, from my years as accompanist and coach for Julius Rudel, at the New York Opera. Then when it comes to memory, I make a kind of chart as I study the score. It would seem complicated to an onlooker, but for me it is a shorthand version of the music. By the time I've gone to that effort, the music is largely in my mind. I just keep going over the rough spots, checking back where necessary and it's mine. That's a wonderful feeling at that point.

Does she conduct all her music from memory?

> I'd like to, for that is how I'm most comfortable. But as a practical matter, I do opera and accompanying (concerts, for example) with a score, since there is an extra element there which can lead to problems that an orchestra piece does not have.

Queler's professional background is as extensive as her training. She has conducted musical productions including both operatic and symphonic literature. A partial list of her operatic conducting appearances would include the following, most in concert version: Operatic Conducting Debut in 1967, Mascagni's Cavalleria in Rusticana; The Opera Orchestra of New York which was founded in 1967; Assistant conductor to Julius Rudel, New York City Opera for five seasons; Puccini's Tosca in 1969; Giodano's Fedora in 1970; Monteverdi's concert version L'Incoronazione di Poppea in 1971; Respighi's Belfagor in 1971; Rossini's William Tell in 1972; Meyerbeer's L'Africana in 1972; Verdi's I Lombardi in 1973; Landonai's Fracesca Da Rimini 1973; Bizet's Pearl Fishers in 1974; Donizetti's

Parisina d'Este in 1974; Verdi's Masnadieri in 1975; Donizetti's La Favorita in 1975; Massenet's Le Cid in 1976; Donizetti's Gemma di Vergy in 1976; Smetana's Dalibor in 1977; Rossini's Tancredi in 1978; and Weber's Oberon in 1978.

On March 8, 1974, Raymond Ericson wrote in the New York Times the following comments on the production of Donizetti's Parisina d'Este*:

> Mrs. Queler led a performance that never flagged and showed off the music as energetically as possible. It will be interesting to see what operatic rarities she decides to revive next season.

Andrew Porter, internationally known music critic, has been one of the many music critics who has diligently pursued the artistic career of the brilliant and amazing Eve Queler. According to Mr. Porter, "She never fails to generate excitement." He wrote the following for the New Yorker, December 29, 1975**:

> Any list, however brief, of the city's notable concerts in recent seasons is likely to include some given by Eve Queler and her Opera Orchestra of New York. In Carnegie Hall, the week before last, Miss Queler showed once again her ability--already admired in performances of Verdi's "I Lombardi" and of Donizetti's "La Favorite"--to present a controversial or uneven work so persuasively that its weaknesses pale before splendors she knows how to reveal. This time, the work was Berlioz's lyric monodrama, or mélologue, "Lélio, ou Le Retour à la Vie." ... Miss Queler paced both the individual numbers and the piece as a whole with a sure romantic instinct.

Byron Belt wrote the following in the Long Island Press, March 9, 1976†:

> Le Cid ... was given a flamingly triumphant performance ... by Eve Queler's Opera Orchestra of

*©1974 by The New York Times Company. Reprinted by permission.
**Reprinted by permission of the publisher.
†Reprinted by permission of the author.

> New York and a stellar cast headed by Grace Bumbry, Placido Domingo and Paul Plishka.... The singing last night was beyond anything heard ... this season and Eve Queler led the performance of her life.... The brilliant work of the soloists, the splendid performances of the orchestra and the chorus were, of course, made possible by the assured, authoritative and impassioned leadership of Eve Queler. It was clear ... that the star-studded audience realized that the conductor is the key to this latest Opera Orchestra of New York's Triumph, and she was given a deserved heroine's reception by the over-flow crowd.

This was quite a change in the media since early in Queler's career male chauvinism had reared its ugly head when the New York Sunday News on November 11, 1970, reported: "Eve Queler has the edge on all other music conductors because she's shapelier than Leopold Stokowski, prettier than Leonard Bernstein, and has better legs than William Steinberg."

The Opera Orchestra of New York gives three professional performances of operas in concert form each season. It would indeed be impossible to rank the various seasons because each one has been outstanding, but an overview of different seasons is in order.

Earlier in 1975, Andrew Porter reviewed two of the Opera Orchestra's performances for the New Yorker (on March 3rd and 10th)*:

> ... nevertheless, such spirited singing, and Miss Queler's fiery conducting, were enough to turn the strictest of judges into an enthusiast, his scruples swept away by the surge of the music.
>
> The Metropolitan's and the City Opera's plugging of Puccini--"Manon Lescaut," "La Bohème," "Tosca," "Madame Butterfly," and "Turandot" are in both repertories, and last week they were playing "Manon Lescaut" on the same day--matters less while Eve Queler and her Opera Orchestra of New York are at hand to expand our experience of grand opera

*Reprinted by permission of the publisher.

> with such things as their "I Masnadieri," reviewed last week, and now, again in Carnegie Hall, "La Favorite." Using the standard text, Miss Queler made a splendid job of it. Miss Queler's command of dramatic pace and her feeling for the natural surge or settle of a vocal line were sure.

It is interesting to note that Mr. Porter suggested some three years later that the Met should invite Eve Queler to take charge of its La Favorite, for she certainly knows how to present a work in the best possible light. Miss Queler's aim, as it has been since her first season, is to resurrect great works which have been withheld from the repertoire "because they are difficult to sing or impossible to stage."

Eve Queler was the first woman to ever conduct an opera that was commercially recorded. Massenet's Le Cid was recorded live at Carnegie Hall on March 8, 1976, by Columbia Masterworks (the three records can be purchased under the Columbia Label number 79300). This was Columbia's premiere recording of Le Cid. The technique of recording live has not been used since Toscanini and the Old National Broadcasting Symphony. They do have some problems with audience noises so Queler uses the following solution:

> We come in the next day and redo the sections which are too bad for commercial purposes--but those few spots are not enough to take away the live-performance spontaneity that we are trying to capture.

Thus far they have recorded Massenet's Le Cid. These operas are not all that rare in Europe, she said, by implication saddened that in the U.S. we tend to concentrate on the standards and thereby miss some pretty wonderful music. Yet, the situation is precisely what is helping to build Ms. Queler's reputation.

On March 10, 1976, Donal Henahan of the New York Times writes of Le Cid*:

> To the great credit of Miss Queler, her performance

made the most of the work's musical appeal, though without hiding its essential dramatic emptiness and unheavenly lengths. Except for about ten minutes worth of music, the score was given complete.

We needed and we got Miss Queler's honest testimony about a work that was widly popular when the Paris Opera was still in the grip of Meyerbeer, but that seems not to have had a major production in this country since 1902 at the Chicago Opera.

Music notes by Shirley Fleming of March 7, 1976, compliment "conductor Eve Queler's Opera Orchestra of New York in making history as usual this season with concert performances of two operas so rare as to be almost extinct. Massenet's Le Cid last seen at the Metropolitan in 1897 and Donizetti's Gemma di Vergy follows." On March 14, 1976, Donizetti's Gemma di Vergy with Eve Queler conducting The Opera Orchestra of New York and Schola Cantorum (Columbia masterpiece [SQ7 79303]). On April 13, 1977, Eve Queler presented what is believed to be the first performance ever in the United States of Puccini's Edgar. Again America's leading lady of opera was recorded (Columbia's Masterpiece M2 34584). Writing for the Philadelphia Inquirer, Daniel Webster offered the following review of Edgar on November 6, 1977*:

> This performance is a strong one, however, and manages to preserve some of the aura of that live performance without collecting the audience noise--except for applause at the end. The engineers have managed to move from the heroic final note of an aria, sure to have drawn applause, to the next section without capturing noise.
>
> Miss Queler's command of the work keeps it lively and even volcanic at times. The orchestra and the Schola Cantorum choir do a lot to uphold the value of a piece that remains a curiosity, but also a vivid prevision of Puccini's best writing.

Other comments include those in The New York Post by David Rosenthal: "the conducting by Eve Queler is striking for its clairty and the sonority it brings to this dusty score"; and those by William Mann in the London Times: "Edgar is given a smart, expert, spirited performance and decently balanced, the audience was very quiet till the applause at the end."

---

*Reprinted by permission of the publisher.

When Miss Queler presented Smetana's Dalibor, Leighton Kerner writing for Voice felt it was the most exciting and important operatic event of the 1976-77 season. Andrew Porter, writing for The New Yorker on January 24, 1977, felt it was a stirring concert performance of that great opera, which has been too long neglected outside Czechoslovakia*:

> Eve Queler has the ability to make an opera go, to set phrases surging and singing out so that listeners are stirred, excited, elevated. She communicates love and warmth and enjoyment--more fully than any of the conductors I have heard at the Met this season. She imposes nothing on the score: the composer's will alone is done. Her performances have the increasingly rare quality of naturalness. Everything seems to move at the right tempo. The singers are neither held back nor driven onward; she seems to breathe with their breath. There was a good orchestra.

In the 1978 season Byron Belt expresses his admiration for Eve Queler's presentation of Weber's Oberon and Rossini's Tancredi, published in Newhouse Newspapers**:

> Oberon is a treasure of lovely music, and the revival by Eve Queler's Opera Orchestra of New York packed Carnegie Hall with an attentive and enthusiastic crowd of admirers.
>
> Miss Queler led her forces with skill and sensitivity, and her expert players and the fine professionally enriched Dessoff choirs provided splendid insights into Weber's classically elegant and romantically expressive score.
>
> Oberon has clearly put New Yorkers once more in debt to Eve Queler and her invaluable organization.

Every time Conductor Eve Queler has directed the Opera Orchestra of New York, the performance ends with a standing ovation in respect and admiration for this truly musical genius.

Mrs. Queler's confident, intuitive feelings for the music she conducts and her exceptionally fine training are ad-

*Reprinted by permission of the publisher

**Reprinted by permission of the author.

mired by both the musicians and the audiences. She envisions her future as permanent conductor of a symphony orchestra. That she has the talent and the resources to accomplish this goal is not the question. Whether she has the opportunity to audition for a conductorship of a prestigious orchestra without reference to her sex, is! Many professional orchestras audition instrumentalists, but not conductors, behind screens so only the ability of the performer is considered in the decision-making process.

Mrs. Queler was the first woman in the United States ever to hold the position of associate conductor of a metropolitan orchestra. She was named to the post of Associate Conductor of the Fort Wayne Philharmonic in 1970, a class B Metropolitan Symphony with a budget of more than $160,000 per year, chosen over four male finalists and one hundred applicants. Maestra Queler was responsible for conducting three subscription concerts, three series for children, and chamber music performances. Her additional duties included guiding the chorus and opera division. An important aspect of her job was the amount of time she spent in public relations because of the need to help adults and children better understand the general aspects of music. She was in demand as a speaker at lunches and dinners, and devoted as much time as possible to press conferences. An enlightened audience is a supportive audience. She held this position for only one season because of the need for the orchestra to have a resident conductor, and she had to commute from New York to Indiana weekly which was too energy consuming and of course, expensive when travel and living costs were included.

She was the only woman out of eight selected by the American Institute of Orchestral Conducting to work with the St. Louis Symphony. This was an enlightening experience: "I'd never conducted symphonic music before and realized then that conducting was my métier. It was my profession." Since Eve Queler was guest conducting before Sarah Caldwell, she has a lengthy and impressive list of first accomplishments. She was the first woman to conduct a full concert with the prestigious Philadelphia Philharmonic Orchestra. During that performance, the audience numbered well over four thousand in a season when only Mr. Ormandy and Mr. Fiedler did as well, and the listeners showed their respect and admiration for Maestra Queler with a standing ovation. How wonderfully deafening the deserved applause must have been for Queler, who has the training, the ability and the talent to conduct one of the five top orchestras in the United States.

She has had many guest appearances in both Europe and the United States which offers her the opportunity to conduct pieces that are not in the repertoire of the Opera Orchestra of New York. Maestra Queler conducted the French Radio and Television Orchestra in 1970. She also conducted a concert at the New York Philharmonic Hall, the first woman to achieve this goal. Eve Queler, the New York Chamber Orchestra and nine singers presented ensemble numbers from eight Mozart operas in 1971 at Philharmonic Hall. In 1972 she conducted a radio performance of Giordano's Fedora in Paris. She conducted the New Philharmonic Orchestra in London, in February 1974 and during the same month made her debut at the Philadelphia Academy of Music, conducting Berlioz's La Damnation de Faust. Guest conductor Eve Queler has received outstanding reviews with every symphony orchestra she has conducted. The Cleveland Orchestra was the first to have two women conductors in the same season. Most other orchestras engage in tokenism and invite one of the three well-known women conductors (Queler, Brico, or Caldwell) each season.

Queler has been a guest director for concerts of the New Jersey Symphony, Hartford Symphony, Cleveland Orchestra, the Montreal Symphony, Philadelphia Orchestra Symphony, San Antonio Symphony, and Lincoln Center's summer Mostly Mozart series; she's also conducted in Providence, Rhode Island; Chattanooga, Tennessee; Lake George, New York; Barcelona, Spain; Nice, France; Las Palmas, Canary Islands; and Puerto Rico.

Robert Pincus, express arts editor for the San Antonio Express wrote the following review on April 14, 1975:

GUEST ARTISTS SUPERB*

> Both San Antonio Symphony guest artists, conductor Eve Queler and violinist Charles Treger, scored spectacular successes Saturday.
>
> Only a few bars into the Wagner overture I noticed how beautifully the orchestra was sounding under Miss Queler's baton. The intonation was gorgeous throughout. What a fine ear she has.
>
> She has a sumptuous feel for bringing out the silken phrase and an unerring sight on design bal-

---

*Reprinted by permission of the author.

anced with detail.

Miss Queler had some interesting things to say about the Wagner. In the quieter sections, her tempos tended to be comparatively slow, but she would accelerate ever so gradually into the dramatic moments.

This was managed with subtle changes; nothing sudden to break the momentum.

Excellent as the overture was, it was in Berlioz' masterpiece where her extraordinary talent came forward. It was a performance that was as intelligently and sensitively conducted as one would want.

All the turbulent, wildly vivid emotions of this revolutionary score were vividly portrayed. It was energetic, invigorating and vital.

Even in the loudest sections, there was no murkiness. Miss Queler's textures were transparent, and this meant she brought out lines often drowned out. This was especially the case with the middle register instruments.

Again her control of tempos and her rhythmic insight were flawless. The orchestra played this virtuoso score magnificently; it performed with a vibrant color.

Comments printed February 10, 1977, in The Hartford Courant, written by James E. Sellars:

QUELER HAS FLUID STYLE*

Guest conductor Eve Queler opened up the sound of the Hartford Symphony Orchestra Wednesday night at the Bushnell Memorial. Her conducting is relaxed, open, and fluent and draws these qualities from her players. She knows how to stretch a downbeat, shape a phrase, and play with the tempo. Her approach was especially fitted to the gorgeously romantic Strauss Die Frau Ohne Schatten (Symphony Fantasy) and the Barber Violin Concerto, which made up the first half of the program.

Ms. Queler got a voluptuous, ardent sound from the orchestra--well balanced, smoothly executed, and rich in detail.

*Reprinted by permission of the author.

Staff writer Donald P. Delany's article in the Trenton Times of March 8, 1977 noted:

CONDUCTOR EVE QUELER WOWS*

> The crowd at Rider was expectant and obviously rooting for Eve Queler, and she did not disappoint. She took command of the orchestra from the first notes and with a smiling authority and striking musicianship she molded a program which was thoroughly satisfying from start to finish.
>
> Her conducting was vigorous, yet sensitive, her beat crisp, but flexible. Her movements on the podium were graceful, and her gestures flowing and expressive without being in any way flamboyant. In short, she has a style which communicates, one which musicians, it would seem, should find easy to follow.
>
> The Firebird music was especially well played. Miss Queler brought out all of the exotic nuances of the work. Nothing was rushed in this, or in any of the other pieces on the program, and it was this quality--her ability to make the music breathe, to let each phrase, each note come through with clarity--which more than anything else made the concert memorable.

The Cleveland Press, on August 1, 1977, published this review by Dick Wootten*:

> The Cleveland Orchestra concert at Blossom Music Center last night was exhilarating and very different. Everyone on stage seemed caught up in the joy of making so much appealing music.
>
> The gang responded to Ms. Queler's urgings from the podium with warmth and precision. It was a kind of a love-in with the audience being the major beneficiary.
>
> Rarely have I heard such a well-balanced and skillfully programmed concert.
>
> She knows what music thrills, stirs and melts an audience.
>
> Ms. Queler had the orchestra in top form throughout the evening. To say that she was in total com-

*Reprinted by permission of the authors.

mand doesn't seem appropriate in her case. One who is in command coaxes and whips. Ms. Queler, I suspect charms instead.

Eve Queler was guest conductor with the Colorado Springs Symphony Orchestra on March 17, 18, and 20 of 1977. She conducted Webern's Passacaglia, Op. I; Schumann's Piano Concerto, Op. 54 in A Minor; and Tchaikovsky's Symphony No. 4, Op. 36 in F Minor. Queler comments "Women conductors face credibility problems. It boils down to accepting leadership from women! I find that whenever I conduct, there is a tremendous interest because many people have never seen a woman conduct--people turn out to look me over."

Eve Queler developed a "training orchestra" to study operatic repertoire in 1978 at the University of Maryland summer session. Through her efforts and guidance, she provided young instrumentalists with a much-needed experience. The orchestra rehearsed from June 19 to July 15, studying the style and scores of such operas as Tristan and Isolde, Bohème, Tosca, Rigoletto and Don Giovanni. Some ninety instrumentalists practiced six hours per day, both under Maestra Queler's baton and at sectional rehearsals with noted guest instructors. Every Friday night, the orchestra held an open rehearsal with singers. The entire summer program culminated with the concert performance of Tristan and Isolde.

When the University of Maryland Summer Session approached Ms. Queler with the idea of establishing an orchestra to study opera repertoire, she was happy on many accounts. "There are excellent programs for training instrumentalists in symphonic repertoire and chamber music, but in opera the player has been ignored," according to Ms. Queler. Opera has been the step-child in most universities and even conservatories--the notable exception being the University of Indiana at Bloomington. Most of the instrumentalists Eve Queler spoke to said that playing opera at school was the "pits," and they tried to be excused from it.

The participants in the University of Maryland's opera workshop were auditioned by Ms. Queler in twelve major cities in the United States. She is a perfectionist who planned the auditions and accomplished the exhausting job of auditioning hundreds of potential participants. She chose the audition pieces with two definite views in mind, the first three were picked because they are so difficult to play and yet rewarding, and the others were chosen also with a view to diversified style. Stephen Sinclair reviewed this workshop for the National Endowment in the November/December 1978 Arts issue of the Cultural Post*:

> The four week workshop climaxed in a concert presentation of Tristan and Isolde after what Queler calls "the way to do it right," with seventeen rehearsals of the full orchestra and at least eight rehearsals of each section.

Jerry Campbell reported on another presentation of Tristan and Isolde for the London Evening Standard on July 20, 1978*. Jess Thomas and Roberta Knie sang the leading roles.

> Eve Queler, an unassuming woman with a will of steel, conducted an orchestra she had selected personally by auditioning hundreds of musicians from coast to coast. Eighty hopefuls applied for one vacancy in the flutes. The sound they made was ravishing.
>
> At the end, as the audience rose and shouted, Maestra! Maestra! Miss Queler made one of the loveliest gestures I have ever seen in a theater. She held up the score of Tristan, to remind us where true genius resides.

The opera received many reviews, and all were in praise of the accomplishments of the participants and the inventiveness of Maestra Queler. This, however, was not to be the only performance, and Queler shared with another audience on New Year's Eve, 1978, a second performance at Carnegie Hall.

Eve Queler correctly diagnosed a "crying need" in America--that of helping instrumentalists to more fully develop their musical careers. That Queler has the talent, experience, and enthusiasm to expend training instrumentalists in operatic repertoire will eventually be reflected throughout the country with more opera, more jobs, and more audiences.

Eve Queler is the best trained, most experienced and

*Reprinted by permission of the authors.

most promising woman conductor in America today. She must not be denied that which is rightfully hers, to conduct from the prestigious podiums in the country. The world awaits you, Maestra Queler. We need your talent and inspiring heights.

Recordings
(Eve Queler and the Opera Orchestra of New York)

Massenet's Le Cid, Columbia Masterpiece, 79300.
Donizetti's Gemma di Vergy Columbia Masterpiece, SQ7 79303.
Puccini's Edgar, Columbia's Masterpiece, M2 34584.

MARGA RICHTER

Composer, Pianist

The first public performance of a composition by Marga Richter took place in a high school auditorium in Robbinsdale, Minnesota, a suburb of Minneapolis. The composer, age 14, was at the piano, accompanying her mother, soprano Inez Chandler Richter. It was not until her fiftieth birthday, however, that she was to sit in Minneapolis' Orchestra Hall and hear a performance of one of her compositions by the Minnesota Orchestra. The piece Lament was composed twenty years earlier, while her mother was dying of cancer.

The critics raved and called for more Richter. Michael Anthony of the Minneapolis Tribune wrote on October 22, 1976*:

> The piece makes a striking effect on first hearing.... It is an early composition of Ms. Richter's and makes one eager to hear her more recent work.

John Harvey, writing for the St. Paul Dispatch and Pioneer Press on October 25, 1976, said*:

> Now that the ice has been broken by this twenty year old work, perhaps it would not be amiss to suggest that we be given the chance to hear a product of the maturity of Richter's undeniable talent.

The journey from Robbinsdale High School to Orchestra Hall had been a long one, interrupted by thirty-three years in New York, where she earned her Master's Degree at the Juilliard School of Music, got married and raised two children.

---

*Reprinted by permission of the authors.

During this period of time the gifted Marga Richter had six of her compositions recorded commercially. Her ballet score had been premiered in Cannes and subsequently performed by three ballet companies on five continents. In addition she had written more than fifty compositions which have been performed and applauded by both audiences and critics throughout the United States.

Richter has been the recipient of many awards, grants, and commissions, including the American Society Composers and Publishers Standard Award for the past twelve years, the National Endowment for the Arts, The Martha Baird Rockefeller Fund, The National Federation of Music Clubs, and Meet the Composer.

The origins of Marga Richter's music reach back to the provincial German city of Einbeck where her grandfather, Richard Richter, was conductor of the municipal orchestra. He was also a composer and many years later Marga played one of his compositions, a piano piece titled Unter den Linden, as a birthday present for her father. She says, "It sounds exactly the way you would expect a piece with that title to sound."

Grandfather Richter, for reasons of his own, refused to allow any of his children to study music, but he was unable to quench his son Paul's innate devotion to the art. Paul was a regular attendant at the local opera house and one evening he heard the beautiful soprano Inez Chandler in a leading role. He was so taken by her that following the performance he rushed backstage and proposed to her on the spot. They were married and moved to Reedsburg, Wisconsin, home of the bride's parents, where their daughter Marga was born. A year later they settled in Minnesota.

Marga grew up in an atmosphere that was saturated with music. Her mother gave private voice lessons, sang in the church choir, and on one glorious occasion she was soloist in an all-Wagner program with the Minneapolis Symphony Orchestra conducted by Eugene Ormandy. Evenings her father would often send his children off to bed to the sound of Beethoven's Pathetique Sonata which he had laboriously taught himself to play. Saturday afternoons were devoted to the broadcasts of the Metropolitan Opera, and if the opera was by Wagner, her father would lock all the doors and allow no one in or out of the house until it was over. (Years later, a fellow composer, trying to explain to a group of performers

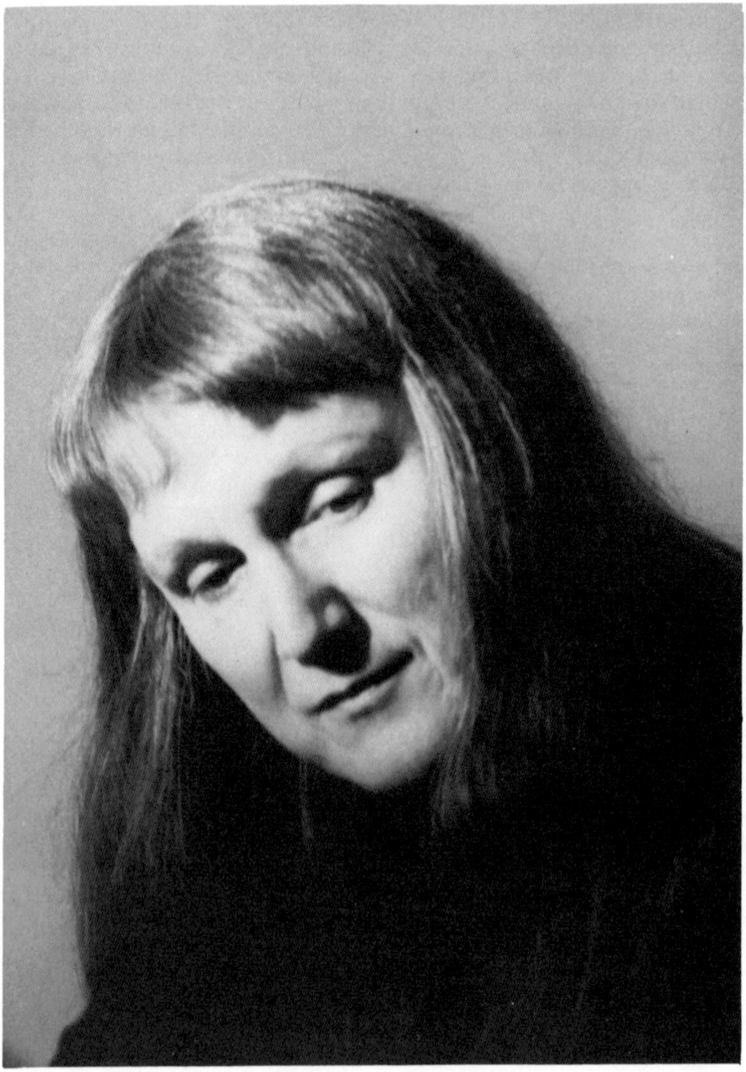

MARGA RICHTER
(Photo by Alan Skelly)

how they should approach one of her compositions said: "Marga's music is like Wagner--it takes a long time to unfold, but it's worth waiting for.")

She began to study piano at the age of three and was writing her own compositions by the age of twelve even though at the time she knew absolutely nothing about music theory. Referring to those early pieces she notes,

> From the beginning I used all twelve tones of the chromatic scale as equals, although at times one tone might be more important than the others, and the music is essentially melodic. I recently looked at one of my early songs and was totally surprised to find that the piano part contains harmonic and melodic elements that I am still using--passages using only consecutive 7th and 9th, including a very dissonant passage in minor 9th with a type of inner figuration which has remained as an element of my later style. This rather amazed me since at that time I had heard very little contemporary music (no Schoenberg, Stravinsky or Bartók for instance) and had played none.

Richter now feels that perhaps her total ignorance of both classical theory and the innovations of the great twentieth-century modernists was all to the good at that stage of her development. "I was free to explore my own personal tonal world without rules or restrictions," she comments. As a result she developed a uniquely individual musical vocabulary which might have been inhibited with too-early exposure to academic training.

The great conductor, Leopold Stokowski, sensed this the one time he heard her music. Richter was seventeen at the time, and a pianist friend of hers performed a composition she had written, Ballet of the Pixilated Penguins, in her debut recital in New York's Town Hall. Says Richter, "I can't imagine anyone doing anything so naive today and getting away with it." The next day this same friend had an audition with Maestro Stokowski. After she had played several standard compositions he asked for something contemporary and the only piece she knew was Richter's Penguins, which she proceeded to play. When she finished Stokowski rushed down the aisle demanding to know who had written it. Upon being told the name and age of the composer, he decreed: "Tell her never to study composition. She will lose something very unique and fresh." Richter, never one to let herself be guided by authority, did eventually study composition, but by then it was too late to destroy her highly individual musical language.

She was a piano major at Juilliard School of Music and studied under Rosalyn Turek, the renowned interpreter of the music of J. S. Bach. Richter credits Madame Tureck as the greatest single influence on her music.

> What she taught me about rhythm was a revelation. She stressed the importance of lightly accenting the first beat of the metrical unit and creating tension in a phrase by understanding and projecting the rhythmic structure. In addition we were taught to incorporate an infinitesimal pause between the beats (the "agogic accent") which creates great rhythmic excitement and interest. This gave me an ingrained sense of rhythm and meter which has greatly influenced my composing.

At this time Richter's only ambition was to become a concert pianist and she was deeply disappointed to learn at the end of her freshman year that Dr. Tureck would resign to devote her career to concertizing. However, Tureck ultimately agreed to continue to teach two students, and Marga was one of them.

Richter was delighted to be studying privately with Tureck but to remain at Juilliard she had to have a major, so she applied to the composition department. Richter says, "I felt the compositions I submitted were not very good and I doubt whether they would be accepted today. But perhaps I was accepted because they could see I was not just a casual songwriter."

She studied compositon with William Bergsma and Vincent Persichetti whose approach to music was very different from hers. She recalls, "Unlike so many composition teachers, they did not try to turn me into weak carbon copies of themselves but helped me learn how to make my own musical ideas into finished pieces."

While still an undergraduate student at Juilliard, three of her compositions were programmed on the Composers Form series in New York. At that time she was the youngest composer ever to be so honored. The program included Sonata for Clarinet and Piano and a song cycle, Transmutation, which are the earliest of her works that are still performed today. Peggy Glanville-Hicks writing for the New York Herald Tribune on February 4, 1951, notes the following*:

> Miss Richter's evolution should be allowed to follow its own inner nature, avoiding formula or systems as much as possible.... The most valuable of her musical attributes are an original sense of rhythm, a sense of drama in choice of materials and, above all, an ability to make her own forms grow from the very nature of her materials and ideas. This is the very essence of composition.

Following graduation from Juilliard, Richter turned first to composing music for modern dance. She wrote scores for James Waring, Irving Burton and Alec Rubin which caught the attention of the dance world, and even more important, of Edward Cole, the brilliant young recording executive. At that time Mr. Cole was in the process of compiling an outstanding catalog of contemporary music for Metro-Goldwyn-Mayer Records. During the next three years, Cole produced two records of Marga Richter performing her own and other contemporary composers' music for children, and she was commissioned by the recording company to write four major works which were performed by outstanding artists of contemporary music.

Alfred Frankenstein, eminent critic of the San Francisco Chronicle, gave lavish praise on December 12, 1957, of the Concerto for Piano and Violins, Cellos and Basses, performed by the gifted William Masselos*:

> I do not recall hearing a new piano concerto with such keen interest since the second concerto of Ravel was unveiled. The strong tawny color of the piece is one of its special virtues; others are its wealth of modal-sounding melody, its crackling energy, and its shrewdly placed contrasts whereby a work of small proportions takes on large importance. Above everything, the concerto communicates a sense of adventure. It goes places. And so does the colossal virtuosity of Masselos.

---

*Reprinted by permission of the authors.

Oliver Daniel, one of the most influential figures on the contemporary music scene at that time, reviewed the Concerto for Saturday Review on December 26, 1959*:

> Wisconsin-born Marga Richter is obviously a fine and sensitive pianist, as previous recordings indicate. Here she establishes herself as a composer and one of no mean gift. She has written a solid work and draws a big sound from her limited orchestra. She is able to be crashing without being a bore. But like many a lady composer she attacks the problem of music (at times) in an almost masculine way. The finest moments, and there are some truly beautiful ones, are those of a more gentle nature.
>
> Marga Richter is one of the young composers who bear watching.

In 1953 Richter married Alan Skelly, who later became Chairman of the Philosophy Department at C. W. Post College on Long Island. They are the parents of two children, Michael and Maureen. Marga devoted many years to her family, and composed only in spare hours. She never regarded her role as wife and mother as a burden. Years later she feels, "I'm glad, I think, that I didn't have commissions coming in and deadlines to meet while the kids were growing up. To tell them, go away I'm busy--I don't think I could have done this. Your kids are only home once, even if you live to be a hundred."

Michael is a pianist who frequently performs his mother's solo works and also plays duo-piano in concert with her. Maureen received a diploma in sitar from Benares Hindu University and introduced her mother to the classical Indian music which was to exert such a strong influence on her later compositions.

In 1964 choreographer Stuart Hodes, who had heard the recording of her Aria and Toccata, requested she expand and orchestrate it for ballet based on the writing of Leonid Andreyev's story "Abyss." The piece was commissioned by the Harkness Ballet and premiered in Cannes, France, and performed by the Harkness Dancers in major cities of Europe, North Africa, Asia, and North and South America. It is now

*Reprinted by permission of the publisher.

part of the repertoires of Joffrey and Boston Ballet Companies.

Although conceived for dance, the score for Abyss is an effective piece of music in its own right. In 1976, it received its first concert performance by the Madison Symphony conducted by Roland Johnson. David Wagner of the Madison Capital Times made the following comments on February 2, 1976*:

> Those Madisonians who attended the Wisconsin Ballet Company's first concert of the season last November in the Civic Center heard Abyss performed on recording, accompanying the complete ballet for which it was designed. Though the music was familiar from that occasion, its performance in a full orchestral version gave listeners the welcome opportunity of examining the music as a work in itself.
>
> There is no doubt about its success as a concert piece. Particularly striking and beautiful Saturday night was the first part, a lyrical viola solo performed over the muted accompaniment of all the other string players in the orchestra by principal violist Sheila Magnuson.
>
> It is rare enough for a viola to take such an extended solo, and Magnuson performed it with an equally rare sensitivity both in the higher reaches of the instrument and especially in the dark, resonant bottom tones, which anticipated with appropriate foreboding the fate of the lovers following the pas de deux which it describes.
>
> The entire work has an independent musical force, and clearly belongs in the standard orchestral repertoire.

Marga Richter decided to set aside all other musical projects in 1968 and devote her time composing a major work for orchestra, a piano concerto, which would incorporate elements of the style and substance of the Indian music to which her daughter had introduced her. She says, "I did not want to try to write authentic Indian music--the Indians do that far better than I could. What I wanted to do was to transfer the melodic and rhythmic beauty and intensity of that kind of

*Reprinted by permission of the publisher.

musical experience to Western instruments, using my own compositional techniques."

It was during this time that Richter also became aware of a new source of inspiration for her music. This included visual stimuli from paintings, landscapes, films, and photographs which began to demand transformation into musical sounds.

She marks February 26, 1968, as the date this new phase of her life began to bear fruit. It was then she came upon an article in Life magazine on the great woman painter Georgia O'Keeffe. Richter recalls, "One look at two of her paintings, Pelvis I and Sky Above Clouds II, and I went to the piano and began to write the concerto. I was totally inspired by the feeling I got from looking at the O'Keeffe clouds --floating, indeterminate, nebulous. The music of that opening section favors the very high and very low registers, and seems to hang aloft with no tone center to pull it down to earth."

Except for the time used in 1971 to write Landscapes of the Mind II for violin and piano for the gifted young virtuoso, Daniel Heifetz, Richter devoted most of the next six years completing the concerto entitled Landscapes of the Mind I. This concerto is far too complex to permit a detailed analysis, but it is a half hour in length, employs a large orchestra which supplements the usual symphonic forces with electric guitar, bass, and an amplified tamboura. The piece is in twelve sections which flow into one another without interruption. The final section, ten minutes in length, is based on the classical Hindu raga, Marva.

Landscapes of the Mind I was premiered on March 19, 1976, with William Masselos as piano soloist and the Tucson Symphony Orchestra conducted by Gregory Miller. It was an immense success with both critics and the audience. Lawrence W. Cheek of the Tucson Citizen called the first section "an undeniable triumph," and wrote on March 20, 1975*:

> The title really suggests the essence of the work ... It seems like a succession of craggy, smoldering mental images parading malignantly past like figures on a Hellenic frieze.

---

*Reprinted by permission of the author.

> Landscapes had a fairly decent reception last night at Music Hall. Miss Richter, in town for the premiere was called up to the stage and warmly applauded.

Ken La Fave, writing in the March 20, 1976, issue of the Arizona Daily Star, said*:

> Happily, last night's audience seemed aware of the fact that Landscapes is a work of vital musical ideas.... They might not have put it that way, and many audience members were openly puzzled about their reactions, but the sense of something important going on was in general attendance.
>
> Ms. Richter is a patient composer. Her ideas happen naturally, and she is content to develop them in a way that does not hurry or deform their organic growth. Landscapes I is in two parts, forcing rhythmic invention which Masselos and a feverish Tucson Symphony Orchestra brought off with flair.
>
> The second section was conceived as a raga, but in the western context it comes off more like a prolonged recitative over a pedal "C." Richter does about everything possible within that limited framework--the final measures are especially powerful--but the constant drone of the "C" comes dangerously close to maddening at times.
>
> Her massive pile-ups of sound are experienced not so much as static dissonances, but as layers of sound, each layer being self-contained consonant.
>
> It is hoped that Landscapes will enjoy repeated performances--it deserves them.

The years devoted to Landscapes I and Landscapes II were the basis of a ten-year continuity of musical thought where she produced six major works on the same or related thematic material. Other works in this group include Blackberry Vines and Winter Fruit (1976), for orchestra; Requiem (1978), for solo piano; Landscapes of the Mind III (1979), for piano trio; and Music for Three Quintets and Orchestra (1979).

Marga Richter's career developed rapidly beginning in 1975. Her children were grown and she was able to devote

*Reprinted by permission of the author.

more time to composing and bringing her music to the attention of musicians. The music world was tiring of the fashions which had dominated the scene for the previous decade and a half and which Richter had firmly resisted in her work. Of course, the women's movement helped the careers of women in traditionally male-occupied positions. The musical profession at large was finally beginning to take women composers seriously and Marga Richter played a part in this development. She was instrumental in founding the League of Women Composers and was a member of the first Board of Directors. In this capacity she organized a number of concerts of music by women, and also represented the League at the annual conventions of the American Symphony Orchestra League. She was also a member of the American Women Composers Incorporation.

Recognition came rapidly; until then only six of her compositions had been published. In March 1975 she was signed to an exclusive publishing contract by the prestigious firm of Carl Fischer, Inc. They agreed to place all of her previously unpublished works in their catalog and to publish all of her new compositions for the next five years.

Grants were to be numerous. The premiere of Landscapes I was made possible by a copying grant from the Martha Baird Rockefeller Foundation; a performance grant allowed the Tucson Symphony the extra rehearsals needed in presenting such a difficult new work; and a grant from the National Endowment for the Arts was awarded. Richter also received a composer grant from the National Endowment to compose Music for Three Quintets and Orchestra. She received a dozen grants from the New York State Council on the Arts through its Meet the Composer program. In 1978 the National Federation of Music Clubs gave her a commission to write Landscapes of the Mind III, to be premiered at their fortieth Biennial Convention.

The music of the talented and gifted Richter was now being performed regularly by outstanding soloists and orchestras and this development was most important to Richter. The Museum of Modern Art in New York presented two concerts entirely of her music in 1975 in addition to performances of her piano music by herself and her son Michael Skelly. The distinguished Karen Phillips, violist, and harpsichordist Leonard Raver also performed her music. Jessye Norman, one of the great singers of our time, discovered Richter's music at this time and has included her songs on recital programs and a broadcast by the British Broadcasting Company, London.

Raver gave the world premiere of her Variations on a Theme by Neithart von Reuenthal for organ, and the well-known critic-at-large Byron Belt wrote the following as it appeared in the Long Island Press on July 12, 1976*:

> Marga Richter was represented by a most attractive world premiere of her Variations on a Theme by Neithart von Reuenthal; identified by Raver as a celebrated Minnesinger of the Middle Ages. As Miss Richter's Variations moved further from the theme itself, the work grew into rich development of sounds that made splendid use of the organ's tonal potentials.

Marga Richter wrote Landscapes of the Mind II for the internationally known violinist Daniel Heifetz. He performed this piece frequently on his tours in the United States and Russia following his New York premiere at Alice Tully Hall in Lincoln Center. Allen Hughes, writing for the New York Times on May 1, 1977, said**:

> Miss Richter's piece, which was given its first New York performance, is written in such a way that it responded to Mr. Heifetz' way of playing, and it made a favorable impression on this listener.... The contrasts of energy and mood are handled adroitly and hold the interest for the twelve minutes or so that the piece lasts.

It is interesting to note a growing enthusiasm of a new generation of musicians for Richter's work. She composed Sonata for Piano in 1954 and it was recorded a year later to critical acclaim. However, it was rarely heard in live performance for the next fifteen years but in 1976-77 three different pianists included it in their programs in New York alone and award-winning pianist Peter Basquin also recorded the sonata on Grenadilla Records number GS1010. Since the Sonata for Piano is available on two recordings, a brief

---

*Reprinted by permission of the author.

**©1977 by The New York Times Company. Reprinted by permission.

analysis of the piece is offered on the album notes by Alan Gregory*:

> The Sonata for Piano is in three movements. The first movement begins with a slow introduction which contains all the material of the movement in germinal form. A somber, percussive development of the opening phrase follows which gradually builds in intensity until it bursts forth into a brilliant, toccata-like section which rises to higher and higher registers and leads to a restatement of the first phrase of the theme with full chordal accompaniment. A quiet, meditative development of the second theme follows. Interruptions by the earlier percussive material gradually become more and more insistent and lead to a complex development of all the elements of the opening statement. Ultimately there is a climactic statement of the full theme in canonic form, followed by a final quiet resolution of all the tensions of the movement.
>
> The second movement is based on a highly chromatic, lyric melody, accompanied initially by an arpeggio figure consisting simply of successive intervals of the minor ninth. The melody is developed against repeated notes and then, repeated chords and tremolos in ninths. It rises gradually to a brilliant climax which encompasses the entire range of the keyboard and subsides to a moving reminiscence of the beginning of the movement.
>
> The finale begins with a surging figure that suggests the percussive passages of the first movement. Now, however, the rhythms are simplified to their essentials and the driving pace is maintained throughout. A final dazzling passage in octaves leads to a last exposure of the opening phrase of the Sonata just before the closing cadence.

Probably the most significant evidence of the dramatic upturn in Richter's career in recent years has been her performances by leading American orchestras. On January 11 and 13, 1976, the ice was finally broken, she performed her first piano concerto with the Oklahoma Symphony conducted by Ainslee Cox.

---

*Reprinted by permission of the author.

Nancy Gilson, music critic for the Oklahoma Journal, wrote on January 12, 1976*:

> Marga Richter, one of the foremost women composers in the United States and co-founder/director of the League of Women Composers presented her Concerto for Piano and Violas, Cellos and Basses. Richter offered precision and grace to the unique and related movements of this intellectual yet mystery-filled piece. At the precise moment the Concerto appears to be a cool and almost technical work, the mood abruptly alters to intense drama and measured emotion.

Marga Richter's music is now performed extensively; for example, Joel Salsman performed the same concerto with the Northwest Chamber Orchestra in Seattle; the world premiere of the concert version of Abyss was performed by the Madison Symphony, conducted by Roland Johnson; Landscapes of the Mind I was presented in Tucson; three performances of Lament were given, with Stanislaw Skrowaczewski conducting the Minnesota Orchestra, followed by performances by the National Gallery Orchestra in Washington, D.C., the Maracaibo Symphony in Venezuela, and the Eastern Music Festival Philharmonic in Greensboro, North Carolina.

In March 1977 Kenneth Schermerhorn conducted two performances of Blackberry Vines and Winter Fruit with the Milwaukee Symphony. This work, an evocation of New England winter landscapes, took its title from Thoreau and was originally commissioned by the Sage City Symphony, a nonprofessional orchestra in Bennington, Vermont, where it was premiered in October 1976 and then performed twice by the Oakland Symphony.

The following is a portion of the review written by Lawrence B. Johnson for High Fidelity/Musical America, in September of 1977**:

> It sprouts simply, with an ostinato runner that issues from two flutes and piccolo and progressively intertwines itself into dense foliage teeming with

---

*Reprinted by permission of the author.

**Reprinted by permission of the publisher.

> instrumental color and rhythmic life. From the engrossing complexity and dramatic pitch of this middle section, in which the ostinato figure takes on many new appearances, all tension is suddenly thrown off and the music begins a long fall through reiterated patterns in the strings. In a formal process akin to chaconne, the strings continuous weaving becomes the backdrop for an imaginative play of brasses and woodwinds--now bold and dominant, now mere innuendoes--until the work melts away.

In three short years Marga Richter's career has moved to a level of recognition that few composers her age, male or female, could match.

Like many other creative women Richter has given much thought to the question of the differences, if any, between the work of male and female artists. In a recent talk she addresses herself to the issue:

> It is fashionable, today, to say that there is none. But in private, the men mostly seem to feel that women's music is weaker, just as they feel we are weaker. For a long time I half believed that myself. Many of the early reviews of my music said things like--it would seem impossible that this pungent and virile composition could be the creation of a woman, or women composers are rare birds, to be sure, but one with as dissonant and biting a style as Marga Richter's is decidedly a shock--I took these as compliments.
>
> Today I feel quite differently. Not long ago, Karel Husa, a Pulitzer Prize winning composer, wrote to me after hearing several of my works covering a fifteen year span and said: 'All of your works have the same qualities: gentleness, deep feeling, long phrasing, contrapuntally clear lines, all very sensitive qualities we do not hear too often, perhaps because they are feminine. I say this as a compliment, as I know these qualities from my home, having four daughters. By this I do not mean that force is not present. One hears it in the Lament as well as the piano-violin work.'*

*Used here courtesy of Karel Husa.

> I take Mr. Husa's statement as a very real compliment, for I think he may have hit upon something. When we have enough music by women to make a study of the question, we may find that women are able to express emotion in a different way. I also feel it may turn out that we construct music differently, when we are being ourselves and not following male models--not worse or better, just differently.
>
> To put it simply, I now say, I don't think men can write music like women--nor vice versa. After all, I am a woman, I express what I am. Therefore it will be different from what a man will express--or any other woman.

Marga Richter has always found it difficult to describe exactly what it is her music expresses. Recently she made an attempt and these are her words:

> There was never a time when I did not think of myself as a musician--first as a pianist then as a composer and music was always a means of expression for me. I am not a verbal person.
>
> In recent years I have come to realize that this must be the reason I never followed any prescribed theory or system or style of composition. Melodic contour, rather than any formula for tonality or serialization, is the fundamental element in my music. The continuous line from the beginning to the end of each piece is what governs the form.
>
> Each new piece is a new experience for me. Most of the thematic relationships occur subconsciously, spontaneously as I play through the piece and allow, coerce, new material to develop. This can be a painfully slow process but when I try to develop new sections by consciously manipulating themes and chords and rhythms, I invariably destroy the work. I have to throw out these constructions and go back to my own system--allowing the music to come from its own mysterious source.
>
> Composing is my response to a constant desire to transform my perceptions and emotions into music. Everything that touches me, everything I become aware of as beautiful or mysterious, or painful, or joyful, or unknowable becomes an immediate or eventual source of inspiration.
>
> A painting, a photograph, a landscape, a skyscape,

a poem, other music, other people--my feelings about all of these things filter through my consciousness and take shape as musical ideas and impulses, which must then be expressed.

Music is the way I speak to the silence of the universe.

Compositions

Marga Richter's compositions are published by Broude Brothers, Belwin-Mills Publishers, Carl Fischer, Carl Fischer Facsimile Edition, and Elkan-Vogel Publishers.

1948 Sonata for Clarinet and Piano
1949 Transmutation, song cycle and piano
1953 Two Chinese Songs, vocal music and piano
1954 Sonata for Piano
1954 She at His Funeral, solo voice and piano
1955 Concerto, for piano, violas, cellos and basses
1955 Three Songs of Madness and Death, vocal
1956 Lament, for stringed orchestra
1957 Aria and Toccata for Viola and Strings, also viola and piano arrangement
1957 Aria and Toccata, solo for viola
1958 String Quartet No. 2
1958 Melodrama, two pianos
1958 Ricercare, brass quartet
1959 Variations on a Sarabande, orchestra
1961 Eight Pieces for Orchestra
1961 Darkening of the Light, solo cello
1963 Psalm 91, mixed chorus
1963 Fragments, solo piano
1964 ABYSS, for orchestra
1964 Variations on a Theme by Latimer, piano four-hands
1964 Suite for Violin and Piano
1964 Three Christmas Songs, soprano, alto, two flutes, piano
1965 Soundings, harpsichord
1965 Seek Him, mixed chorus acappella
1967 Bird of Yearning, orchestra, twenty-seven minutes complete, fifteen-minutes concert version. Also scored for reduced orchestra
1971 Landscapes of the Mind II, violin and piano
1971 Remembrances, solo-piano
1974 One for Two and Two for Three, trombone duet and trio
1974 Landscapes of the Mind I, piano concerto

1974 Short Prelude in Baroque Style, solo piano
1974 Variations on a Theme by Neithart von Reuenthal, organ
1975 Pastorale, for two oboes
1976 Blackberry Vines and Winter Fruit, orchestra
1976 Fragments, orchestra
1976 Bird of Yearning, solo piano
1978 Music for Three Quintets and Orchestra, Wind Quintet: Flute, Oboe, Clarinet, Horn, Bassoon. String Quintet: two violins, viola, cello, bass. Brass Quintet: two trumpets, horn, trombone, bass
1978 Requiem, solo piano
1979 Landscapes of the Mind III, piano, cello, violin
1979 Trio, piano, violin, cello

Recording

Sonata for Piano, Peter Basquin, pianist, Grenadilla Records Number GS1010.

LOUISE TALMA

Composer, Performer, Professor

Dean of American Women Composers, Louise Talma, was the first woman to win the Sibelius Award in composition; the first woman to have been twice awarded a Guggenheim Fellowship in composition; the first American woman to have a major work staged in a major opera house in Europe; the first woman to be elected to the Music Department of the National Institute of Arts and Letters, and the only American to teach at Fontainebleau summers, from 1936 to 1939 and in 1978. Louise Talma has had an extraordinarily rich life in music. She is an excellent composer, an inspiring teacher, and a charming intelligent person.

Born in 1906, Louise Talma was reared by a single parent following the death of her father when she was an infant. Her mother was an operatic singer who gave music lessons to financially survive. There was little money for the young Louise, but her mother managed to provide numerous opportunities for her daughter to attend concerts by ghost writing reviews for a friend who was a critic for a newspaper. They attended many concerts each week receiving free tickets from the critic for writing the review.

Louise Talma's first piano lesson was given by her mother when she was five years old. As a teenager, she was fascinated with chemistry and took a course at Columbia University. She would have majored in this field had her mother not been ill, but she wisely realized that she would have to support herself, and music was the only field she knew.

Talma studied at the Institute of Musical Art in New York (1922-1930) where she studied composition with Howard Brockway and theory with George Wedge and Helen Whily, counterpoint and fugue with Percy Goetschius. She also studied at Columbia University (1923-1933) and at New York University (1930-1931). She was at the Fontainebleau School of Music for seventeen summers where she studied composition, harmony, fugue, counterpoint, and organ with Nadia Boulanger, and piano with Isidore Philipp. Her studies were demanding, and Talma spent many years developing her talent and expanding her musical horizons. Dedication to the study of musical expression and awareness prepared her to create phenomenal compositions, rich in design and orchestration.

When Louise Talma went to Fontainebleau, it was to study piano with Isidore Philipp. The first two summers, she pursued the study of the keyboard with determined dedication to what was then her first love, perfection of her piano technique. During those two summers, her curiosity was challenged by comments in conversation with fellow students studying with Nadia Boulanger, who claimed that she was missing the best part of school. She felt that since she had already studied theory, harmony, counterpoint, and composition there was certainly no need to repeat the same studies. That was until she met the astounding Nadia Boulanger, who reviewed a composition the young Talma had written for piano and strings. That meeting with Miss Boulanger was to be the spark that would change the direction of Louise Talma's career, for the world renowned Nadia Boulanger discovered the creative possibilities inherent in the young Talma.

Louise Talma was absolutely amazed at the ability of Nadia Boulanger. She says of this master teacher: "She read my score, immediately identified it as the Scriabin School, then played the first page without ever turning back the pages and offered critical suggestions--she had a fabulous memory. She told me that I should develop my talent, but it would be a period of study because my training must be solid and complete."

So, Louise Talma began the study of theory, harmony, counterpoint and fugue over again with Boulanger. The lessons were both group and individual, and for several summers Miss Talma studied both composition and piano before finally deciding to pursue only composition, (although of course she continued to practice and perform piano repertoire).

Nadia Boulanger never imposed any style on her students; however, Louise Talma and other students were aware of Boulanger's enormous enthusiasm for Igor Stravinsky's music. Many of his scores were discussed and studied in depth

LOUISE TALMA
(Photo by Vincent Gonzales)

long before they were even published. This did indeed influence the young Talma.

Louise Talma vividly described her meeting with the musical genius Stravinsky. Miss Boulanger requested that Talma escort him to classes. "I immediately began to plan my conversation, for it would take a least ten minutes to walk from the hotel, across the court yard, to the classroom. Mr. Stravinsky was known to be a very stern man, and when I told him that I hoped he would talk about the Firebird Suite for the class, he smiled, turned to me, and said that it would take at least two weeks for him to review his own work."

Professor Talma taught theory and ear training at the Manhattan School of Music (1926-1928) and joined the faculty of Hunter College in 1928 where she taught various musical subjects during her tenure and was promoted to full professor in 1952.

When Louise Talma applied for her first Guggenheim Fellowship, it was at the insistence of her beloved teacher Nadia Boulanger. She had never applied for a foundation grant, and at that time she had no published music. She did, however, have excellent recommendations, including Boulanger's, on which to base her request. The date for announcements of recipients passed and many of her contemporaries received negative responses, but Talma heard nothing. Finally, days and days later, she received a registered letter at seven o'clock in the morning. "I was ecstatic, I had a Guggenheim, and when you live alone, who do you talk to at seven a.m.? I just needed to talk, so finally I called my doctor friend and said 'I got it, I got it!' Of course, she didn't know what I was talking about, so you can imagine what her reaction was. That was a most exciting time in my career."

Louise Talma composed Toccata for Orchestra and dedicated it to Reginald Stewart, conductor of the Baltimore Symphony Orchestra. It was premiered under Stewart's baton in 1945, and in 1946 Talma was awarded the Juilliard Publication Award for this composition.

The Toccata opens with an immensely exciting trumpet fanfare eventually supported by strings and woodwinds. It is a rich, beautiful work, with a statement of the theme played by violins and violas accompanied by a scrambling figure in the lower strings. The structure of the rhythm of the theme dominates a somewhat Latin-Jazz syntax, based on dotted quarter note, dotted quarter note, quarter note. The exciting structural strength leads into a new section that exploits different rhythms and begins pianissimo, but remains spirited. A delightful chattering between strings and woodwinds evolves halfway through the composition that stimulates the hearing of the audience and is followed by the marvelous addition of brass and percussion instruments that continue almost uninterrupted until the end. (The composition has been recorded by the Imperial Philharmonic Orchestra of Tokyo, conducted by William Strickland, on the Composer's Recording, Inc., 170 West 74th Street, New York, N.Y. recording number CRS-SRD 145.)

Alleluia in Form of Toccata for Piano was written in 1945 by Talma and is published by Carl Fischer. There are two recordings of this composition, the first recorded by the pianist Sahan Arzruni for Musical Heritage Society (number 1843), and the second record by Nancy Fierro for Avant Records (AV number 1012).

Illinois Wesleyan University Collegiate Choir commissioned Louise Talma in 1954-55 and she composed La Corona based on Holy Sonnets by John Donne, for a cappella mixed chorus. According to Miss Talma, "The seven Corona sonnets of John Donne were first brought to my attention by Donald Aird, at that time conductor of the Berkeley Chamber Singers. I was immediately drawn to them by reason of the circular form in which the last line of each sonnet is used as the first line of the next one, and the last line of the last sonnet is the first line of the first sonnet. This presented highly interesting possibilities for musical variations." The work was composed over a period of two summers, mostly at the MacDowell Colony. Miss Talma dedicated the work to Donald Aird and Lloyd Pfautsch. In 1960 the Marjorie Peabody Waite Award from the National Institute of the Arts and Letters included funds for a recording of La Corona by the Dorian Chorale recorded by Composers Recordings (number 187).

Miss Talma's most discussed work has been her opera The Alcestiad, adapted from Thornton Wilder's play Life in the Sun. Mr. Wilder wrote the libretto by reshaping the work and asked Louise Talma to compose the music. "You must find music for Apollo and tender music for the mad Tiresias." The Alcestiad received its world premiere on March 1, 1962, at Frankfurt-am-Main, and Talma was the first American woman to have a major work staged in a major opera house in Europe.

Mr. Wilder and Miss Talma met at the famous MacDowell Colony in New Hampshire in the early nineteen-fifties. When Thornton Wilder first approached Louise Talma to collaborate with him for an opera, she was flabbergasted because she had always been in awe of his greatness as a man and a writer. Wilder heard a short piano composition Alleluia that Miss Talma had composed and decided she must compose the music for him. At first she declined, and he asked her, "If you ever change your mind, let me know." A year later she heard from him, and they met for a drink at the Algonquin Hotel. There she said "Okay, if you are willing to take a chance on me, let's go ahead."

This meeting was just the beginning, and they corresponded over the project the next year. The following three years, she and Wilder met four times a year in various places throughout the world, she would play the music she had composed, and they would discuss the opera. He never criticized or made suggestions about the music. He would say, "Fine, fine Louise, that's just the way I like it." It took Louise Talma almost five years to compose and score the opera, based on the legend of Alcestis, an ancient Greek woman whose devotion to the god Apollo wins her redemption from Hades by Hercules. She received a Senior Fulbright Research Grant in 1955-1956 and spent ten months in Rome working on the opera.

Both Talma and Wilder were present at the world premiere and received a twenty-minute ovation and took several bows. The audience shouted, "Louise! Louise! And she was the heroine of the evening, responding graciously from the stage, wearing a long, black sequined gown, spectacles, a spray of white orchids and an enormous, radiant smile. The day after the premiere the critic of the Hanover Anzeiger wrote:

> Louise Talma ... is everywhere at home, in tonal as well as atonal practice. She makes use of twelve-tone rows, and she shows herself at times inspired by the late impressionism of Stravinsky, also of Bartók. Clearly visible are her abhorrence of every melodic banality and the refinement of her orchestration.

Professor Talma received the Marjorie Peabody Waite Award from the National Institute of Arts and Letters with the citation "To Louise Talma whose personal, highly controlled and beautifully-shaped music has gained a new cogency and dramatic effectiveness in the opera she made of Thornton Wilder's The Alcestiad."

Composing is essentially an intellectual craft that develops on the subconscious level and through a period of time until conditions are ideal for the manifestation of the conscious mind to deal with the process. Louise Talma's extensive and impressive education provided her with all the tools necessary to produce artistic musical compositions that have freshness and a quality that exhibits imaginative conceptions. Compositions result from manipulation of learned sound materials according to native talent, personal resources, and intense labor.

In 1962, in honor of Boulanger's seventy-fifth birthday, Talma wrote Sonata for Violin and Piano. The premiere was performed in April of 1963 at Judson Hall by David Sackson, violin, and by the composer at the piano. Michall Brozen wrote the following comment in the June issue 1963 of High Fidelity/Musical America*:

> The Sonata is in a sparse and dissonant style that is yet attractive, perhaps because the harmonies are more resonant than contemporary composers often allow themselves. Details are well thought out, and the entire work seems to unfold from the opening measures. Mr. Sackson and Miss Talma gave it a fine reading.

Professor Talma is a corporate member of the Edward MacDowell Association which annually raises monies for commissions and scholarships to help defray the expenses of young aspiring creative artists who live in residence at the MacDowell Colony where they can work under ideal conditions, including comfort and quiet atmosphere. Louise Talma has been associated with the famous MacDowell Colony for over thirty years. As early as 1943, she wrote her first piano sonata there.

Twenty-eight years later her symphonic work com-

---

*Reprinted by permission of the publisher. All rights reserved.

missioned by the MacDowell Club of Milwaukee The Tolling Bell for baritone and orchestra had its world premiere by the Milwaukee Symphony Orchestra with Kenneth Schermerhorn conducting and William Metcalf as the baritone soloist. This composition was nominated for the Pulitzer Prize. On January 29, 1979, the American Composers Orchestra, Lukas Foss Conductor, John Reardon soloist, performed The Tolling Bell at Alice Tully Hall, Lincoln Center for the Performing Arts. Louise Talma described her composition as follows:

> The first and third parts are meditative in character; the second is dramatic. The texts, on the nature of existence, are taken from Shakespeare, Marlowe, and Donne. The title is derived from the famous lines of John Donne which come at the close of the work: "No man is an island entire of itself.... Ask not for whom the bell tolls, it tolls for thee."

As I listened that evening to the Tolling Bell (subtitled Triptych for baritone and orchestra), I heard the thunderous applause, and watched the response of the talented Louise Talma, I could not help but feel a deep and sincere sense of destiny. Louise Talma's need to financially support herself as a teenager gave the world of music an opportunity to share her creative abilities--she is a musical genius. (Had she the necessary money, she would have studied chemistry). Following the performance, Miss Talma was surrounded by a large group of admirers including many of her present students at Hunter College. She holds the title of distinguished professor which, simply stated, means she is past the mandatory retirement age and receives no money for teaching!

In 1968, Louise Talma composed Three Duologues for clarinet and piano. The piece was premiered at Town Hall by twenty-three-year-old clarinetist Michael Webster accompanied by his father Beveridge Webster on the piano. Mr. Webster, Sr., is well known and respected in music circles, and his son proved to be a fine and sensitive musician who performed with perfection and confidence the composition that Talma had dedicated to him. The opening movement was written in serial style that developed short episodes within larger sections, and the middle movement was a haunting and brooding piece of night music that was immediately recognized as the highlight of the program.

Louise Talma's ability to meld words and sounds into

imaginative and creative listening experiences has long been held in esteem. One of her finest examples of choral-orchestra compositions was built on the words and quotations of the late President John F. Kennedy. There are many memorials to President Kennedy, and Talma's composition will always remain in a respected position among the many tributes because of the expression of deep personal qualities and beautiful tonal combinations.

Allen Hughes wrote the following review for the New York Times on May 13, 1968*:

> The work entitled A Time to Remember was composed by Louise Talma, a member of the Hunter College music faculty. It is about twenty minutes long, is scored for three spatially separated choirs and chamber orchestra. Its five sections--First Day, A Time for Every Purpose, The Way of Peace, Last Day, and Invocation proceeded without pause. The work has a ceremonial quality and is both tasteful and dignified. The music, essentially uncomplicated, is easy to listen to. It comes to a climax in the Last Day over the relentless drum beat. The emotional import of the composition will enhance its appeal to large choral groups.

Talma's virtuosity as a respected and nationally recognized composer was reflected in a concert of her music on February 4, 1974, at The Museum of the Philadelphia Civic Center by the Pennsylvania Chamber Chorus and the Amado String Quarter with Louis Salemno conducting. Voices of Peace for mixed chorus and strings was premiered, and the intoxicatingly beautiful combinations were enthusiastically received by the audience. The remainder of the program included String Quartet, Piano Sonata No. 2 played by Herbert Rogers and the Violin and Piano Sonata performed by Daniel Stepnor and Professor Talma. It is always a treat to hear the composer participate in public performances, and the audience was not to be denied; Stepner and Talma offered a welcomed and fascinating performance.

Professor Louise Talma's distinguished teaching career spanned a period of fifty years, almost all of them as a faculty member at Hunter College in New York City. Some professors are great teachers of theory and technique, but do not have the talent to create compositions of lasting value. Some composers are talented in the creative field, but are unable to impart their knowledge in the classroom. Louise Talma was a master of both as reflected by her compositions and hundreds of students who were directly influenced by her teaching of piano-playing, sight-reading, theory, harmony, counterpoint, fugue and analysis.

That she was demanding of her students and insisted on the highest standards are virtues that are not hers alone, but are part of the teaching profession. What she does possess is the unique ability to activate the creative thinking process of the students who in turn demand of themselves critical intensity of study.

Professor Talma's humanistic qualities have strongly influenced her teaching. She understands and relates not only to society's needs and resources, but encourages growth and obliterating of ignorance. Louise Talma has a deep compassion for people and always made time in her busy schedule to offer extra help and guidance for the student in need.

One of the finest tributes to Louise Talma's long and distinguished career was the concert conducted by Lukas Foss at Hunter College on March 5, 1977. Again, an entire program was devoted to the music of Louise Talma--a rare evening of pure musical delight not often afforded an audience. The music was sensitive, solid, lyrical and beautifully designed. The concert included Sonata No. 2 for piano, Summer Sounds a chamber work, Terre de France song cycle for soprano and piano, All the Days of My Life and Voices of Peace, both cantatas. Professor Talma's social messages contained in her vocal music are thought-provoking and an excellent means of communicating humanism. Miss Talma and Lukas Foss joined in an encore, Four Hand Fun, that provided the audience with a lighthearted and amusing end to a long-to-be-remembered evening.

Louise Talma has received many awards, grants, and commissions that have provided her an opportunity to compose music to share with people. She has been most appreciative of the opportunities provided her by foundations. Professor Talma said, "You can't describe a painting, you have to see it; and words do not convey a piece of music, you must hear it."

In March of 1976, Miss Talma was guest of the Yale Music School's Samuel Simon Sanford Fellowship Program following in the path of such notable men as Eugene Ormandy, William Steinberg and others. Her program included a lecture-discussion, excerpts from Talma-Wilder opera The Alcestiad, Sonata for violin and piano, Piano Sonata No. 2, and four of the Six Etudes for piano. Miss Talma received the prestigious commemorative medallion which accompanies the invitation.

Miss Talma is concerned because many composers receive commissions to write music, but it is very difficult to receive commissions to record music. It is especially difficult to receive funds to record a large orchestral composition or a full opera. She speaks of a crying need in America to preserve the music that is part of our culture. When wars and politics are long forgotten, the arts will live on if they are preserved.

Dean of American women composers and a recognized American contemporary composer, Louise Talma has prodigiously pursued a dual career of teaching and composing. She has willingly given of her time, energy and talents, as well as developing a legacy for the American History of Music. Her compositional thinking embraces many changes and yet it remains subtle to the listening audience. Miss Talma's music is well worth hearing. She is a master.

The following is a partial list of awards and honors given to Louise Talma in recognition of her outstanding accomplishments:

Isaac Newton Seligman Prize for Composition, Institute of Musical Art, 1927, 1928, 1929.
Pleyel Prize for Piano, Fontainebleau School of Music, 1927.
Presser Prize for Piano, Fontainebleau School of Music, 1928.
National Federation of Music Clubs, winner of the Eastern inter-state Piano contest, 1927.
Joseph H. Bearns Prize for Composition, Columbus University, 1932. ($1200)
Society for the Advancement of Women in the Liberal Professions, Paris, Prize for Composition, 1937.
Stovall Prize for Composition, Fontainebleau School of Music, 1938, 1939.
Juilliard Publication Award for Toccata for Orchestra, 1946.
Two Guggenheim Fellowships, 1946, 1947.
North American Prize of $1000 for Piano Sonata No. 1, 1947.

French Government "Prix d'Excellence de Composition," 1951.
Elected to Phi Beta Kappa, Nu Chapter, Hunter College, 1953.
Senior Fulbright Research Grant, ten months in Rome, to compose The Alcestiad, 1955-56.
Koussevitzky Music Foundation Commission for a work of chamber music, 1959.
Marjorie Peabody Waite Award from the National Institute of Arts and Letters, 1960.
National Federation of Music Clubs, Award "for advancing national and world culture through distinguished service to Music," 1963.
National Association for American Composers and Conductors, Award "for outstanding service to American Music," 1963.
Sibelius Medal for Composition from the Harriet Cohen International Awards, London, 1963.
$7500 sabbatical leave grant, awarded May 20, 1966, by the National Endowment for the Arts of the National Foundation on the Arts and the Humanities, Washington, D.C.
First woman composer elected to the National Institute of Arts and Letters, Jan., 1974.
$3750 Fellowship Grant from the National Endowment for the Arts, Feb., 1975.
Clark Lecturer, Scripps College, Claremont, California, March, 1975.
Certificate of Merit, Sigma Alpha Iota, August, 1975.
Samuel Simons Sanford Fellow, Yale University, March, 1976.
Made a member of the President's Circle, Hunter College, February, 1977.

She is a corporate member of the Edward MacDowell Association, a member of the American Society of Composers, Authors and Publishers, a member of the Board of Trustees of the Fontainebleau Fine Arts and Music Association, she was a member of the Board of Directors of the League of Composers, International Society for Contemporary Music, and a charter member of the American Society of University Composers.

The citation read at her induction into the National Institute of Arts and Letters, May 22, 1974, as the first woman composer ever to be elected to this society:

> LOUISE TALMA, composer, born in France in 1906. Louise Talma's music is distinguished by a strongly contrapuntal style. Her works are in a variety of forms, including opera. Many of her admirers, who had grown accustomed to seeing or hearing her

referred to as one of our foremost women composers, have noticed with pleasure in recent years that she is being referred to more and more often without any qualification at all as one of our foremost composers.

Recordings

Toccata for Orchestra, Imperial Orchestra of Tokyo, William Strickland conductor, Number CRI-SRD 145.

La Corona (seven sonnets by John Donne), scored for a cappella mixed chorus and commissioned by Illinois Wesleyan University Collegiate Choir, Number CRS 187.

Three Duologues, for clarinet and piano performed by Michael Webster, Clarinetist, Beveridge Webster, pianist, Number CRS-SD 374.

Let's Touch the Sky, published by Westminster Choral Series (three poems by e. e. cummings), scored for mixed chorus, flute, oboe, performed by the Gregg Smith Singers, VOX Company, SVBX Number 5353.

Alleluia in Form of a Toccata for Piano, performed by Nancy Fierro, pianist, Avant Record Company, Number 1012.

Alleluia in Form of a Toccata for Piano, performed by Sahan Arzruni, Musical Heritage Society, Number 1843.

Six Etudes for Piano, performed by Beveridge Webster, Desto Label Number 7117.

America Sings, recorded in the Gregg Smith Collection, put out by VOX (SVBX 5353).

Recordings of Louise Talma's music are available at these addresses:

Composers Recording, Inc., 170 West 74th Street, New York, N. Y.

VOX Records, c/o Turnabout, c/o Moss Music Group, 211 East Forty-Third Street, New York, N. Y. 10017.

Avant Records, c/o Crystal Records, P. O. Box 65661, Los Angeles, Cal. 90065.

Musical Heritage Society, 14 Park Road, Tinton Falls, N. J. 07724.

Desto Records, c/o CMS, 14 Warren Street, New York, N. Y. 10007.

Compositions

Following is a partial list of Louise Talma's compositions; principal publishers are Carl Fischer, Hinshaw Publishers, C. F. Peters, G. Schirmer, and Edition Musicus.

1939	In Principio Erat Verbum (St. John), mixed chorus and organ
1939	Four-handed Fun, piano four hands (two piano version published by Carl Fischer, 1949)
1941	One need not be a Chamber to be Haunted (Emily Dickinson), soprano and piano
1943	Carmina Mariana (Ave Maria, Regina Caeli, Salve Regina), two soprano voices and piano
1943	Piano Sonata No. 1
1943-45	Terre de France, song cycle, soprano and piano
1944	Toccata for Orchestra
1945	Alleluia in Form of Toccata for Piano
1945	Leap before you Look (W. H. Auden), Letter to St. Peter (Elma Dean), two songs for soprano and piano
1946	Wedding Piece. Where Thou Goest I Go, Canon for Organ
1946	Pied Beauty, Spring and Fall (Gerard Manley Hopkins), two songs for soprano and piano
1946-48	The Divine Flame, Oratorio (The Bible and Missal) for mixed chorus and orchestra, mezzo-soprano and baritone
1946-50	Two Sonnets (Gerard Manley Hopkins), baritone and piano
1949	Pastoral Prelude, for piano
1950-51	The Leaden Echo and the Golden Echo (Gerard Manley Hopkins), mixed double chorus, soprano solo and piano
1951	Song and Dance, violin and piano
1952	Let's Touch the Sky (three poems by e. e. cummings), mixed chorus, flute, oboe, clarinet, No. 3, W. W. Norton Anthology of Choral Music
1953-54	Six Etudes for Piano
1954	String Quartet
1954-55	La Corona (Seven Sonnets by John Donne), a cappella mixed chorus
1954-55	Piano Sonata No. 2
1955	Three Bagatelles for Piano
1955-58	The Alcestiad, opera in three acts, text by Thornton Wilder
1955-62	Passacaglia and Fugue for Piano
1960	Birthday Song (Edmund Spenser), tenor, flute, viola
1962	Sonata for Violin and Piano
1963-65	All the Days of My Life (Bible), Cantata for tenor, clarinet, violoncello, piano, percussion
1963-64	Dialogues for Piano and Orchestra
1966-67	A Time to Remember (text from speeches by John F. Kennedy and Biblical and literary quotations

used therein. Prologue and Epilogue from "A Thousand Days" by Arthur M. Schlesinger, Jr.), mixed choirs and orchestra

1967-68 Three Duologues for Clarinet and Piano

1967-69 The Tolling Bell (Shakespeare, Marlowe, Donne), Triptych for baritone and orchestra

1969-73 Summer Sounds, Quintet for clarinet, 2 violins, viola, violoncello (Carl Fischer 1975)

1973 Voices of Peace (the Missal, the Bible, St. Francis of Assisi, Gerard Manley Hopkins), mixed chorus and strings

1973 Rain Song, soprano and piano

1944-74 Soundshots, 20 short pieces for piano

1974-76 Have You Heard? Do You Know? Divertimento in seven scenes, text by Louise Talma, for soprano, mezzo-soprano, tenor and instrumental ensemble

1976-77 Celebration (excerpts from the Psalms, Desiderata, Salutation of the Dawn, the Metta Sutra, Horace-Dryden Book III Code 29) Women's Chorus and small orchestra

1977- Textures for Piano, commissioned by the International Society for Contemporary Music for Beveridge Webster's seventieth birthday

1978 Psalm 84, a cappella mixed chorus. Commissioned by the Corpus Christi Church of New York

1978-79 Diadem (texts taken from Confucius and Medieval Lapidaries). Tenor, flute, clarinet, violin, violoncello and piano. Commissioned by the Da Capo Chamber Players

ROSALYN TURECK

Concert Artist, Conductor, Master Teacher, Author

Dr. Rosalyn Tureck is the recipient of four honorary doctorate degrees, plus the prestigious Miriam Sacher Visiting Fellowship to Oxford University in England. She was the first woman invited to conduct the New York Philharmonic Orchestra in a subscription concert in 1958 and has conducted major orchestras on four continents as well as appearing as soloist. She founded the International Bach Society in 1966 and formed the Composers of Today Inc. in 1948. Madame Tureck has a distinguished career as a concert artist on piano, harpsichord, organ and clavichord, is a Bach specialist, an editor of several publications, an author, and a professor of master classes throughout the world. Her honorary doctorate degrees in music were received from Colby College in 1964, Roosevelt University in 1968, Wilson College in 1968, and prestigious Oxford University in 1977.

Rosalyn Tureck was born in 1914 in Chicago, Illinois, the youngest of three daughters of Samuel and Monya Tureck, and the first generation American in a musical family of Russian and Turkish background. At the age of four, she demonstrated her gift of perfect pitch by imitating her sister's piano pieces and her musical career was launched.

As a child protégée, she made her debut in two solo recitals in Chicago at the age of nine and at the age of twelve, when she was soloist with the Chicago Symphony Orchestra. When Rosalyn Tureck was thirteen she won first prize over 15,000 school-age contestants in the Greater Chicago Playing Tournament; at fourteen she performed her first all-Bach recital and concentrated not only on piano but harpsichord, clavichord, and organ; and at the age of sixteen she won a four-year fellowship to Juilliard School of Music.

ROSALYN TURECK
(Photo by Christian Steiner)

Beginning at the age of ten, Tureck received outstanding keyboard instruction and as a young girl combined these lessons with her own study of the history of music, theory and related topics. She was an amazing person even as a young child and the growth of her intellectual capacity and musical ability has firmly established her in the spotlight of twentieth-century genius.

Her first teacher, Sophia Brilliant-Liven, was a Russian immigrant who had been a teaching assistant to the great Anton Rubinstein. Mrs. Liven was more than a keyboard teacher to the young girl, since she also provided Tureck with many opportunities to meet the finest Russian instrumentalists of the time. During the four years she studied with Liven she absorbed a tremendous amount of knowledge from the visits and conversations of the touring musicians often entertained by her teacher. These guests included such notable men as Leopold Aver, Ossip Gabrilowitsch and Leo Theremin; Tureck performed for all of them.

Her early love of Bach was supported by her second teacher, Jan Chiapusso, a Bach scholar with whom she had two lessons each week. Assigned a Bach Prelude and Fugue for her first lesson with him, she returned two days later, handed the music to him and to his astonishment played it through from memory without a flaw. Chiapusso felt she had extraordinary insight for her age and declared, "You must specialize in Bach." This was the first time that Rosalyn Tureck realized she was doing something unusual. During her first year of study with Jan Chiapusso she gave two all-Bach recitals in Chicago and the following year at the age of sixteen won a four-year scholarship with Olga Samaroff at Juilliard School of Music. She overwhelmed the audition committee by playing sixteen Bach Preludes and Fugues in addition to the works of Beethoven, Chopin, Paganini and Liszt. In addition to all the repertoire studied she researched embellishments, methods of transcribers and antique instruments.

Rosalyn Tureck experienced a revelation just before her seventeenth birthday. "I had to form new ways of thinking about music, new keyboard techniques of phrasing, dynamics, touch and endless means of performance. I had to create a totally new tonal and physical piano technique to match this deeper perception of what Bach's music and structure really is. My teacher Olga Samaroff thought it was marvelous but impossible to carry through. I could not possibly go back because I had found a new world. I had to create a new technique for playing the piano and for realizing Bach's structures in a valid and authentical way."

From that moment, Rosalyn Tureck's development was a painstaking process of working, playing, thinking and searching into the infinite concept and meaning of Bach's music. Olga Samaroff told Tureck, "I am cheating Juilliard by taking you as a student for there is nothing for me to help you with." She then made arrangements for the talented Tureck to be presented before the distinguished faculty at Juilliard after her second year at the school, in order for them to help decide whether Tureck should take the direction as a Bach performer or concentrate on the 19th and 20th century repertoire.

Following her second year at Juilliard, the talented Tureck was presented for examination by the distinguished faculty including Josef Lhevinne, James Friskin, Ernest Hutcheson and other notable members. She performed many compositions and the faculty decided Tureck could play it all and recommended, "Begin your career as a performer on all standard repertoire and you will have great success." Josef Lhevinne added, "You have time until you are forty years old to establish a speciality."

Madame Tureck has praised Samaroff and remarks, "She must receive credit for she was a very fine musician and taught me to be non-imitative as a teacher, for her attitude of teaching in a non-imitative way was to influence me and I shall be forever grateful."

Rosalyn Tureck did not realize until she was fourteen years old that Bach was supposed to be more difficult, she says, "I just learned it all." In fact, "I did not plan to start my adult concert career until I was thirty years old." Her career plans were to change abruptly when her teachers entered her in two competitions at the age of twenty. The gifted Rosalyn Tureck won the greatest contest of the time, The Schubert Memorial Award and with this award made an auspicious New York debut, playing the Brahms' B♭ Concerto with Eugene Ormandy and the Philadelphia Orchestra. Rosalyn Tureck was twenty years old and had a career on her hands. This was to be the sunrise for the brilliant and talented young woman, and some forty years later this career would still be shining and in great demand.

A year earlier at nineteen, she also made it to the

finals of the Naumburg Competition and presented an all-Bach program at her last performance. She lost. Some of the judges felt that no performer could possibly make a career of all-Bach! (Many of the faculty at Juilliard had made similar comments to her.)

Madame Tureck gave her first all-Bach series of six weekly concerts in New York at the age of twenty-two, and included all forty-eight Preludes and Fugues, the Goldberg Variations and other works. She was honored for her astonishing accomplishments with the first Town Hall Endowment Award for the "most distinguished performance of the New York Season." The award was presented by the President of Town Hall, Walter W. Naumberg who after the presentation apologized for the decision made at the Naumberg Contest three years earlier.

At age twenty-two Rosalyn Tureck performed her series of three all-Bach concerts on the West Coast at California Institute of Technology. This performance was to profoundly influence the young woman for here she would meet and converse with many of the great scientific men of the twentieth century. She was invited to meet with the Stammtisch group for their weekly Wednesday evening dinner, a practice long established where this internationally recognized group of scientists invited guests to dine and converse with them on various topics. Some of the group included Robert J. Oppenheimer, Hugo Benioff, Russell Bertrand, and Richard Chase Tolman, who asked her questions concerning the quantity and quality of tone on the piano.

She had made a study on the quality and quantity of sound as it relates to the piano and presented her views to the members of the Stammtisch group. She demonstrated her theory on a piano and received approval of her ideas. She worked with Hugo Benioff whenever she was in California helping him to perfect the electronic piano now built by Baldwin Company. When she first met Benioff he had only one note perfected.

Madame Tureck went to Europe in the 1950's and it was there that she first achieved the widespread recognition and position of eminence she now commands in the world of music at large. She comments, "I had recognition in America before I went to Europe but not on the same mass scale. I performed for fifteen hundred people at Town Hall but, in London the audience numbered three thousand."

Her extraordinary success is evident in the hundreds of reviews on four continents. A list of headlines could easily be endless, but throughout the world the genius Tureck received high praise.

These headlines proved Madame Tureck's teachers at Juilliard and the judges at the Naumburg Competition wrong when they insisted that she could never make a career with the music of Bach, and it would be pure folly to try since there was no listening audience ready to hear all-Bach programs. Standing ovations in sold-out houses throughout Europe began in 1954, and still continues today wherever Madame Tureck performs.

In 1956 Dr. Tureck conducted her first series of concerts of concerto and orchestral performances of Bach with the Collegium Musicum in Copenhagen. She then conducted the great Philharmonic Orchestra of London at Festival Hall in 1957 and the Scottish National Orchestra in Edinburgh and Glasgow.

Madame Tureck discusses her first impressions of conducting: "I had done so much research in the field of Bach that I felt I could conduct, and get results more quickly at rehearsals and with more validity than conductors who had not made Bach their speciality. I walked out to my first rehearsal, lifted my hands, brought them down for the downbeat and by God they all came in. The first sound that came with the downbeat was the most thrilling moment of my life and the series of four concerts was a great success. No one realized that it was the first time I had conducted."

There never was a male-female relationship problem when Tureck conducted. She never experienced a bad incident, and there developed an extraordinary relationship of love and respect for this first-rate musician. Again, one must remember that most musicians respect the ability of the conductor and the gender is of no importance.

In 1958 she returned to the United States for her first tour in five years and was greeted by audiences with a standing ovation on her entrance on the Town Hall stage in New York. Madame Tureck conducted the New York Philharmonic Orchestra at Carnegie Hall in their regular series in four appearances, and history was made by her being the first woman ever to conduct this major orchestra. Newsweek

Magazine featured an interesting review of Rosalyn Tureck in the December 29, 1958, issue titled Do It Yourself*:

> Although the graceful lines of her black dress hid Rosalyn Tureck's purposeful step as she walked out on the stage of Carnegie Hall one night last week, it was evident that the noted pianist had more on her mind than simply playing another of her celebrated Bach programs. She was to perform both the Bach D Minor and G Minor Concertos, yes; but she was also going to conduct the New York Philharmonic as she did so--and that was something no other woman had ever done before a Philharmonic subscription audience.
>
> While the dual nature of Miss Tureck's assignment kept her at the piano instead of up on the podium, she was in full command. With head bobbing like a metronome, she kept the orchestra in hand and forcefully demonstrated the Bach style for which she stands--"a full rich articulated sound."

Since the 1950's Madame Tureck has not only appeared as soloist with leading orchestras in the world but has conducted them also. In addition to the previous mentioned guest conducting appearances, she has been a guest on the podiums of the Washington National Symphony, Syracuse Symphony Orchestra and in Israel with both Israel Philharmonic, the Kol Israel Orchestra and the Scottish National Orchestra. Her credentials as the world's leading interpreter of the music of Bach has placed her on a pedestal and opened the doors to guest conducting throughout the world. She was the first woman to conduct each of these orchestras.

This creative and talented woman founded the Tureck Bach Players in England, a chamber orchestra that has received great acclaim. Dr. Tureck has been presented in her own weekend Bach Festival at Glyndebourne where she not only conducted her orchestra but in addition, performed solo recitals. The Tureck Bach Players performed throughout England and Ireland.

Tureck explains, "I'm interested in concepts and form

involving many centuries. I studied Bach of my own choice, some people think playing Bach is limited. As a performer, conductor, and artist I know that is absolute nonsense."

Madame Tureck's interest in contemporary music has never wavered. As a performer she has often programmed major contemporary works including Aaron Copland and Roger Sessions, and always played for the composer first. As a result of this interest, she founded Composers of Today Inc. in 1948 to help contemporary composers. She says, "I felt that concert artists did not know enough about contemporary music and felt they had very little dialogue with the composer. A concert artist might play a premiere, but this was sometimes only a way to get a concert with a symphony orchestra or a recording so I created the society to bridge the gap between composer and performer, and encourage interest between them."

Rosalyn Tureck willingly gave not only of her time and effort to provide an avenue for contemporary music, but during the first year she used her own beautiful apartment on Riverside Drive in New York to host the concerts. Attendance was by invitation only and represented both musicians and composers and was limited to one hundred and fifty people. One must give special credit to this gifted lady for few people of her caliber and international stature would ever consider finding time in their busy schedules to reach out and provide a means to encourage young struggling composers. She is a humanist as well as a musical giant.

At one of the four concerts given in the first year at Riverside Drive the power was cut off in the building and everyone had to climb eleven flights of stairs. According to Madame Tureck, "Milton Babbitt, known as a twelve-tone composer, walked up twelve flights of stairs and then back down one."

Attendance at one of these concerts was considered a privilege by the musical elite in both the United States and Europe. Many Europeans planned their trips to the United States around the concert dates and the New York Times called Rosalyn Tureck and asked for an invitation. After the first year the concerts became too big to be held in her apartment and she was given, as a contribution, Town Hall Club to use for future performances. The audiences were very large and still by invitation only.

These concerts provided an opportunity for newly published work and unpublished work to be performed and the audiences heard music that would otherwise never have been a part of the established concert season. Of course, the hand-picked audiences included the finest members of the musical world at that time including composers, performers, publishers, musicologists, professors, and other notable representatives.

A sample of the music performed by Composers of Today Inc. includes:

Composition	Composer	Performer(s)
Fifth Piano Sonata	Jack Beeson	John Kirkpatrick
Song Cycle	Milton Babbitt	Bethany Beardslee Jacques Monod
Second Piano Sonata	Roger Sessions	Beveridge Webster
Studies for Violin and Piano	Dallapiccola	Ruggiero Ricci Michael Field
Second String Quartet	Ralph Shapey	The Juilliard String Quartet
Sonata for Violin and Piano	Joseph Tal	Zwi Zeitlin Robert Starer
Sonatina for Solo Clarinet	Hans Erich Apostel	Eric Simon
Nos I and II "Ile de Feu"	Olivier Messiaen	Joseph Bloch
Sonata for Violin	Paul Ben-Haim	Zwi Zeitlin
Trio for Violin, Clarinet & Piano	Ernest Krenek	Roman Totenberg Eric Simon Edward Stuermann
A Short Service for tenor voice and Trumpet	Julia Perry	Robert Price Ronald Kutic
Khirgiz Suite for Violin & Piano	Alan Hovhaness	Ruggiero Ricci Mitchell Andrews
Songs from the Book of Hanging Gardens--Voice and Piano	Harold Schoenberg	Rose Bampton Russell Sherman

The concerts continued for several seasons until Madame Tureck's busy European Concert schedule prevented her from being in the United States to continue her effort. This accomplishment will forever be a part of the twentieth-century history of music. Her goals were of the highest standards, and the composers and performers were for a short time finally reaching out to combine their talents, thanks to the insightful and idealistic Madame Tureck.

In keeping with a lifelong devotion to scholarship and to the highest ideals in art, Madame Tureck also founded the International Bach Society, Inc. in 1966. The Society was created for the purpose of establishing a world center for the studies in the interpretation and performance of the music of Johann Sebastian Bach. Its aims are to provide opportunity for the exchange of ideas of persons professionally connected with Bach's music, to raise the standards of performance, to provide professional musicians and gifted students with opportunities for advanced studies in Bach style, and to make available auditing opportunities for teachers, students and laymen.

Membership is open to professional performers, musicologists, teachers, students and laymen. Charters are granted to music societies, teachers' associations and other musical organizations as branches of the International Bach Society.

Participants at past annual International Congresses have included some of the foremost scholars, musicians and composers in all phases of music. The distinguished participants have included Karl Geiringer, William Dowd, William Newman, Frederick Neuman, Theo Nederpelt (of Holland) as well as Professor Chou Wen Chung of Columbia University, and Teo Tin Chaun of Singapore. This Society provides a unique opportunity for gifted performers on strings, winds, harpsichord, clavichord, as well as solo and choral singers who audition for International Bach Society Performance Awards. Season winners become Performing Participants at the Congress events and receive coaching from Rosalyn Tureck and the staff of the collegia. Madame Tureck lectures, demonstrates through performance and conducts open rehearsals and Master Classes.

In 1973 Tureck made available a series of continuing recordings of the past International Bach Society Congress events for general distribution, Composers of Today Inc. and her own private recording of her public performances. The IBS recordings consist of lectures and performing illustrations by her and by her invited guests. The recordings are accompanied by a booklet of visual materials of music scores and illustrations of the music performed and discussed, embellishment charts, and illustrations of pertinent musical instruments. Dr. Tureck has provided a means to share the expertise of these events with countless numbers of interested music lovers, teachers, performers and artists. (The tape cassettes and visual materials are available from the International Bach Society, Inc. 165 West 57th Street, New York, N.Y. 10019.)

Dr. Rosalyn Tureck's interest in Bach has no equal. Her conviction that Bach is a composer of deep significance for our time has been given dramatic expression each year at the IBS events by an evening devoted to Bach and the Contemporary Scene.

For instance, imagine hearing Bach's F minor Sinfonia (Three Part Invention) played on four different instruments invented and perfected over a period of three hundred years. The diminutive delicacy of the clavichord, the provocative aggression of the harpsichord, the distinct lyrical romanticism of the piano and finally the Moog Synthesizer with all its possible sonic capabilities.

Dr. Tureck was only ten years old when she heard an entire concert given by electronic instrument pioneer Leo Theremin in Chicago. At age sixteen, she won the Theremin fellowship to study with him. She concentrated on two of his instruments: the Theremin, which is played by moving the hands in relation to two antennae and a keyboard instrument somewhat similar to the synthesizer as it is known today. It was on this keyboard electronic instrument that Rosalyn Tureck gave the first performance of Bach's music in her New York debut in Carnegie Hall while still a student at Juilliard. At the IBS events Dr. Tureck has also performed on other electronic instruments, and in 1971, she expanded this contemporary view of Bach to include an evening of Bach and Rock.

As a result of Madame Tureck's concert tour in Singapore she presented an evening of Bach and Chinese Music in 1971. She is the only person in the world who has brought forth this original research in Asian cultures and found in them a legitimate basis for comparison. The Chinese music was performed by Teo Tin Chaun, concertmaster of the Chinese Orchestra of the National Theatre of Singapore. He performed on the Erh-hu, a traditional two-stringed Chinese instrument, held upright on the knee and played with a bow.

Again as a result of her concert tour in India, Dr. Tureck was able to give a program on Embellishment in Indian Music and Bach with Jon Higgins as co-lecturer and performer. In 1971 she toured India, Hong Kong and Singapore, giving the first all-Bach recitals ever heard in those areas to sold-out houses. In New Delhi, Prime Minister Indira Gandhi invited her to a state dinner so they might have the opportunity to discuss the subject of music in India. In Bombay a group of leading Indian musicians gave a private concert for her on Indian instruments: the surbahar, the been, the tabla, the sitar and others. There, too, the great sitar player Willayat Kahn gave her a private concert, as did his well-known brother in Calcutta. In Madras she was treated to a private concert by one of India's great dancers.

The talented Rosalyn Tureck's teaching career is extensive. She has taught many Master Classes throughout the world and has been a professor at a number of private and public colleges and universities.

Her Master Classes include Washington University, 1963/64; University of Connecticut, 1967; University of California, San Diego, 1967-70; International Bach Society, Inc., 1967--; Roosevelt University, 1969; Peabody College, 1972; West Chester College, 1976; Oxford University, Oxford Music Festival, 1976; Queens University, Kingston, Ontario, 1977; University of Maryland, 1977; International Society for Music Education Convention, 1978; American Music Scholarship Association Annual Competition, 1978; International Festival of Music (Barcelona, Spain) 1978, Curtis Institute 1979. She has lectured at the University of Chicago, Wichita State University, Oxford University, England etc.

Her academic appointments (U. S.) include Philadelphia Conservatory of Music, 1935-42; Mannes College of Music, 1940-44; Juilliard School of Music, 1943-55; Columbia University, 1953-1955; Visiting Professor of Music, Washington University (St. Louis), 1963-64; and Professor of Music, University of California, San Diego, 1966-1972. She was a lecturer at the University of Cincinnati, 1963; University of California, San Diego, Regents Lecturer 1966; University of Chicago, 1966; University of Connecticut, 1967; Roosevelt University, 1969; Georgia Southern University, 1970; Peabody College, 1972; Institute for Special Studies, Juilliard School of Music, 1972; Metropolitan Museum of Art (New York) 1969, 1970; International Bach Society, Inc. 1967-1972; Spanish Ministry of Music, Madrid, 1973; Columbia University, 1977;

University of Calgary, 1978; International Society for Music Education Conference, 1978; Emory University, 1979. Her academic appointments in England include Visiting Fellow, St. Hilda's College, 1974, Honorary Life Fellow, St. Hilda's College, Oxford University, 1974--; Visiting Fellow, Wolfson College, Oxford University, 1975--. She also lectured at University of London, 1955-56.

Aspiring artists from all over the world seek out Madame Tureck to study privately and in Master Classes. Her principles of teaching are explained by her, "I teach from deep principles of structure, I work in research with manuscripts and editions which cover two hundred years involving music form and more. My teaching applies to all kinds of music and all instruments. I teach antique instruments, such as the harpsichord, clavichord, and also string instruments, piano, and classical guitar. I work with orchestras and choruses and vocal soloists."

Rosalyn Tureck has always edited Bach's music for her own performance, and she is now working on it for publication. In preparing her edition for publication by Shirmer Music, Inc. of Bach's Italian Concerto, she will have printed for the first time in the history of music a text with performance instructions based on performance practices edited for both the piano and harpsichord. This is the first of an ongoing series to be published by G. Schirmer, Inc.

Dr. Rosalyn Tureck is a very erudite woman and a profilic writer. Her book An Introduction to the Performance of Bach (in three volumes) was published in 1959 by Oxford University Press and attests to her scholarship. It has since been published in translation in Japanese and Spanish. She was editor of Bach-Sarabande, C Minor in 1950, Paganini, Moto Perpeto in 1950, and Bach Keyboard Works in 1977. She contributes to a variety of magazines and has written articles that are of significant value to the field of music. When Albert Schweitzer (one of the first heralds of the modern renaissance of Bach) died, the Saturday Review invited Rosalyn Tureck to write its obituary evaluation of him as a Bach musician and authority.

In November 1972, Dr. Tureck published an interesting and lengthy article in Current Musicology (no. 14) titled "Toward Unity of Performance and Musicology." Every serious student of music should be required to read this treatise. She develops the relationship of musicology and performance by 1) examining this relationship in light of her own experience performing; 2) a brief analysis of the nature of each activity; and 3) a few remarks on the interaction of the two disciplines. The final paragraph summarizes the article*:

> The artist-performer must be concerned with forging the sum of all these parts into a great whole with depth of feeling and unobstructed freedom of communication. Such a marriage, though rare, is capable of producing great beauty and arrives as close to the composer's thoughts as is humanly possible. This achievement is difficult on every level; it combines the musicological labor of scholar with the technical and musical development of the gifted performer; it demands a talent for merging the two into an artistic unity; and it is quickened into life only by the precious spiritual gift of giving oneself with reverence and love.

Madame Tureck has contributed numerous articles to Current Musicology, New York; Making Music, London; Music and Letters, London; New Statesman, London; Saturday Review, New York; and Hi-Fi/Musical America, New York.

Honor and awards for an artist of Rosalyn Tureck's stature are many and varied. They include Honorary Member of Advisory Council for the Music Library, Hebrew University; First prize, Greater Chicago Piano Playing Tournament; Winner, Schubert Memorial Contest; Phi Beta Award for Excellence; Honorary Member, Societé Johann Sebastian Bach de Belgique, Bruxelles; First Town Hall Endowment Award; Honorary Member Guildhall School of Music (an honor rarely accorded an American); a bronze head of her, sculpted by Sir Jacob Epstein, the renowned sculptor, was the beginning of Royal Festival Hall's now notable sculpture collection. Of the nine bronze heads in existence, Epstein gave her one as a gift, the original plaster cast is owned by the Museum of Modern Art (New York), one is in the Philadelphia Art Museum, and the others are in private collections.

Madame Tureck has been a friend and colleague of some of the most respected and honored men of the twentieth century. Her friends include Nobel Prize Winners Otto Loewi, Austria; Niels Bohr, Denmark; Isidor Isaac Rabi, United

---

*Reprinted by permission of the publisher and author.

States, Harold C. Urey, United States; and many other famous scientists and artists in both America and Europe.

Rosalyn Tureck must be considered one of the most amazing individuals of the twentieth century, her scholarly contributions, her total commitment to the world of musicology, her deep and abiding sense of musical direction and her willingness to share her expertise places her, at the peak of the mountain of intellectual giants. She comments, "Bach's music is the greatest ever written. It is the highest in intellect, the highest in spirituality, the deepest emotionally, the most difficult in structure and in performance, the most challenging. With these qualities, I wish to spend my life and with nothing less."

Through her many activities, her lectures, her published books, her scholarly involvement, her innovative activities and most of all her performances (live and recorded), there will be a treasured collection in the history of music. Madame Tureck has recorded for the following companies: Decca, Brunswick, Odeon, Allegro, Capitol and Columbia Masterworks. Her earlier recordings were with Decca and as they are no longer in existence, the records have become collectors' items. Her recent recordings are with Columbia Masterworks. The first of these (to be released in June 1979) is the Goldberg Variations and Aria and Ten Variations in the Italian Style (number 79-750143). Her second album, Chromatic Fantasia and Fugue, Italian Concerto and Four Duets from Book Three of the Clavierubung, will be released in 1980.

NANCY VAN DE VATE

Composer, Professor

Dr. Nancy Van de Vate is a composer, professor, academic dean, articulate Past President of the Southeastern Composers' League, and Founder and Chairperson of the executive board of the International League of Women Composers Inc. She is on the Board of Directors New England Women's Symphony, the Advisory Board of Women in American Music; A Bibliography, and the Board of Directors Mariska Aldrich Library of Rare Music. Dr. Van de Vate is Past President Concordium Hawaii Chamber Music Series and the author of several provocative articles on women in twentieth-century musical life.

Nancy Van de Vate was born in New Jersey in 1930. She was a piano major at Eastman School of Music where she received the Rochester Prize scholarship and the George Eastman scholarship. She transferred to Wellesley College in Massachusetts where she graduated with a Bachelor of Arts Degree, with a major in theory. She was recognized as a Wellesley College Scholar. Her Master's Degree in composition was awarded by the University of Mississippi, and her Doctorate of Music, with a major in composition, was earned at Florida State University.

She has been a recipient of numerous awards based on her talent and versatility as a composer in a variety of musical forms including orchestra, chorus, ensembles for strings, woodwinds, brass, piano, mixed ensembles, voice, and tape. She expresses through her music the ethical, philosophical, and emotional issues identifiable with the twentieth century. Her music represents the questioning, agreeing, arguing, and altering tone of events. The results are exciting and leave an indelible imprint with the listener.

Van de Vate moved to Oxford, Mississippi, with her

husband and three-month-old baby in 1955. The constraints of a young family--limited time, energy, financial resources and professional contact--convinced her that performance was no longer a feasible outlet for her professional ambitions. At that time, composition seemed like an activity which did not demand the daily level of physical and mental activity that practicing an instrument does. She comments, "I changed to composition, then became so totally engrossed in it that I never again wished to direct the major part of my time and energy to any other aspect of music."

The parameters of Van de Vate's music range from serious, expressive and highly personal, to witty, experimental and highly objective. One needs only to compare and contrast her String Trio for Amateur Players with Suite for Solo Violin to readily grasp and immediately hear the irreconcilable differences and the obvious changes in musical vocabulary. Suite for Solo Violin combines the elements and forms of the past with twentieth-century procedures. Strongly atonal and based on the row technique, Van de Vate artistically combines a series of modernistic gestures, rich sounds that are produced by the actual striking of the body of the instrument with new and strangely exciting tonal sounds produced by playing below the bridge of the violin. String Trio for Amateur Players is a completely tonal composition, lyrically beautiful and emotionally passionate. The talented composer wrote the entire piece for strings playing in the first position.

Dr. Van de Vate has been the recipient of six standard ASCAP (American Society of Composers Authors and Publishers) awards for serious compositions between 1973-79. The awards are important since they provide the artist with stipends which permit some freedom from the mundane functions of daily routine. Composer Van de Vate received two resident awards to the Ossabow Island Project and Yaddo, which provides the artist a place and undisturbed time for actual composing. Candidates must have already had performed work of high artistic merit, and have other projects underway. Artistic merit, rather than popular appeal, is the standard of judgment. Yaddo, located in historic Saratoga Springs, New York, is an artist's paradise consisting of beautiful residential buildings, surrounded by formal rose gardens and lovely statues.

Awards include first place in 1975 at the prestigious Delius Composition Contest for Quintet for Brass; third prize

NANCY VAN DE VATE

in the Stowe Competition for String Trio; two awards in 1979 from the NLAPW (National League of American Pen Women); first prize and honorable mention respectively for her art songs Cradelsong and The Earth Is So Lovely, both for soprano and piano; first prize in the NLAPW Mid Administration Congress Composer's Competition for Four Somber Songs, a cycle for mezzo and piano.

Her commissions include the Knoxville Choral Society for An American Essay, a work for large chorus and instruments; The Music Teachers National Association for Letter to a Friend's Loneliness, for soprano and string quartet; The University of Redlands New Music Ensemble for Incidental Piece for Three Saxes; and, Eugene Bondi, Assistant Principal Cellist of The Honolulu Symphony Orchestra for Music for Student String Quartets.

Most composers are influenced by the faculty of the composition department in indergraduate and graduate colleges and Nancy Van de Vate reflects on these experiences:

> During the middle 1950's most of the composers trained at the Eastman School of music wrote in the Bernard Rogers, Howard Hanson pan-diatonic style. The teachers I had, tried to make me into that model, but for some reason I was never very good at it. I did try hard, however, and ultimately became a pretty good contrapuntist but more in the style of Bartók. My music is more chromatic and harmonically intense than the pan-diatonic school. My style--lyric, often straightforwardly melodic, much chromatic inflection, tense, frequently dissonant, structurally oriented, always very intense in mood, becoming more coloristic in recent years, more pointillistic. I much admire Varèse, whose music I wish I had discovered earlier in life. I would like to combine Bartók's marvelous linear writing with Varèse's concept of "sound mass or sound structure," his sense of continuity fascinates me--because it is not linear but it is certainly there. I also admire Penderecki and George Crumb. I do not wish to compose totally organized music, in the sense of totally serialized music, although occasionally I do use a pitch series.

In 1966 Nancy Van de Vate's composition was premiered among the bright new works heard at the forum presented by the University of Alabama and the Southeastern Composers League. The forum presented two days of exciting new music and discussions. She was the only women composer presented at the forum. J. F. Goossen, writing for the Tuscaloosa-Alabama News on May 2, 1966, commented on her Sonata for Viola and Piano*:

> In her Viola Sonata, Nancy Van de Vate probed deeply, particularly in the slow sections, yet provided vivid contrast in the more rapid music.
>
> This year's forum, while not radical in the accepted sense, did reveal some strong new talents and the continued growth of established ones. Performances were on the whole well above minimum standards, and in some cases truly virtuoso. The vigorous life of music in this region seems secure.

The Music Review in The NATS Bulletin (Feb. /March of 1971, Vol. XXVII, No. 3, page 42) written by Hadley Crawford offered the following**:

> Two Songs: (1) Death Is the Chilly Night, (2) Loneliness, Nancy Van de Vate. Published by Waterloo Music Company, medium voice and piano.
>
> The first song is set to a poem by Heinrich Heine and the second to a text by Rainer M. Rilke, both translated to English by Kate Flores. On our copy only the English text is presented. It is very singable. The songs are difficult enough to demand musicianship but not extremely so. Each are less than two minutes long.
>
> Each of these songs are mood pictures, achieved with restraint and good taste. The first creates a sharp contrast between Death Is the Chilly Night and Life Is the Torrid Day. The ending text: "Above my bed there grows a tree where sings a young nightingale."

Van de Vate's commission, in 1971, from the Knoxville Choral Society resulted in An American Essay scored for large chorus and instruments. The premiere performance was reviewed by Evelyn Miller and published in the May 2, 1972, issue of the Knoxville News-Sentinel†:

---

*Reprinted by permission of the publisher.
**Reprinted by permission of the publisher.
†Reprinted by permission of The Knoxville News-Sentinel Co.

> The Knoxville Choral Society Chorale and its conductor, J. B. Lyle made a three point landing, musically speaking, at the chorale's Spring Concert at UT Music Hall.
>
> For the first time the Chorale sang a work commissioned by the Society; the composer, Nancy Van de Vate, heard the first performance of her composition; and Mr. Lyle conducted the premiere performance for the first time. It was an achievement of great stature for the Chorale, the composer and the conductor.
>
> Mrs. Van de Vates's work entitled An American Essay is the setting of poems from Walt Whitman's Leaves of Grass. She selected poems of strength and eloquence, rooted in America by a poet who passionately loved the warp and woof of his country.
>
> The words could have been written yesterday, especially the Sobbing of the Bells which expresses the "sad reverberations" of the news of President Garfield's death following wounds by an assassin's bullet.
>
> Mrs. Van de Vate's setting of the poems is strongly rhythmic, melodic lines are often angular, harmonies are clashing but the dissonances are exciting, purposeful and full of suspense. The words must be flung out with great intensity. Mr. Lyle guided his singers through the manuscript score with musicianly skill, excellent diction, no ragged edges.
>
> The City of Ships which opens the work and the last one, Sobbing of the Bells, are the finest in the group. Patrolling Barnegat grows wearisome from too much repetition of words and phrases, backtracking and surging forward but even so this technic well described the lashing of a stormy sea.
>
> Mrs. Van de Vate writes well for chorus although she occasionally pushes the sopranos to an uncomfortable pitch and holds them there. This was especially noticeable in To the East and to the West which was sung as a solo by Janice Clark. Mrs. Clark conquered the high tessitura with full, true voice.

Every composer must have the opportunity to hear her compositions for this is how creativity flourishes, imaginative concepts are developed and expanded through the process. Dr. Van de Vate explains, "Music composition is really an urban occupation, you must be where there are performers and audiences to hear your music. My own style was hampered by being in a rural environment, which was the point of my article Notes from a Bearded Lady. There simply are few composers from places like South Dakota, North Dakota, Utah, Wyoming, Arkansas, and Nevada; it is just too rural." She continues,

> Of course, academic composition is different, for you go where the job is. The Southeastern Composers League, for example, has over one hundred members the majority of whom have doctorate degrees in composing. That group includes about half of all the composers in the region. They do suffer from some isolation but it is not as acute if they are members of music departments. However, women composers have been largely excluded in the area of college teaching, too. The College Music Society reported in 1970, only sixty-seven women teaching composition, full or part-time, in the whole country. The housewife in Oxford, Mississippi or Knoxville, Tennessee who is also trying to be a serious composer doesn't have much going for her except, it heightens her survival technique.
>
> Many factors influence a composer. I don't think being in New York City solves all problems for it can also destroy a composer. The tendency is to feel that other people are looking over your shoulder and perhaps to respond too much to current trends and fads. It is not easy, to go your own way, in the midst of a musical environment that is mandating that you go in another direction.
>
> My style was considered far too advanced for the South, far too conservative for New York City--there is such a style rift. Composers tend to pitch themselves with one camp or another, aleatory (chance), tonal, serial and there is some comfort belonging to one school, but if you are in the middle you have less ideology to defend your music. Acceptance of style is largely regional, what is accepted in big cities often will not go in less urban places.

Beginning in the 1970's Nancy Van de Vate's compositions were extensively performed throughout the United States: Six Etudes for Solo Viola was premiered at the Lincoln Center in New York, by Jacob Glick; Trio for Strings received two performances, in Oak Ridge and Knoxville, Tennessee; Quintet for Brass was premiered at the University of Jacksonville, Florida: String Quartet received its first performance at the New Music Festival at Memphis (Tennessee) State University; Psalm 121 for mixed chorus was performed at St. John's Church in Knoxville; and Radio Station WROL in Knoxville featured two programs, City of Ships and The Sobbing of the Bells from An American Essay and Inventions I and II for magnetic tape; Quintet for flute, oboe, clarinet, cello, and piano premiered at the Bicentennial Concert of New Music at the University of Hawaii in Honolulu; Incidental Piece for Three Saxes by the New Music Ensemble at the University of Redlands in California; How Goes the Night? for women's voices, performed at the Unitarian Church of Honolulu; Letter to a Friend's Loneliness for string quartet and soprano, presented at Johnson City, Tennessee; and Music for Viola, Percussion and Piano in Honolulu.

Mark Blechner reviewed the sixth concert of Meet the Woman Composer for High Fidelity/Musical America (March 1977)*:

> Militant women musicians literally went underground on December 3. It was the sixth concert in the series "Meet the Woman Composer," and the setting was the basement of the New School, where the acoustics are dismal. There was plenty of heated rhetoric at this event proclaiming women's power, but these vehement gestures received little support from the music, by Nancy Van de Vate, founder and chairperson of the League of Women Composers, and by Tui St. George Tucker.
>
> The main stumbling block to these composers is an obsession with avant-garde techniques at the cost of sincere expression. This is especially true of Mrs. Van de Vate. Her Suite for Solo Violin, which began like the Berg Violin Concerto, turned into a shopping list of modernist gestures, like beating the violin's body and playing below the bridge. This was a sad waste, since Mrs. Van de Vate does have substantial musical talent, as was demonstrated by her frankly tonal String Trio for Amateur Players. Who would have thought that strings, playing in the

*Reprinted by permission of the publisher.

> first position, could yield such passion and drama? It is no small irony that this work, written for trios, should be the only one on the program that professionals might cherish.

In the August 1977 issue of High Fidelity/Musical America, Dr. Nancy Van de Vate wrote the following letter in response to Mr. Blechner's review*:

> To The Editor:
>
> As music critic (The Hawaii Observer), I can understand the temptation to let a catchy phrase supersede judgment in discussing music. However, when the reviewer's tendency to overstate converts criticism into caricature, it represents a lapse of professional taste.
>
> In the March 1977 issue of Musical America ("Van de Vate, Tucker," page MA-26), Mark Blechner refers to "militant women musicians." In point of fact, the League of Women Composers is an advocacy group, not a "militant" organization. We might be more effective if we were militant, but we are not, any more than Common Cause, Amnesty International, or any consumers' advocacy groups.
>
> Mr. Blechner says "there was plenty of heated rhetoric at this event proclaiming women's power." ("Influence" would have been a better word, perhaps.) It was brought out that women are rarely conductors of large orchestras or chairpersons of large music departments, and musicians who can confer no professional advantage on other musicians are not usually on the receiving end of such advantage. That is the nature of influence, whether it happens to be male or female.
>
> Meet the Composer, which sponsored the New School series, Meet the Woman Composer, stipulates that composers whose music is performed answer questions from the audience. When those questions are concerned with the professional status of women, they should be answered honestly. No one involved in the series intended to use it as a soapbox, and it is regrettable that facts set forth about women in

*Reprinted by permission of the publisher.

> composition struck Mr. Blechner as no more than feminist rhetoric
>
> In music criticism, the success or failure of a composer's work is not usually tied to his or her politics. Whether my music is good or bad has little to do with my views as a feminist, although it has much to do with the opportunities afforded or denied me as a woman composer. The sociology of music is a fascinating subject and one on which very little has been written. However, it needs to be treated responsibly.
>
> Caricaturing "women's libbers" is still, unfortunately, socially acceptable, just as a generation ago one could still deride the aspirations of blacks. Women composers look forward to a time when critics respond to their music without attributing its possible short-comings to their politics.

In 1978, Music with a Difference, a series of concerts by women composers, was co-founded by Dr. Van de Vate and Dorothy Stein, director of the adult programs at the University YWCA of Honolulu. The series has included music by Clara Schumann, Daria Semegen, Ruth Shaw Wylie, Virginia Kendrick, Gladys Rich, Marcia Cohen, Cecile Chaminade, Marga Richter, Jay Anderson and Van de Vate.

Ben Hyams, classical music writer for Honolulu magazine wrote an article in the March 1979 issue on "Music Composed by Women"*:

> "Vive la Difference!" was the cry that threw the French National Assembly into an uproar when, in a debate over a certain male-versus-female issue, someone had the bad taste to ask what difference it made.
>
> In Honolulu today, in a sort of "off-Broadway" concert series called Music with a Difference, two determined ladies are fighting the cause of the woman composer. Only music composed by women is performed. "I would prefer to have presented it as a straightforward music series," said Nancy Van de Vate," and I don't think anyone would have noticed that it was all by women composers. You couldn't tell from listening to the music."

---

*Reprinted by permission of the author.

Mrs. Van de Vate was co-founder of the concerts with Dorothy Stein, director of adult programs at the University YWCA, where they are held. The two met at a Concordium concert and agreed women needed more recognition in music and the series was set up with the Y as sponsor and the International League of Women Composers cooperating. The result is a musical adventure far from the mainstream. Seekers after the unusual will find in it new sounds to stimulate the ear and challenge the mind.

KAIM's Betty Anderson baffled Mrs. Stein with the question: "Are there really women who write music?" By way of living proof, Mrs. Stein took Mrs. Van de Vate to the radio station and Miss Anderson then taped nine broadcast interviews with them so they could present their case and open some listeners' eyes, or ears. "I would like to see more people become aware that there are plenty of women writing music," said Mrs. Van de Vate, "so that I will stop being treated as a bit of a freak. It is just what I happen to do for a living, as opposed to being a seamstress or a journalist or decorator."

Radio stations in our country would do a fine public service if they broadcast music composed by women. It would not only enlighten the listening public but would broaden the base for the music directors. The British Broadcasting Company has for years presented music of both men and women and the United States could well follow that example.

Nancy Van de Vate has a seemingly boundless supply of energy and her accomplishments in music, teaching, writing, and working for national organizations could easily exhaust two people. She not only expands creative awareness but expounds on social issues. The December-January 1973-74 issue of Symphony News published her article "Every Good Boy (Composer) Does Fine," which presents the plight of women composers and the problems and issues they face. The first paragraph immediately amazes the reader*:

During the summer and early fall of 1972, WUOT-FM, a serious music station of Knoxville, Tennes-

*Reprinted by permission of the publisher.

> see, broadcast every recorded work by a woman composer. I mean every recorded serious work, everything that one thousand years of music writing and one hundred years of recording have produced. This series of programs was conceived by Norris Dryer, music director of the station, who received an award of merit from the National Federation of Music Clubs for the Project.
>
> Seven hours of broadcast time included them all.

In the article Van de Vate clearily defines the obstacles and offers possible solutions, for example, the Schwann catalog lists only twenty-four female composers, women are not taken seriously, and there must be remedies for this gross neglect and they should be institutional and collective.

Nancy Van de Vate wrote an intriguing article in July 1975 published by the International Musician entitled "Notes From a Bearded Lady: The American Women Composer." A short excerpt from this lengthy and well-written article follows*:

> Most of the standard avenues for obtaining performances of their works have not been open to women. (Broad boulevards of symphony and operatic performances, commissions and recordings.) In the past every city and town had its music club of genteel ladies who would listen to sentimental songs by women or works for solo piano. Church choirs have provided outlets for edifying anthems, and educational publishers have accepted teaching pieces by women, with triple names. But serious compositional aspirations have been about as welcome in woman as beards and for the same reason.

The article presents excellent food for thought and action, anonymity in the submission of scores for all competitions and awards, quality would be the sole basis for judgment, and the music performed by major orchestras would be based on this quality, not the "old boy" syndrome, since no major symphony orchestras, in the United States, are conducted by women.

*Reprinted by permission of the publisher.

The subjugation of women in the field of conducting and composing is finally elapsing into a slow and complete death. One is presently watching the last bastion of male chauvinism crumble in the field of music. "The American Woman Composer: Some Sour Notes," written by Nancy Van de Vate, was published by High Fidelity/Musical America June 1975. This article answers an important and often asked question: Why have there been no great women composers?*

> Originality is normally the concomitant of style change in music. One or two major talents will articulate the features of a new style. They will be remembered as great artists, seminal thinkers, important influences. Women composers are never permitted to rise to this level. They are scarcely able to win recognition as dutiful followers, let alone as leaders. The male musical innovator may survive initial rejection, but among women initial rejection leads inevitably to ultimate obscurity, for they are not heard. Composers who are routinely denied performance may have bold new ideas, but unfortunately the public will not hear them.
>
> The line between eccentricity and originality is never clear. The composer, however, will be tolerated, and his eccentricities will at least make their way to an initial performance. No woman composer has succeeded in establishing herself to this extent. She cannot persist in her eccentricity--or her originality--for her claim to professionalism is not secure. No wonder, then, that women composers are not boldly innovative.
>
> The rapidity of style change during the last decade has worked a peculiar hardship on the contemporary woman composer. She must first of all demonstrate her conpetence in one of the accepted idioms. The absence of performance opportunities, however, means that many years may elapse between the creation of a work and its presentation to the public. By then it may be regarded as stylistically regressive, and she must start all over again in a new idiom.
>
> This problem is, of course, faced by male com-

*Reprinted by permission of the publisher.

posers also, but limited performance opportunities for women and the profession's limited tolerance for their work makes it far more acute for the latter.

This talented musician-composer is a prognostic writer of current issues relative to the creative arts and specifically to the status of women composers. That she has had the audacity to question the establishment in national publications has obviously ruffled the bristles of many adherents to the "old boy" syndrome. She has had the courage and the ability to speak out and is projected as a heroine. No passive male ever produced needed changes in society, and we should expect the same of our females. Active assertive people are leaders, and there should be no sexual differentiation. People and organizations are not infallible, changes should be inherent and when they are not, then one must challenge.

Nancy Van de Vate has challenged the National Endowment for the Arts and the John F. Kennedy Center-Rockefeller Foundation International Competition for Excellence in the performance of American music. Her concern is outlined in the exchange of letters between Howard Klein (John F. Kennedy Center--Rockefeller Foundation), Doris Hays, and herself. The letters were published in the August 21, 1978, issue of the League of Women Composers Newsletter*:

April 11, 1978

Dear Ms. Hays:

Thank you for your letter of March 5 regarding the John F. Kennedy Center-Rockefeller International Competitions for Excellence in the Performance of American Music.

I am sorry you feel our short list seems biased against women composers. But we asked our panel not to list composers but compositions which were stage worthy and neglected. The composer's name was the result of having chosen a title. Were we to have placed emphasis on the composer, I assure you the list would have looked different. Perhaps you are familiar with the composers represented on Recorded Anthology of American Music, including some you mentioned.

*Reprinted by permission of the publisher.

I hope that this clarifies the selection of repertory for the competition.

Yours sincerely,
Howard Klein

April 17, 1978

Dear Mr. Klein:

Thank you for your letter of April 11, in attempting to clarify how the repertoire list was made for the Kennedy Center-Rockefeller Foundation Competition.... Unfortunately, your letter leaves me even more mystified as to how compositions were chosen.

You wrote that compositions were selected by title. But if say a Sonata No 1 were listed, it could either be Ives or Vivian Fine; if Six Etudes were listed they could be by John Cage, or by Louise Talma. Titles must be backed up by a human creator in order to be identified. And how was the preselection of titles arrived at, by whom and from what other list, which titles were given to the repertoire selection panel? And to the criteria of "stage worthy and neglected"--the neglected women composers of this country could provide you with enough stage-worthy music to complete an entire repertoire list. If neglect is one of your criterion, you failed utterly to take advantage of the obvious neglect and seeming discrimination which women creators encounter in finding avenues of performance.

I should genuinely appreciate being enlightened about the selection process for the competition repertoire. Future competitions will produce other repertoire lists. Perhaps there is some way you can avoid the present paradox of neglected compositions by neglected women composers being omitted from among the neglected titles by male composers?

Sincerely,
Doris Hays

May 19, 1978

Dear Mr. Klein:

The League of Women Composers wishes to express

its concern with the lack of representation of works by women in the Kennedy-Rockefeller Foundation . . .

We have been advised that next year's competition will be in the area of vocal music. Women composers have devoted much of their efforts to music for voice, and we would hope that some of their excellent works in this medium will be selected for next year's repertory list. If there is any way in which the League can assist in directing the selection panel to works by women, please do not hesitate to contact us.

The League hopes that the presumption of egalitarianism which should characterize any project associated with the Kennedy Center will extend to representation of the creative works of women.

Yours sincerely,
Nancy Van de Vate, Chairperson

June 6, 1978

Dear Ms. Van de Vate:

We deeply appreciate the concern of the League to promote the cause of women composers. It is a goal shared by the Rockefeller Foundation and any right thinking organization. But you are also doubtless aware of the problems that surround the whole issue of American composers, leaving aside for the moment subgroups among them. I believe what you are asking for is equity, and it is what we are desperately trying to achieve, first for American composers. We are not exactly alone in trying to help American artists but sometimes it feels as though we are. In our Recorded Anthology of American Music, we note the inclusion of works by women which had never been recorded before. We think our record on the subject is not too bad. We also feel that we are making progress by putting together the lists of American compositions for piano, voice, and soon strings. And we are taking great pains to locate works for those lists, a time-consuming and expensive process in which the Foundation is the lone pioneer. In compiling those lists we are going directly to the performers, not to composers, a policy we shall continue. You may be assured that women have figured into our selection process from the beginning and will continue to do so.

Sincerely yours,
Howard Klein

Ms. Ellen Buchwalter of the Rockefeller Foundation telephoned me on April 12, 1979, as the result of my written request to verify the contents of Mr. Klein's letters. She said, "The content was correct; however, the letters alone did not reflect a true picture." She sent a brochure of the 1979 competition*:

> John F. Kennedy Center-Rockefeller Foundation International Competitions for Excellence in the Performance of American Music, 1979 Vocal Competition. Purpose: Competitions are intended to stimulate a greater interest on the part of performers, teachers and students in the large body of recital music written by American composers since 1900. It is hoped that by identifying and calling attention to skilled performers of this literature through competitive awards more of the rich heritage of 20th-century music by Americans will be discovered and appreciated, and more works from this body of music will win places in the standard repertory. The competitions are administered by the John F. Kennedy Center for the Performing Arts in Washington, D.C. The 1978 competition was for pianists. The 1979 competition is for singers. The 1980 competition will be for violinists.

For this competition, a list of forty-two American composers was published by the Foundation. There were five women composers recognized on the repertory list: Mrs. H. H. A. Beach, Ruth Crawford (Seeger), Miriam Gideon, Cathy Berberian, and Louise Talma. There was no indication how the composers were selected. "Singers of both sexes, of any age and nationality, are eligible. Judging for the competition will be done by an international jury of musicians" (states the brochure). There is no indication of how the judges are chosen.

Dr. Nancy Van de Vate is totally committed to any

*Reprinted by permission of the publisher.

endeavor that she accepts, no matter how large or powerful the organization might be or how minute the results. In April 1976 two articles appeared in Musical America: in Nancy Van de Vate's, "The National Endowment: Playing Favorites," the composer sees geographic bias in some NEA awards. The second article was written, as requested by the editor of the magazine, by the director of the Music Programs for the National Endowment for the Arts, Mr. Walter F. Anderson. The title was "Decisions Are Objective." The articles are much too long to present again; however, one can only question, Why would the director of America's most powerful and prestigious art foundation publicly respond to Nancy Van de Vate's charges? It can only be surmised that a sensitive and vulnerable spot might have been punctured. There are no immediate winners in an exchange of positions presented in these articles. Yet, the fact that time and critical thoughts were exchanged can only mean there is an honesty of effort involved.

The International League of Women Composers is an organization devoted to expanding opportunities for women in composition. Dr. Van de Vate is chairperson of the executive board. The principle aim of the organization is to obtain more commissions, recordings and orchestral performances for women composers of serious music. Membership is open to any woman whose seriousness of purpose has been demonstrated in one of the following ways: 1) by any single degree in composition (if the degree is not recent, some evidence of recent activity should be offered), 2) by holding a current teaching position in composition at the college level, 3) by having had a work performed at a recognized symposium or by a professional group, 4) by having had a serious work published, or 5) by submitting two compositions to the executive board for review.

The League has come into being at a time when opportunity was never greater for dispelling the old and unfair tradition of neglect of the woman composer. They believe the future of women in composition depends upon effective collective action.

Dr. Van de Vate has also been an active member of American Society of Composers, Authors and Publishers; American Society of University Composers; College Music Society, National Association of Composers, USA: Southeastern Composers' League, President, 1973-75, Secretary, 1965-68, 1970-73, Editor, Music Now, 1965-68, 1970-73; League of

Women Composers, Chairperson, Executive, 1975- ; and Popular Culture Association, Southern Region, Tennessee State Coordinator 1972-74.

Professor Van de Vate has been a faculty member at the University of Mississippi, Memphis State University, the University of Tennessee, Knoxville College, Maryville College, the University of Hawaii and Hawaii Loa College, where she is presently Dean of Academic Affairs and Associate Professor of Music.

In her young life Nancy Van de Vate has contributed more effort to family, teaching, composing, and certain human social issues than seems possible. She is a model for twentieth-century women who choose to combine a career with family responsibilities. It can be successfully accomplished if the individual is as talented, well-educated, confident, organized and dedicated as Nancy Van de Vate.

Compositions

A partial list of Nancy Van de Vate's compositions follows. They are published by Theodore Presser Company, Southern Music Company, Waterloo Associated Music Publishers, Manuscript Publications, Summy-Birchard, American Society of University Composers, and Journal of Music Scores.

1957 Adagio for Orchestra for two flutes, two oboes, two clarinets, two trumpets, tuba, tympani and strings
1958 Psalm 121 (mixed a cappella)
1958 Variations for Chamber Orchestra for flute, oboe, clarinet, bassoon and strings
1959 How Fares the Night? (women's voices and piano)
1960 Short Suite for Brass Quartet for two trumpets, trombone and bass trombone
1960 Two Songs for medium voice: Death Is the Chilly Night and Loneliness
1960 Youthful Age (soprano)
1962 Cradlesong (soprano)
1962 The Earth Is So Lovely (mezzo)
1964 Diversion for Brass for two trumpets, horn, trombone or euphonium
1964 Sonata for viola and piano
1964 Woodwind Quartet for flute, oboe, clarinet and bassoon
1968 Concerto for Piano and Orchestra for piccolo, two flutes, two oboes, two clarinets, four horns in F,

two trumpets, three trombones, tuba, tympani, triangle, cymbal, bass drum and strings

1969 Six Etudes for solo viola (arr. for violin also)
1969 String Quartet No. 1
1970 Four Somber Songs (a cycle for mezzo and piano)
1970 Sonata for oboe and piano
1970 The Pond (mixed a cappella)
1972 An American Essay (mixed voices, piano and percussion--2 players)
1972 To the East and To the West (high voice)
1973 Three Sound Pieces for Brass and Percussion for two trumpets, two horns, two trombones, tuba and six percussion players
1974 Quintet for Brass for two trumpets, horn, trombone and tuba
1974 Trio for strings
1975 Quintet for flute, oboe, clarinet, cello and piano
1975 Suite for Solo Violin (arr. for viola also)
1976 Concert piece for Cello and Small Orchestra for eight violins, four violas, four cellos, two double bass, piano, two celestas, and five percussion players
1976 Letter to a Friend's Loneliness for string quartet and soprano
1976 Music for Viola, Percussion and Piano (one percussion player)
1976 Incidental Piece for three saxes (E♭ alto)
1977 Music for Student String Quartet
1978 Nine Preludes for piano
1978 Sonata for piano
1979 Cantata for Women's Voices (SSAA), piccolo, flute, B♭ clarinet, tympani, suspended cymbal, tambourine (percussion)

Recording

Music for Viola, Percussion and Piano, Grenadilla Records.

INDEX